THE GRACIOUS WORD, YEAR C

The Gracious Word
Year C

COMMENTARY ON
SUNDAY AND
HOLY DAY
READINGS

Wilfrid J. Harrington OP

INTRODUCTIONS TO
THE LITURGICAL SEASONS

Philip Gleeson OP

DOMINICAN PUBLICATIONS

First published (1997) by
Dominican Publications
42 Parnell Square
Dublin 1

ISBN 1-871552-63-X

British Library Cataloguing in Publications Data.
A cataloguing record for this book is available from the British Library.

Copyright © (1997) the authors and Dominican Publications

Cover design by
David Cooke

Printed in the Republic of Ireland by
Colour Books Ltd, Baldoyle, Co. Dublin.

Contents

Contributors

Wilfrid J. Harrington OP, author of forty books on the Bible, lectures in Scripture at the Dominican *studium*, Tallaght, at the Milltown Institute of Theology and Philosophy, and at Trinity College, Dublin. He is a regular contributor to summer schools at St Mary's College, Winooski, Vermont, and at Gonzaga University, Spokane, Washington, U.S.A.

Philip Gleeson OP lectures in dogmatics and liturgy at Tallaght and at the Milltown Institute. He also contributes to courses at the Irish Institute of Pastoral Liturgy.

Michael Biggs (1928-1993), whose wood-cuts appear on pages 71, 72, 74, 78, 90, and 91, was a sculptor with a special interest in lettering. His work can be seem in the Proclamation of Independence outside the General Post Office and in the Garden of Remembrance, both in Dublin, and in very many churches – including Holy Cross Dominican Church, Sligo (foundation stone), St Michael's, Dun Laoghaire, St Patrick's College of Education, Dublin, Holy Cross Abbey, Co. Tipperary, and, pre-eminently, St Macartan's Cathedral, Monaghan.

Introduction

The three-volume *The Saving Word* [1] with scriptural commentary on the Sunday and feastday readings and accompanying relevant patristic texts and Church documents has served its purpose. It is now felt that a presentation of the Scripture commentaries alone would be welcome.

What is on offer is by no means a mere reprint of the earlier commentaries. All the material has been thoroughly revised — in large measure rewritten.

Besides, there are significant new features. Among these are quite full introductions to the Gospels and shorter introductions to the major biblical writings. We offer a lengthy treatment of the infancy narratives of Matthew and Luke, obviously of special interest at Christmastide. And there is an analysis of the distinctive features of the passion narratives – of special relevance for preaching in Holy Week. And, something quite new, courtesy of my confrere Philip Gleeson, splendid introductions to the liturgical seasons. In short, this is, essentially, a new work.

Wilfrid J. Harrington OP

---

1. Wilfrid Harrington, Thomas Halton, Michael Krupa, Austin Flannery, three volumes (Wilmington, DE / Dublin: M. Glazier / Dominican Publications, 1980-1982).

Advent

Introduction to the Liturgical Season

The readings for Advent are a proclamation of hope, and a call to live Christian lives. They focus in a particularly moving way on the child of God whose birth will be celebrated at Christmas. They are full of the paradox of power and weakness which is one of the abiding themes of the liturgy of this time.

GOSPELS

The Gospels all point towards Jesus. He is the one who will come at the end of time, the one for whom John prepared the way and to whom he bore witness, the one whose coming was made known to Elizabeth.

FIRST READINGS

The First Readings are prophetic passages, especially from Isaiah, about the Messiah and the messianic times. They help to give Advent its own particular flavour. They express the messianic hope of God's people, they give resonance to John the Baptist's call to conversion, they take up the theme of rejoicing (*Gaudete* Sunday), and they recall the promise made to the house of David.

SECOND READINGS

The Second Readings are in harmony with the Gospels and First Readings. They look forward to the coming of the Lord at the end of time, they contain expressions of hope and urge people to live Christian lives, they speak of Christian joy, and, on the fourth Sunday, they present Christ, the one who came into the world to do the will of the Father.

Philip Gleeson OP

Advent

FIRST SUNDAY OF ADVENT

First Reading   Jer 33:14-16

It is likely that this passage, significantly missing in the Septuagint, is a later, adapted version of an authentic oracle of the prophet already given in Jerusalem 23:5-6. There, as a conclusion to his oracles against the kings of Judah (21:1123:8), Jeremiah gives three messianic oracles (23:1-4, 5-6, 7-8); the second of these looks to a personal Messiah: 'Behold, the days are coming, says the Lord, when I will raise up for David a righteous branch, and he shall reign as king and deal wisely, and shall execute justice and righteousness in the land' (23:5). The term 'branch,' derived from Isaiah 11:1, designates the Messiah (see Zechariah 3:8; 6:12).

The new reign will be marked, to an eminent degree, by wisdom, justice and righteousness and, in the days of the new king the reunited land will again know peace: 'In those days Judah will be saved, and Jerusalem will live in safety' (v. 16). The name of the Messiah is 'Yahweh is our righteousness' in deliberate contrast to the last pathetic king of Judah – Zedekiah, a living contradiction of the meaning of his own name ('my righteousness is Yahweh'). In the adapted oracle the New Jerusalem has taken the place of Israel and is now called by the new name of the messianic king (33:16). This hopeful oracle does find place in the 'Book of Consolation' (Jer 30-33).

The prophet takes his stand on God's word: a time must and will come when his promise to his people will be accomplished. The day will dawn when the Son of David will stand among his people and when the New Jerusalem will stand forth as the true city of God. The oracle fittingly introduces the season of Advent, of preparation. For Jesus is the 'root of David' (Rev 5:5), who will inaugurate the new Jerusalem, the veritable kingdom of God (21:9-27).

Second Reading   1 Thess 3:12 4:2

Paul visited Thessalonica for the first time in the course of his second missionary journey, probably in the year 50 A.D. He preached with success; but after a stay of no more than two or three months he was forced, by Jewish opposition, to leave the town. In his concern for a Church that had so soon been left to itself, he sent Timothy to visit it. The latter returned to Corinth with a comforting report (3:6-10); the first part of our reading is Paul's heartfelt prayer for the future progress of his converts.

He prays that the Lord Jesus, the immediate source of growth in love, may bring these Christians to a deepening of love within their community, a love that will then reach out to all people. For love must begin as love of one another, as love of the brothers and sisters. When a community is truly a community of mutual love it will then flow over in love for others. It can then also love where it finds no answering love – the love of enemies. But, one insists, this charity must begin at home: it must be learned in the school of Christian brotherly/sisterly love. Such love is the motivation of Paul's concern for the Thessalonians: he is not paternalistic but loves them as brothers and sisters. If their brotherly/sisterly love does increase and abound, then, indeed, they will have nothing to fear when they stand before the judgment seat of God. They will be gathered together by the Lord at his coming, for it is he who will bring about in them growth and goodness.

Paul exhorts them *in* the Lord Jesus and reminds them that he has instructed them *through* the Lord Jesus; he exhorts and instructs in the spirit of the Lord and with his authority. But Paul is not taking refuge behind the authority of the Lord: it is, especially, from his own way of life that they have learned how one ought to live in order to please God. He has authority, as an apostle, but that authority is reinforced by the authenticity of his life. In our day we begin to understand very well that pastoral authority is only effective – indeed is only acknowledged – if the pastor is sincere, if one's pastoral concern rings true.

Gospel   Lk 21:25-28.34-36

The three synoptists have each an 'eschatological' or 'apocalyptic' discourse: Mk 13:1-37; Mt 24:1-51; Lk 21:5-36. Luke alone, as well, treats of the *parousia*, the glorious return of Jesus, by itself (17:22-37). In chapter 21 he makes a clear distinction between the destruction of Jerusalem (21:5-24) and the End (21:25-36). In short, he handles two distinct themes. One is historical – the destruction of Jerusalem and the victory of the gospel. The other is eschatological – the end of this age and the *parousia* of the Son of Man. He does so because he is conscious of the delay of the *parousia* (no longer sharing the earliest expectation that it was around the corner) and because he is convinced that Christians must adjust to a long period of waiting and persecution. The two passages that make up our reading concern the coming of the Son of Man and a call to watchfulness.

Luke's apocalyptic description (21:25-27) is couched in Old Testament language; it has been influenced especially by Isaiah 13:10 and

Psalm 65:8. Cosmic signs and distress on earth are the stock accompaniment of a divine intervention and especially of the divine judgement of humankind. The cloud which accompanies Old Testament theophanies not only veils the glory of God (Hab 3:4; Ps 18:11) but also manifests it (Ex 34:5). The cloud of the *parousia* will reveal Jesus' hitherto hidden glory, which is the glory of God. He comes in the cloud, the vehicle of God, to effect the divine work of judgment and redemption. We must not forget that all this is apocalyptic imagery. The *parousia* really means that there is a goal to the divine plan working itself out in history, a plan that is accomplished in and through the incarnate Son, the Alpha and the Omega, the beginning and the end (Rev 22:13).

Christians need not fear: the cosmic events which will terrify the nations will indicate to the followers of Christ that the time of persecution is ending – their 'redemption' (a Pauline word) is *drawing near*. They have been liberated, set free from sin, by Christ. But they must not be presumptuous (21:34-36). Christians must be constantly on their guard against dissipation and absorption in worldly affairs (see 8:14; 12:22; 17:26-30): the end will come suddenly, and upon all without distinction. Vigilance and prayer (see 18:1) will win for them strength to support the dangers and temptations of the last trials and will enable them to stand (among the redeemed) in the presence of the Son of Man come in his glory. The *parousia* may be delayed, but it will eventually involve us all. How one lives here and now determines how one will 'stand before the Son of Man.' These words of Luke, apparently so remote, are not at all without reference to our day-to-day lives. For trials can strike us suddenly, at any time; and the need of prayer is always with us. (See Thirty-Third Sunday of the Year, pp. 222-223.)

SECOND SUNDAY OF ADVENT

First Reading   Bar 5:1-9

The little book of Baruch, though attributed to Jeremiah's disciple and secretary, is very much later; it is a compilation from about the beginning of the second century B.C. The section of interest to us here is the discourse of exhortation and consolation, 4:5–5:9. In his address to the people of Israel (4:5-9) the poet reminds them that the affliction of the exile had come upon them because they had provoked the eternal God who had made them and because they had grieved Jerusalem their mother. Then Zion speaks (4:9-29): she reminds her children of the suffering they had caused her by their rebelliousness and of the petitions she had addressed to the Everlasting on their behalf. Her cries have been heard and she foretells their speedy return. The Everlasting replies by the mouth of the prophet and makes known to Zion that her sorrows are ended and that her children will be restored to her (4:30-5:9); our reading comprises the conclusion of that comforting oracle.

Jerusalem can, at last, forget the suffering of the past; she can, instead, wear the gloriously resplendent garment of God's saving action on her behalf. She can put on the robe of righteousness: God has removed her sin and made her 'just'; she can wear a crown inscribed with his name. Peace will reign in the wake of righteousness; her glory will derive from her godliness, her pure worship of God. 'Peace' and 'Glory' will be her attributes and her very name. Jerusalem will know the joy of having her exiled children restored to her. Indeed, as in Isaiah 40:3-4, God will level out a highway to facilitate the return; and he will give the travellers pleasant shade along the way. Indeed, he himself will lead them back, lead them in the 'light of his glory' – the effect of his saving presence. His intervention on their behalf is motivated by his mercy and by his saving righteousness. In short, there is the promise of restoration: Jerusalem will be reinstated, but in a glory surpassing any she had known. It is messianic restoration.

Second Reading
Phil 1:3-6.8-11

This is the opening of one of the three Pauline letters (1:1 - 3:1 plus 4:2-9) which make up Philippians. Its central message is a call for unity and perseverance and for unwavering witness to the truth. Permeated by the deep affection that bound him to Philippi it is, with Philemon, the most personal of all Paul's letters. Paul's remembrance of the Philippians leads to thanksgiving on their account: for the fervour with which they have accepted the gospel from the beginning.

In his assurance of prayer for them he strikes the note of joy that will ring throughout the whole epistle. They have not only received the good news but have played their part in preaching the gospel. They had participated in this work by supporting Paul (4:14-16) and by their suffering for the gospel (1:29-30); but Paul surely means that they would have been also, in a more direct fashion, fellow-workers of his. He is confident that God will bring to perfection the good work he has begun in them; they will have their reward – to be 'with the Lord' (1 Thess 4:17; 5:10) – at the glorious coming of Christ, the *parousia*. Paul can declare that he loves his converts with the warmth and selflessness of Jesus' love for them. He prays that their growth in union with Christ will bring them an increased personal knowledge of the Christian reality. He prays especially that they may have true discernment, a refined and keen awareness, that they may be able to assess and approve what really matters. Clearly, he wants them to be mature and responsible.

Christian living cannot be a matter of blind or wooden adherence to a code of morals; it lays upon every Christian the demand of personal decision. The goal of their endeavours is righteousness before God. Yet, this is no achievement of theirs but comes only through union with Christ. Their truly Christian lives redound to the glory of the Father.

Gospel   Lk 3:1-6

The infancy narrative of Luke (chapters 1-2) had introduced the Messiah and his herald and had indicated a first manifestation of both; now the time has come for a public manifestation, a proclamation that the age of fulfilment has begun. So John steps forward to prepare the way, to open the hearts of men and women.

Luke is at great pains to date exactly the ministry of the Baptist (3:1-2); his real purpose is thereby to date the beginning of our Lord's ministry. His elaborate synchronization, which illustrates the political situation in Palestine, serves to set the gospel event in the framework of world history (see 1:5). The fifteenth year of Tiberias is, likely, 27/28 AD, and Pilate was procurator 26-36 AD. Herod Antipas, son of Herod the Great and Malthake, was tetrarch of Galilee (and Peraea), 4 BC to 39 AD. Philip, son of Herod the Great and Cleopatra (not the famous Egyptian queen) was tetrarch of territories north-east of the sea of Galilee from 4 BC to 34 AD. Lysanias (not of Herod's family) was tetrarch of Abilene (north-west of Damascus) until 37 AD. Caiaphas was high priest from 18 to 16 AD; he was son-in-law of Annas and had been high priest from 6-15 AD. The latter's influence was very great (five of his sons and his son-in-law had been high priests) and that is why Luke can associate him with Caiaphas and speak of 'the high priesthood of Annas and Caiaphas' (see Jn 18:13-24; Acts 4:6).

In the manner of the Old Testament prophets, John (who had already been marked as a prophet, 1:15) is now solemnly called to his mission (see Jer 1:1,5,11; Hos 1:1; Joel 1:1). The 'wilderness' and 'all the region around the Jordan' (vv. 2-3) most likely refer to the same area north of the Dead Sea, in the neighbourhood of Jericho. John is presented as an itinerant preacher whose message was repentance with a view to forgiveness of sins, an anticipation of the Christian message (24:47). Luke, unlike Mark and Matthew, continues the quotation of Isaiah on to verse 5 (Is 40:3-5) and so introduces a universalist note ('all flesh'); see 2:30-32. The Hebrew of Isaiah 40:3 reads: 'A voice cries out: "In the wilderness prepare the way of the Lord".' But the evangelist follows the Septuagint rendering and sees in the Baptist a prophetic voice crying in the wilderness. John is the link between the old covenant and the new, but he himself belongs to the former (7:28; 16:16).

What is one to make of such a passage as Luke 3:1-6 in a Sunday liturgy? It is a reminder that Christianity is a historical religion, an affair of people who live in a real world of political structures and religious institutions. It is a reminder that Christianity has its roots in Israel, that it can never, with impunity, ignore its heritage. And it is a reminder that the message of Christ is, even more insistently than that of his precursor, a call to *metanoia*, a comforting assurance of the forgiveness of sins and a promise of salvation.

THIRD SUNDAY OF ADVENT

First Reading   Zeph 3:14-18

The oracles of Zephaniah date from the second half of the seventh century BC, just prior to the ministry of Jeremiah. Like Amos before him, Zephaniah warned his readers of the 'Day of Yahweh,' a universal catastrophe that will sweep away Judah and the nations. The chastisement of the nations, already begun, should be a warning to Judah, but the 'shameless nation' will not take heed. Yet a remnant will be faithful, a people 'humble and lowly' (3:12f), the *anawim* – the poor of Yahweh who will inherit the kingdom of God (Mt 5:3). Our passage contains part of the prophet's promises to them.

Jerusalem is bidden to rejoice because her salvation is at hand. Yahweh himself stands in their midst, the king and protector of his people. Under his leadership the nation will suffer no evil within nor fear any enemy without. There can be no place for 'weak hands' – no place for discouragement. This king, this victorious warrior, is none other than the bridegroom who gives new life to his bride by the very fervour of his love. Therefore is there all the more cause for rejoicing. The image of loving bridegroom, here as elsewhere, tempers the concept of the awful majesty of God. For Israel, Yahweh was always personal and close at hand, a God who steadfastly loves his unworthy and unfaithful bride.

The presence of God among his people is emphasized by the repetition of 'in your midst' (literally 'in your womb') in verses 15,17. The passage has notably influenced Luke 1:28-31. Mary is bidden 'Do not fear' as was Zion (Lk 1:30; Zeph 3:16). The prophetic text also explains the tautology of Luke: 'You will conceive *in your womb*' an echo of a phrase which, we have noted, occurs twice in the passage of Zephaniah.

Second Reading   Phil 4:4-7

This is part of the concluding portion of the letter whose opening passage was read on the previous Sunday. The conclusion (4:2-9), in the nature of a postscript, addresses an appeal for unity to specific individuals and is rounded off with a number of general counsels. The central section (vv. 4-7) calls on Christians to rejoice in the Lord, to be free from anxiety and to live in a spirit of prayer and thanksgiving. In this way they will win the peace of God. 'Joy' is a key-word of the epistle (1:18, 25; 2:2, 17f, 28f; 3:1; 4:1; 4, 10). It is not a natural joy – it is 'in the Lord'; it is a basic condition of Christian life, for Christians are called to rejoice always. It is a quality of peace and gentleness and kindness flowing from a deep inner conviction of faith. It ought to be a Christian quality that the world can recognize. More often, however, the world will be impatient of Christian attitudes and standards and way of life; Christians have need of patience and understanding. Perhaps, more importantly, forbearance must begin at home. A Christian community will not display to the world an aspect of 'joy' if there is lack of understanding and meanness within itself.

'The Lord is at hand.' Though we cannot share the tremendous expectancy of our earliest brothers and sisters, we can be assured as they that the Lord is our secure future, as he is our present support. If the joy, based on faith, is a reality in our lives, there can be no place for anxiety. Christians can turn to God their *Abba*, their loving and understanding Father, with simplicity and confidence. They can, and ought, without any attempt to 'prepare a brief,' make their requests known to him and leave them in his understanding hands. Importantly, they must not forget to thank him for his goodness, for all they have received. In this atmosphere of humble trust they will find that the peace of God will stand guard over their hearts and minds. This is a peace that passes human understanding because it cannot be attained by human efforts. It can prevail over our doubts and over questionings and keep us faithful in the steadfast following of Christ.

Gospel

Lk 3:10-18

Luke has the Baptist begin his preaching by warning that the axe of God's judgment already threatens the fruitless tree of Judaism though there is yet time for repentance. But if there is no change of heart the tree will be cut down and cast into the fire: those who fail to grasp this opportunity cannot expect to escape punishment (3:7-9). A modern exegete has an apposite comment on vv. 7-9 which underlines their relevance and their challenge:

> The axe is heading downstroke in any society that thinks these words are an invitation merely to distribute Christmas food baskets, handouts of castoff clothes, or money. Any one who is insensitive to the broadening gulf between the prosperous and the economically disadvantaged deserves to know that prophets did not risk their necks for petty moralizing of that sort. A call to repentance, an across-the-board review of respectable resources for injustice, prejudice, and indifference to the needs of human beings – this is what set apart true prophets from the bogus. (Danker, p. 88)

Then, in a passage peculiar to him (vv. 10-14) and which reveals his interest in the universal aspect of redemption and also his 'social' concern, the evangelist explains the character of the repentance required as a preparation for the kingdom. It is a thoroughgoing conversion finding expression in the observance of the commandments and in works of charity. This teaching reflects the exhortations of the Old Testament prophets, while v. 11 suggests the sharing of property in the primitive Jerusalem Church (Acts 2:44-45). The recommendation to tax collectors and to soldiers (most likely troops of Herod Antipas in whose territory John was preaching) is more specific in view of the special temptation of their way of life.

Verse 15 is also peculiar to Luke and provides the psychological setting, the air of expectancy. The common opinion that John was the Messiah, a view explicitly rejected by the Baptist himself, is also reflected in the Fourth Gospel (see John 1:19-20, 26-27); both John and Luke emphasize the subordinate role of the Baptist. This verse serves to turn the statement on baptism (vv. 16-17) into a disclaimer of messianic dignity. John declares himself unworthy to be a slave of the coming Messiah: and the water baptism of John is only a preparation for the Messiah's baptism with its bestowal of the Holy Spirit (see Acts 1:5; 11:16). Spirit and fire stand in apposition ('the fire of the Spirit') and refer to the outpouring of the Holy Spirit of Acts 2:3. Verse 17 shows the Messiah in his role as judge: he will separate grain – the new Israel which he will gather to himself – from chaff. According to the primitive method, still in practice among Palestinian Arabs, the threshed grain is tossed into the air so that the wind blows aside the chaff (to be gathered and later burned). The fire (not that of v. 16) is the final wrath of God (Is 66:24).

Verses 16-17 raise the vexed question of the relationship between the Baptist and Jesus. John's 'coming one' is unlikely to be Jesus (though, for Luke, he surely is); and his view of the role of the 'coming one' does not really match the practice of Jesus. Verse 18 is a summary description of John's preaching: he 'evangelized' the people.

FOURTH SUNDAY OF ADVENT

First Reading   Mic 5:1-4

Micah was a late eighth-century prophet, a contemporary of Hosea and Isaiah. In this oracle he announces the Ruler from Bethlehem who will bring peace. The circumstances of the oracle are those of Isaiah 11:1-9 – the siege of Jerusalem by Sennacherib in 701 BC. Zion is threatened and the Davidic dynasty is in jeopardy, but salvation will come from little Ephrathah (Bethlehem), the birthplace of David. Ephrathah, the name of the clan to which David's father Jesse belonged (1 Sam 17:12), was also used as the name for Bethlehem (Gen 35:19; 48:7) – 'Bethlehem' here is likely to be a later addition making the identification clear. Though the village of Bethlehem is insignificant in comparison with the splendour of Jerusalem, yet the promised ruler will not come from the capital but from the humbler background. This ruler is a Davidic prince whose origin ('from of old') goes back to the beginning of the Davidic dynasty three centuries earlier.

The prophet gives the assurance that another 'ruler in Israel' will come from the ancient Davidic line; the dynasty will not end with Hezekiah, despite the threat of Assyria. But until the new ruler will emerge, Israel will be subject to other nations; when he begins his rule the scattered exiles will be gathered together and the divided people will become one again. All will come to pass 'when she who is in labour has brought forth.' This is, very likely, an allusion to the mother of Immanuel, Is 7:14 , and must share that other text's uncertainty of interpretation. At any rate, Micah 5:1-4, like Isaiah 11:1-19, is some thirty years later than the Immanuel prophecy. It seems not unlikely that Isaiah, disillusioned with Hezekiah (the Immanuel of 7:14) looks to a future Messiah; similarly, Micah may, perhaps, look to the mother of the Messiah whom he describes in the following verse. The ruler will be the faithful shepherd of his flock, fully equipped by God for that office. With such a leader, so endowed, the people will have security, and he will bring the messianic blessing of peace. The oracle certainly has to do with the messianic dynasty of David, and so is an authentically messianic oracle. It proclaims the coming of the Prince of Peace. And the woman of verse 2 is the mother of the ideal king to come, the mother of the Messiah within the perspective of the line of David.

Second Reading   Heb 10:5-10

The whole Letter to the Hebrews is, structurally, a combination of doctrinal exposition and parentheses (admonition, exhortation) in alternating passages; our reading is part of a doctrinal passage (10:1-18). It presents Jesus, High Priest, as the source of eternal salvation. The author opens his argument by asserting that because the Mosaic law contains but a shadow of the future benefits and not the reality of these things, it can never, by the constant repetition of the same sacrifices year after year, perfect those who seek to draw near to God. These sacrifices not only did not purify from sin, but their very repetition was a constant reminder of sin. And, anyhow, it was quite impossible that the blood of animals should take away guilt.

Psalm 40 had predicted the ineffectiveness of all levitical sacrifices, and had announced instead the value of obedience. The author puts verses 7-9 of this psalm in the mouth of Christ; his entry into the world is thus explicitly presented as redemptive (Heb 10:5-7). Verses 8-10 are a comment on the psalm-text, developing its application to Christ. They state that Christ has undone the old order and brought in the new. He has done so by expressing his willingness, through his obedience and sacrifice of self, to bring about the reconciliation between God and his people – something that the levitical sacrifices could never achieve. The sacrifice of Christ, though instinct with obedience, is not metaphorical but real – it is the sacrifice of his body, the laying down of his life. And it is the will of God that this obedience unto death be our sanctifying sacrifice offered once for all. The accent is on the will of God; it is by virtue of Christ's adherence to this will that his immolation is agreeable to the Father.

Gospel   Lk 1:39-45

In the structure of the Lucan infancy narrative, this passage, 'The Visitation,' is a complementary episode, a pendant to the diptych of

annunciations (1:1-38). Mary is portrayed as making her way in haste
– a haste inspired by friendship and charity but yet more by her
recognition of a divine invitation. At Mary's greeting Elizabeth felt the
infant Baptist stir in her womb – John, while still in the womb, is
precursor (1:17) of the Lord. Enlightened by the prophetic Spirit, she
concluded that Mary is to be mother of 'the Lord.' That is why Mary
is 'blessed among women,' a Hebraism, meaning the most blessed of
all women. Elizabeth went on to praise Mary's unhesitating acquiescence in God's plan for her – her great faith: 'And blessed is she who
believed ... '

The Infancy Narratives

Matthew 1-2; Luke 1-2

The Infancy Narratives of Matthew and Luke have had a notable influence on Christian tradition and have put a profound mark on Christian art. The long Christian appreciation of them has not been misplaced. We had sensed that there was something special here – that these texts said quite a lot more than they appeared to say. In our day we have, happily, come to realise that both infancy narratives – which are wholly independent of each other – are, first and foremost, christological statements. It is along this line, and only here, that we can grasp their true meaning. An overall look at these texts is appropriate as an introduction to the readings of Christmastide.

Matthew 1-2

Matthew and Luke shared a twofold tradition: Jesus' home was Nazareth; Jesus was descendant of David and, as such, appropriately born in Bethlehem. Reconciliation of these traditions has influenced the shape of their narratives. For Matthew, Jesus' birth in Bethlehem offered no problem; in his view, Bethlehem was home of Joseph and Mary. He has to move Jesus from Bethlehem to Nazareth. For Luke, on the other hand, the home of Joseph and Mary was Nazareth; he has to arrange to have Jesus born in Bethlehem. This contrived reconciliation, by each evangelist, of the dominant Nazareth tradition (throughout the gospels Jesus is counted a Nazarene) with the Bethlehem tradition would suggest that birth at Bethlehem is to be taken as a theologoumenon (a theological affirmation related as an historical event) – in this case an affirmation of the Davidic descent of Jesus.

In building his infancy narrative Matthew has made use of two main blocks of material: a cycle of angelic dream appearances and the Magi story. The material has been thoroughly edited by Matthew but the two blocks are still recognizably distinct. Angelic dream appearances: 1:20-25; 2:13-15; 2:19-23. It is evident that Joseph wears the cloak of the famous patriarch Joseph, especially in his being a man of dreams and in his going down into Egypt. The Magi story: 2:1-12. As it stands, this is a self-contained story, with no mention of Joseph. Matthew composed its sequel (2:16-18) when he combined it with the flight into Egypt episode.

A feature of Matthew's gospel is his use of formula citations which sit loosely in their context; they are particularly frequent in his infancy narrative: 1:22-23; 2:5-6; 2:15; 2:17-18; 2:23. Matthew has recognized the applicability of particular Old Testament texts to particular incidents in Jesus' career. He introduced them because they fit his theology of the oneness of God's plan and because they help to bring out, for his Christian readers, who and what Jesus is. Thus, the five infancy narrative citations tell us that the virginally-conceived Jesus is God-with-us, that as son of David he was, fittingly, born in Bethlehem, that, in being called out of Egypt, he re-enacted the Exodus of his people, that he suffered the Exile of his people, and that as the Nazorean he began his saving work.

THE GENEALOGY OF JESUS (1:1-17)

The Old Testament, especially Genesis and 1 Chronicles, makes skilful use of genealogies. In his turn, Matthew finds his genealogy to be an effective way of establishing the identity of Jesus. He traces Jesus' ancestry back to David and Abraham. In particular, he shows that the one whom Christians proclaim as 'Messiah' can be correctly claimed to be 'son of David'. The sequences of fourteen generations suggest that Jesus was born at the 'right' time.

Two features of the genealogy are of special interest: (1) The formula 'A was the father of B' (literally 'A begot B') is interrupted in v. 16. It is not said that 'Joseph was the father of Jesus,' rather: 'Joseph, the husband of Mary, of her was begotten Jesus, called the Messiah.' (2) The other feature, closely related to the first, is the unexpected presence of four women: Tamar, Rahab, Ruth, Bathsheba ('the wife of Uriah'). The point is that, in the Old Testament and especially in Jewish tradition, there was something irregular in the union of these women with their partners yet all four of them continued the lineage of the Messiah. Indeed they played such an important role that they were regarded as manifestly instruments of the Spirit. Clearly, then, they foreshadow the role of Mary. There was something 'irregular' about her relation with Joseph and she is 'with child of the Holy Spirit' (2:18). In that line of the Messiah Matthew had clearly seen the hand of God. We might add that it simply is not possible to reconcile this genealogy with that of Lk 3:23-38. But both of them tell us how to evaluate Jesus: theologically he is 'son of David,' 'son of Abraham,' (Matthew) and 'Son of God' (Luke).

THE BIRTH OF JESUS (1:18-25)

Joseph and Mary were betrothed. In Jewish society, bethrothal was something far more serious than our marriage engagement. Betrothal was really a marriage contract, except that the partners had not begun to live together. Joseph discovered that his betrothed was pregnant. 'Of the Holy Spirit' is Matthew's nod to the reader; Joseph was not aware of that factor and was in a quandary. He was a 'righteous'man, that is, Law-observant. He assumed that Mary had been unfaithful. The death penalty for adultery (Deut 22:23-27) was not then, if it ever had been, in force; divorce was the answer. This was the course Joseph decided on – except that he wanted to divorce her 'quietly.' It is not clear how he could have hoped to achieve this. And divorce would not have helped Mary at all. She would have been left on her own to bear her baby – in a thoroughly disapproving society. The 'righteous' man, Joseph, was a confused man. He desperately wanted to do the decent thing, but his 'solution' was no solution at all.

Happily for him – and for Mary – God took a hand. In a dream, all was made clear. Mary was not an unfaithful bride but a wholly privileged instrument of God. Her child, of divine parenthood, would be Saviour; he is the one who 'will save his people from their sins.' And here Matthew throws in his formula-citation. He looked to Is 7:14 (in the Greek) and found there a word of promise: 'the virgin would bear a son.' That son will be Emmanuel, God-with-us. Cleverly, Matthew has anticipated the close of his gospel: 'Remember, I am with you always' (Mt 28:20). In that unique child of Mary, a first-century Palestinian Jew, we meet our God. Paul has put it in his inimitable fashion: 'God was in Christ, reconciling the world to himself' (2 Cor 5:19).

THE MAGI STORY (2:1-12)

In this narrative, Matthew has cast back into the infancy the reactions that, historically, greeted the proclamation of the risen Lord: some believed and paid homage; others rejected the message and the preachers. In other words, christological revelation was followed by proclamation and by the twofold reaction of acceptance-homage and rejection-persecution. But this had been prepared for in the ministry of Jesus. The same pattern is presented in the infancy narrative.

There seems little point in looking for the homeland of the Magi – whom Matthew seemingly would regard as astrologers of some sort. Nor is there any point in looking to a comet, a supernova, or a planetary conjunction to account for 'his star' (1:2). A star which rises, goes before, and comes to rest over a place is no natural phenomenon but a miraculous (more precisely, a symbolic) star. More to he point is the fact that, for Matthew, the Magi represent the Gentiles, fittingly alerted not by an angel (as Luke's Jewish shepherds) but by a star. The liturgical tradition of the feast of Epiphany has caught Matthew's intent. The Magis' role as prefiguring the acceptance of Gentiles into the Christian community points toward the universal character of the gospel. Jesus is functioning as son of Abraham.

The Balaam narrative of Numbers 22-24, embroidered with Jewish tradition, would, skilfully used by Matthew, appear to have been the inspiration of the magi story. Balaam was summoned by Balak 'from the east' to curse Israel. Significantly, Philo calls him a *magos*. Similarly, Herod tried to use the magi for his own ends. In his oracle Balaam had declared: 'A star shall come out of Jacob, and a sceptre shall rise out of Israel' (Num 24:17). Here, credibly, is 'his star' (Mt 2:2).

FLIGHT AND RETURN (2:13-23)

The next two episodes are coloured by the story of Moses in Egypt – again as elaborated in Jewish tradition – and also echo the Exodus motif. The basic story line in 2:13-15 concerns the rescue of the child saviour from the machinations of the wicked king by flight into Egypt. Jewish tradition, as we find it, for example, in Josephus, had it that the Pharaoh of the Exodus had been forewarned by one of his 'sacred scribes' of the birth of a Hebrew who would constitute a threat to the Egyptian kingdom. Pharaoh and the whole of Egypt were filled with dread (see Mt 2:3). Pharaoh's plan was frustrated by a warning communicated in a dream to Moses' father. The parallels between this Jewish legend and the pre-Matthean infancy narrative are manifest. Read against the background of Exodus 1-2, Jesus emerges as a Moses-figure. The Hosea quotation – 'Out of Egypt have I called my son' – refers to the exodus of Israel from Egypt. Matthew sees that Jesus relives the history of his people: not only the exodus but the previous going down into Egypt.

The story line in 2:16-18, involving the massacre of the male children in Bethlehem, echoes Pharaoh's decree against the male infants of the Hebrews. Matthew, with his formula citation of Jeremiah 31:15, works in another theme: that of the Babylonian Exile. Again, Jesus is associated with a tragic event of his people. The names in the three formula citations: Bethlehem (the city of David), Egypt (the land of the Exodus) and Ramah (the mourning place of the Exile) are theologically suggestive. The final episode (2:19-23), too, gives us three significant names: Israel, Galilee and Nazareth. The 'citation' here is really not such: Matthew is playing on the name Nazareth.

Quite likely, he is thinking both of the *neser*, 'branch,' of Is 11:1 and of *nazir* – one consecrated or made holy to God. At any rate he knows that this son of David, Son of God, is none other than Jesus the Nazorean.

> As Matthew narrates the infancy narrative, it is the place where the Old Testament and the Gospel meet. If he brought forward some themes from the Old Testament with which to clothe the infant Jesus, he also brought back from the Gospel some evaluations of Jesus by the Christian community: son of David, son of Abraham, and messianic Son of God. He attaches the basic Gospel revelation, 'You are the Christ, the Son of the living God' (16:16) to the conception of Jesus. He has this revelation proclaimed to Gentiles and Jews, to be received by the former and rejected by the authorities among the latter. (Raymond E. Brown, *The Birth of the Messiah*. 231).

Luke 1-2

Luke, writing consciously in the style of the Greek Bible (the LXX), composed his narrative, broadly, in the shape of two diptychs: prophecies of the birth of John the Baptist and Jesus and narratives of the birth of both.

PROPHECY OF JOHN'S BIRTH (1:5-25)

The introduction (1:5-7) gives four items of information. The first three – time setting in the reign of Herod the Great, the names Zechariah and Elizabeth, their priestly descent – are items of tradition. The other, that they were aged and Elizabeth barren, reflects the stories of Abraham and Sarah, Elkanah and Hannah. Thus, the birth of John the Baptist is in continuity with the births of famous figures in the salvific history of Israel.

The pattern of annunciation (1:8-23) reflects that announcing Ishmael (Gen 16), Isaac (Gen 17) and Samson (Jdg 13) and carries echoes of Daniel 8:16-27; 9:21-23. The Lucan angel is named Gabriel (as in Daniel). The verses 15-17, which prophetically characterize the adult Baptist as an ascetic prophet calling upon Israel to repent, are culled from the ministry portrayal of him – 3:1-3; 7:24-35. The sign, required by the literary pattern, is dumbness, suggested by Dan 10:15. Since Elizabeth's pregnancy is going to be a sign for Mary (1:36) her seclusion (1:24-25) underlines its sign-value since no one could have known of her pregnancy. For Zechariah and Elizabeth, Luke has looked to the Old Testament models of Abraham and Sarah; for the infant Baptist he drew on the description of John in the gospel story of the ministry. He has portrayed the Baptist in conscious parallel to Jesus – taking consistent care to keep the former on a lower level.

PROPHECY OF JESUS' BIRTH (1:26-38)

The structure again follows faithfully the pattern of angelic annunciations of birth. Hence, material not explained by the literary pattern is significant: the peculiar manner of conception (virginal), identity of the child (vv 32-33, 35), the portrait of Mary in vv 34 and 38. In 1:32-33 Jesus is described as the Davidic Messiah in terms taken from 2 Sam 7:9-16. The only thing specifically Christian here is that Jesus has been identified as that promised Messiah. Luke uses the technique of Mary's question and Gabriel's answer to point to the true identity of the Davidic Messiah: together they speak Luke's christological message. The Messiah is God's Son and his conception is not through marital intercourse (Mary) but through the Holy Spirit (Gabriel). It is Luke's dramatic version of an early christological formula, such as that in Romans 1:3-4.

The portrait of Mary in 1:38 is shaped from Luke's account of her in the ministry (8:19-21); as one who hears and does the will of God she is truly 'servant of the Lord.' Against the patriarchal background of Luke's biblical tradition, his focus on Mary is striking. It carries a typical Lucan message.

> In contrast to Zechariah, we notice, Mary holds no official position among the people, she is not described as 'righteous' in terms of observing Torah, and her experience does not take place in a cultic setting. She is among the most powerless people in her society: she is young in a world that values age; female in a world ruled by men; poor in a stratified economy. Furthermore, she has neither husband nor child to validate her existence. That she should have found 'favour with God' and be 'highly gifted' shows Luke's understanding of God's activity as surprising and often paradoxical, almost always reversing human expectations. (Luke T. Johnson, *Luke*. 39).

MARY VISITS ELIZABETH (1:39-56)

In the structure of the Lucan infancy narrative this passage 'The Visitation', is a complementary episode, a pendant to the diptych of annunciations (1:5-38). Elizabeth is granted the perception not only that Mary is with child but that her child is the Messiah. Her canticle in praise of Mary (1:42-45) echoes Old Teastament motifs and anticipates motifs that will be found in the gospel (11:27-28). This narrative serves as a hinge between the two birth stories of John and of Jesus. And this meeting of women illustrates their respective situations. Elizabeth's pregnancy was not only a sign for Mary; it was also an invitation. The 'haste' of Mary was inspired by friendship and charity.

At Mary's greeting Elizabeth felt the infant stir within her – John, while still in the womb, is precursor (1:17) of the Lord. Enlightened by the prophetic Spirit she concluded that Mary is to be mother of 'the Lord.' That is why Mary is 'blessed among women' – the most blessed of women. Elizabeth went on to praise Mary's unhesitating acquiescence in God's plan for her – her great faith: 'And blessed is she who believed ... ' The song of Mary (1:46-55) moves from the reversal of Mary's condition from lowliness to exaltation (vv 47-49), to a general statement of God's mercy (50), on to a recital of his past and present reversals (51-53) and to a final statement on his mercy to Israel in fulfilment of his promise to Abraham (54-55). In some sort, throughout, Mary is representative of Israel.

THE BIRTH OF JOHN (1:57-80)

The birth of John marked the fulfilment of the angel's message to Zechariah. Circumcision was prescribed for the eighth day after birth. Elizabeth, to the consternation of relatives who had objected to her choice of name, was supported by her husband: the child's name was John. At that Zechariah found himself able to speak again. The infancy story of the Baptist closes (1:80) with a 'refrain of growth' indicating his physical and spiritual development. In typical Lucan style, reference to John's sojourn in the desert prepares the way for his next appearance (3:2). The canticle of Zechariah (1:68-79) begins with the fulfilment of God's promised visitation of his people and then focuses on John's role as 'prophet of the Most High.'

THE BIRTH OF JESUS (2:1-21)

The setting (2:1-7) is necessitated in part by Luke's assumption that Joseph and Mary lived in Nazareth before Jesus was born; for Matthew, their home was in Bethlehem. Luke has to get Mary to Bethlehem for the birth of Jesus there. His stratagem is the census of Quirinius and he is certainly confused in his account of the census – an unhistorical event as he relates it. But, then, it may be that we have tended to take Luke too literally. His prime interest would seem to lie in the fact that the mighty Augustus was, unwittingly, an instrument of the Lord. Through his decree it came to pass that Jesus the Messiah was born in the town of David. When we look at it dispassionately we must admit that what we had taken to be the Lucan picture of many distant descendants of David crowding into the insignificant Bethlehem is not very likely – still less likely as following on a policy of the practical Romans. What Luke wants to show is that Jesus was born in the hometown of David as one who belonged there – not in lodgings like an alien. Manger and swaddling clothes (2:12) symbolize God's care and protection.

From the first, Mary is the caring mother, solicitously wrapping her baby and laying him in a manger-cradle. Luke is not suggesting anything miraculous about the birth – merely insisting that the 'servant of the Lord' is, in her loving care, reflecting God's care. In the annunciation to the shepherds (2:8-14) heaven and earth touch. The angels interpret the event and give it its true meaning: this child is Saviour, Messiah and Lord. The form of the proclamation (vv 10-11) and the canticle, the Gloria (v. 14), would seem, again, to glance at Augustus who, architect of the *pax Augusta*, was hailed as Saviour. Jesus, not he, Luke asserts, is Saviour and bringer of peace.

In the reaction (2:15-20) to birth and heavenly proclamation the shepherds are forerunners of future believers who will glorify God for what they had heard and will praise God for what they had seen. In this third part of the passage all the protagonists, Mary, Joseph, baby and the shepherds come together. Yet, only one figure constitutes a bridge from the infancy narrative to the ministry of Jesus, and that is Mary, his mother. She is that by being a believer and disciple (Lk 8:19-21; 11:27-28; Acts 1:12-14). This is what Luke intends by his declaration: Mary 'treasured all these words and pondered them in her heart' (2:19). One should look to the parallel assertion in 2:51 – 'his mother treasured all these things in her heart.' She, like the Twelve, will come to full understanding when Jesus will have risen from the dead. Until then, in the obscurity of faith, she pondered those puzzling events. It is a misunderstanding of Luke's purpose, and of his literary achievement, to claim, as some have argued, that these statements point to Mary as source of the evangelist's narrative. Luke had access to some traditions but the infancy narrative, as we have it, is his creation.

THE PRESENTATION (2:22-40)

We have seen that the Matthean magi story displayed the magi as reacting with acceptance and homage to the proclamation of the Messiah. Luke's shepherds play a similar role. But the magi story has two elements missing in the Lucan story up to now: the positive response of Gentiles and the rejection of the new-born Messiah. These are supplied in Simeon's double oracle (2:29-32, 34-35). In the setting of this episode (2:22-24) Luke has combined two different Israelite customs: (1) consecration or presentation of the child to the Lord (Ex 13:1, 11-16); (2) purification of the mother after the birth of a child (Lev 12:1-8). Luke's text gives evidence of his general knowledge of these customs and his inaccurate grasp of details. Simeon's Nunc Dimittis introduces the theme of salvation for the Gentiles (see Is 42:6; 52:10). In the second oracle (2:34-45) Simeon anticipates the rejection of Jesus by the Jewish authorities and the rejection of the Christian mission to Israel as described in Acts.

> As in the *Magnificat*, Mary is here portrayed as a personification of the people of Israel. Israel will be divided, and so will Mary's soul be run through by a sword ... At the level of human drama, the revelatory significance of Jesus will not be obvious to all nor accepted by all. Jesus will be a 'sign of contradiction' (Luke T. Johnson, *Luke*, 57).

THE BOY JESUS IN THE TEMPLE (2:41-52)

This passage, concerning the twelve-year old Jesus, is hardly an infancy narrative and the repeated conclusion v. 52 (see v. 40) marks is as an addition. Originally, the story seemed to situate the 'christological moment' in Jesus' youth: here we have Jesus saying of himself what the heavenly voice will say at baptism. Obviously, for Luke, the punchline is v. 49: 'Did you not know that I must be in my Father's house?' Jesus, in his first spoken words in Luke's gospel, himself announces who he is: he is the one totally committed to God, his Father. By stressing Mary's lack of understanding (v. 50) Luke makes the historically accurate assertion that the christology of Jesus as God's Son was not perceived until after the resurrection.

> Luke is giving us a perceptive theological insight into history; there was a continuity from the infant Jesus to the boy Jesus to the Jesus of the ministry to the risen Jesus; and when Christian disciples like Mary believed in Jesus as God's Son after the resurrection, they were finding adequate expression for institutions that had begun long before (Brown, *The Birth of the Messiah*, 494).

The infancy narratives are independent of each other and are stylistically markedly distinct. They are concerned with quite different episodes. All the more striking, then, is their total theological agreement. For Matthew, as for Luke, Jesus, virginally conceived, is son of David and Son of God. He is Saviour of Jew and Gentile and destined to meet with acceptance and rejection. The whole is part of a divine plan long prepared in the salvific history of Israel. The Christian instinct has always reached beyond the surface of these narratives.

Christmastide

Introduction to the Liturgical Season

The readings for the Christmas season are full of joy at the light shining in the darkness, the revelation of God's love. They are an invitation to live in the light. At the heart of the whole season is the humanity of our God.

GOSPELS

The central Gospel for this season is the Prologue of John, which is read at Mass during the day on Christmas Day itself, and also on the second Sunday after Christmas. But we also see the bright pictures painted by Matthew and Luke: the beginning of the Gospel according to Matthew, that is, the genealogy, the annunciation made to Joseph, the birth and naming of Jesus (Christmas vigil Mass); Luke's account of the birth of Jesus and the angels singing for joy (midnight Mass), and his account of the shepherds worshipping the child, and Mary turning things over in her heart (Mass at dawn).

On the feast of the Holy Family, the Gospel this year tells of the finding of the child Jesus in the temple.

On the solemnity of Mary, Mother of God (the Octave of the Nativity), the Gospel again puts us in the company of the shepherds, looking at Mary, Joseph, and the Child, and it goes on to tell us that on the eighth day the child was circumcised and given the name, 'Jesus'.

On the Epiphany, the Gospel is that of the Magi, the traditional Roman reading for this day. Then, on the feast of the Baptism of the Lord, the last day of the Christmas season, we move on to the Luke's description of the baptism of Jesus, the beloved Son, on whom the Spirit descended.

FIRST READINGS

Isaiah, so prominent during Advent, continues to be heard during the Christmas season. On Christmas Day, the Masses include readings from Isaiah which express delight at the wedding of God and God's people (vigil Mass) and proclaim a message of light and joy.

On the Epiphany, the First Reading is the traditional Roman one, the passage from Isaiah about kings and camels and gifts of gold and incense.

On the Baptism of the Lord, there is a passage from Isaiah about the beloved servant; the *ad libitum* Reading is the consoling message that the glory of God shall be revealed.

Besides these readings from Isaiah, the First Readings include Ecclesiasticus in praise of family virtue (Holy Family). This year, the *ad libitum* First Reading for the Holy Family puts before us the example of an Old Testament family – Hannah, Elkanah, and Samuel. Numbers teaches us to invoke the name of God in blessing (Solemnity of Mary, Octave of Christmas). Ecclesiasticus meditates on divine Wisdom rejoicing in God's presence and taking root in God's people (second Sunday after Christmas).

SECOND READINGS

The Second Readings harmonize with the Gospels and First Readings. On Christmas Day they include a passage from Acts, giving Paul's proclamation of Jesus as the fulfilment of the promise to the house of David (vigil Mass), two passages from Titus about the revelation of God's grace and God's kindness (midnight and dawn), and one from Hebrews about the revelation of the radiant light of God's glory (Mass during the day).

On the Feast of the Holy Family, Ephesians speaks about family virtues, and First John reflects on our own status as God's children (*ad libitum* reading).

On the Solemnity of Mary Mother of God, the Octave of Christmas, Galatians speaks of the child, born of a woman, and of the Spirit who enables us to call God, "Abba".

On the second Sunday after Christmas, Ephesians is on the theme of our adoption in Jesus.

On the Epiphany, Ephesians announces the revelation of the mystery that pagans now share in the inheritance of God's people.

Finally, on the Baptism of the Lord, the Second Reading, from Acts, contains part of Peter's address to Cornelius and his household, about the beginning of the ministry of Jesus, anointed with the Spirit and with power. The *ad libitum* Second Reading is from First John about the water of rebirth, and the Holy Spirit.

Philip Gleeson OP

Christmastide

CHRISTMAS: MASS AT MIDNIGHT

First Reading
Is 9:1-7

This reading presents the child who is born to us as the complete ruler who will inaugurate a reign of unending peace (*shalom* – wholeness of life) and justice. Historically, the oracle was spoken on the occasion of the deportation of the people of Israel (the northern kingdom) in 732 B.C. It implies that salvation will be a reward of faithfulness as only those who have sown and waited patiently share in the harvest, and only those who have fought share the spoils of battle. The sufferings of the people are invoked in the opening lines: they have 'walked in darkness,' 'lived in a land of deep darkness,' 'been burdened by the yoke,' and felt the 'rod' of the taskmaster. These images of oppression are countered by the promise of light, joy and freedom that will come with the accession of a new Davidic king.

The composite throne-name of the royal child is prophetic: he possesses, to an eminent degree, the virtues of the heroes of his race – the wisdom of Solomon, the valour of David, the dedication of Moses and the prophets. Christian tradition and liturgy, in applying these titles to Jesus, acknowledge that he is the Emmanuel: God-with-us.

Second Reading
Tit 2:11-14

This passage from a letter written by a later admirer of Paul reminds us that we are moving on many levels when we speak about the coming of Christ. Even as on Christmas night we recall his first coming some two thousand years ago, we are still waiting for his final coming at the end of time (one way of expressing our conviction that God's saving plan moves towards a goal). There is the coming of Christ to each individual in the course of his or her life.

The purpose of God's freely-bestowed grace is not to take Christian men and women out of the world but to empower them effectively to renounce vice and to live virtuous lives 'in this world.' Beginning at Bethlehem and culminating on the cross, the process continues down the ages and will reach its perfection with the final 'manifestation of the glory of the great God and our Saviour Jesus Christ.' Our gracious God will have spoken his final word – word of salvation.

Gospel   Lk 2:1-14

The setting is necessitated in part by Luke's assumption that Joseph and Mary lived in Nazareth before Jesus was born; for Matthew their home was Bethlehem. Luke has to get Mary to Bethlehem for the birth of Jesus there. His stratagem is the census of Quirinius and he is certainly confused in his account of the census – an unhistorical event as he relates it. But, then, it may be that we have tended to take Luke too literally. His prime interest would seem to lie in the fact that the mighty Augustus was, unwittingly, an instrument of the Lord. Through his decree it came to pass that Jesus the Messiah was born in the town of David. When we look at it dispassionately we must admit that what we had taken to be the Lucan picture of many distant descendants of David crowding into the insignificant Bethlehem is not very likely – still less likely as following on a policy of the practical Romans. What Luke wants to show is that Jesus was born in the city of David as one who belonged there – not in lodgings like an alien. Manger and swaddling clothes (2:12) symbolize God's care and protection.

From the first, Mary is the caring mother, solicitously wrapping her baby and laying him in a manger-cradle. Luke is not suggesting anything miraculous about the birth – merely insisting that the 'handmaid of the Lord' is, in her loving care, reflecting God's care.

In the annunciation to the shepherds (2: 8-14) heaven and earth touch. The angels interpret the event and give it its true meaning: this child is Saviour, Messiah and Lord. The form of the proclamation (vv. 10-11) and the canticle, the *Gloria* (2:14), would seem, again, to glance at Augustus who, architect of the *pax Augusta*, was hailed as Saviour. Jesus, not he, Luke asserts, is Saviour and bringer of peace (*shalom*).

Apart from symbolism, the simple circumstances of Jesus' birth are eloquent. He was born in poverty and the very first invited to share in the joy of Mary and Joseph were simple country folk, shepherds guarding their sheep. In our day Latin America has rediscovered this privilege of the poor.

CHRISTMAS DAY: MASS AT DAWN

First Reading   Is 62:11-12

The context is the joyful return of the exiles from Babylon and the restoration of Jerusalem, the 'daughter of Zion.' The city is no longer to be named 'forsaken' but is now 'sought out' – object of love. The people who live in Zion are God's 'holy people', 'the redeemed of the Lord.

All the titles used in this reading can be applied to the Church, the new people of God, a holy people redeemed by the Lord, a people no longer abandoned, the community of salvation. It requires prayerful insight to see the Church in such terms. It needs faith to see beneath the human and the sinful to the deeper reality of a holy people of God.

Second Reading
Tit 3:4-7

Quite undeservedly, God has lavished his goodness and loving kindness upon Christians – his loving kindness concretely manifested in Jesus. Before Christ came all were in the same state, ignorant, misled and enslaved by passions. But God freely, and without any merit on our part, sent his Son to cleanse and renew us. This author, a disciple of Paul, echoes a constant teaching of Paul: the call to salvation is a gratuitous act of God, independent of our deeds. Confronted with such generosity there is no place for self-righteousness; our response to God's Christmas gift must be one of humble thankfulness and acceptance.

The idea of the Spirit being poured out is a prophetic one (see Joel 3:1); it signifies the abundance of messianic blessings which were to appear in the eschatological era. This era has now arrived with the coming of Christ.

Gospel
Lk 2:15-20

This is a continuation of the passage read at midnight Mass. In their reaction to the heavenly proclamation of birth the shepherds are forerunners of future believers who will glorify God for what they had heard and will praise God for what they had seen.

Here all the protagonists – Mary, Joseph, baby and the shepherds – all come together. Yet, only one figure constitutes a bridge from the infancy narrative to the ministry of Jesus, and that is Mary, his mother. She is that by being a believer and disciple (Lk 8:19-21; 11:27-28; Acts 1:12-14). This is what Luke intends by his declaration: Mary 'treasured all these things and pondered them in her heart' (2:19). One should look to the parallel assertion in 2:51 – 'His mother treasured all these things in her heart.' She, like the Twelve, will come to full understanding when Jesus will have risen from the dead. Until then, in the obscurity of faith, she pondered those puzzling events. It is a misunderstanding of Luke's purpose, and of his literary achievement, to claim, as some have argued, that these statements point to Mary as source of the evangelist's narrative. Luke had access to some traditions, but the infancy gospel, as we have it, is his creation.

The picture of Mary here is that of a loving and capable mother. Jesus was in very good hands. Furthermore, she is a deeply thoughtful woman. And she is a woman of faith who lived her life in faith.

CHRISTMAS DAY: MASS DURING THE DAY

First Reading   Is 52:7-10

The first lines of today's reading are familiar to us from Paul's use of them in Romans 10:15. A messenger ran along the mountain ridges to bring the good news of the return of the exiles from Babylon. His task is to proclaim salvation and peace. From now on, God is king and his reign will mean peace and prosperity. Watchmen on the ruined walls of Jerusalem take up the joyful message of the herald and announce it to the city: Jerusalem will be restored. The term for 'good news' in Greek is *euaggelion*, that is, 'gospel'. Here we see the true meaning of Gospel: it is the news of God's liberation. There is a note of universality; the event will not be of significance only for Israel. God's saving work will be so striking that 'all the ends of the earth shall see the salvation of our God.' We Christmas Christians must grasp the important truth that our salvation in Christ is in direct continuity with God's saving work in Israel.

Second Reading   Heb 1:1-6

Fittingly, in the second reading and in the gospel reading, two powerful texts, two prologues to writings of paramount christological importance, are brought together in this Mass of Christmas Day. 'Long ago God spoke to our ancestors in many and various ways': the Old Testament is the word of God; God spoke, but fragmentarily, through prophets. Now he 'has spoken' – once for all; and not any more by a prophet but through the Son. God has spoken his final word because this Son is the reflection of God's glory and bears the very stamp of his nature. High Priest of the new covenant, he has achieved purification of sin: in the Son and only in the Son was sin wholly expiated. We Christians do not listen for a whisper of angels. We hearken to the Word: 'the reflection of God's glory and the exact imprint of God's very being.'

Gospel
Jn 1:1-18

The sublime prologue of John's gospel takes up the theme of the second reading and puts it in unmistakable Johannine terms. God has spoken his final word – the Word-made-flesh who has pitched his tent among us. The first part of the prologue (vv. 1-11) speaks about the Son in metaphor, as a 'Word' who brings 'life' from God and as 'light' in so far as he is revealer of God. The second part (vv. 12-18), in more concrete language (Jesus Christ, the Father) describes the positive response to Christ, and the life of Christians as children of God. (See Second Sunday after Christmas.)

THE HOLY FAMILY
SUNDAY WITHIN THE OCTAVE OF CHRISTMAS

First Reading
Sir 3:2-6.12-14

Ben Sirach (author of Sirach or Ecclesiasticus) has the down-to-earth aim of teaching piety and morality and his book is an important witness to the moral outlook of Judaism shortly before the Maccabean age, that is to say, in the early second century B.C. The spirituality of the book is grounded in faith in the God of the covenant, a faith which shows itself in cult and in the practice of justice and mercy. Thus ben Sirach exhorts to humility and kindness to the poor. He denounces pride, sins of the tongue, adultery, covetousness and sloth. The book, in short, abounds in practical religious counsels. Our passage is typical.

One of the more attractive characteristics of earlier, more traditional societies was the care and regard they showed for the elderly. The text of this reading is a commentary on the command to honour father and mother (Ex 20:12; Deut 5:16). Too often we think of the fourth commandment merely in terms of obedience on the part of younger children. Of much greater importance is the obligation of grown children to ensure that their aged parents have a peaceful and comfortable old age so that they can live their final years in dignity. Although the father is the centre of attention here (as one might expect in a patriarchal culture) the advice offered certainly does apply to both parents.

First Reading *ad libitum*
1 Sam 1:20-22.24-28

A story of the dedication to the Lord of the future prophet Samuel. A barren Hannah had prayed for a child (1 Sam 1:9-18); the answer to her prayer is the birth of a son (vv. 9-20). In response to Hannah's vow (v.11), she and her husband Elkanah resolved to dedicate the boy to the service of the Lord. In due course they brought the child to the sanctuary of Shiloh and handed him over to the care of the priest Eli. In 2:1-10 an appropriate hymn is put on the lips of Hannah – a hymn that has manifestly coloured the *Magnificat* (Lk 1:46-55). Hannah, barren and childless, had long suffered the taunts of her rival – Elkanah's other wife. Hannah is the typical oppressed woman of Israel – or of any culture or time. Samuel, the Lord's gift, is a token of God's preferential option for the poor.

Second Reading   Col 3:12-21

This charming passage, with its image of dressing afresh (after the tattered rags of hate and division have been stripped off, 3:5-11) conveys the harmonious atmosphere of a truly Christian community – moving on to the peace of a Christian household. As 'chosen, holy, beloved', Christians are designated as the people of the new covenant. With special stress on mutual forgiveness the author faithfully echoes an exigent demand of Jesus (notably in the Lord's prayer, Mt 6:12-15; Lk 11:4; and in the parable of the unforgiving servant, Mt 18:32-35). Christians are recipients of unbounded divine forgiveness. But if we do not, generously, extend forgiveness to others, we have not really learned to know our loving Lord.

Above all, they must put on love. Almost every descriptive list of virtues in the New Testament culminates in *agapé*, that special brand of brotherly and sisterly love which Jesus singled out as the very hallmark of discipleship (Jn 13:35). The verses, Colossians 3:15-17, show the positive face of morality in a most attracticve light. The 'peace' of Christ is inward security and contentment – the Lord's legacy to his Church. Verse 16 gives a glimpse of a Christian assembly at prayer. 'Do everything in the name of the Lord Jesus.' Doing things in his name reminds us of our belonging to him as members of his body, branches of his vine, empowered to act as his ambassadors in the world.

The Christian community spirit must not be only reflected in the home: it ought to begin there. Yet the demands here in vv. 18-21 leave us uncomfortable: wives are to 'be subject', husbands are 'not to be harsh,' children are 'to obey in everything,' fathers are 'not to provoke' their children – a far cry from the sublimity of vv. 12-17. These demands are time-conditioned, reflecting the outlook and presuppositions of another age and of another culture than ours. Significantly, v. 22 goes on to the master-slave relationship. Here is no fixed immutable ethic, binding for all time. The first part of the reading, rather than its close, truly depicts the atmosphere of the Christian family.

Second Reading *ad libitum* 1 Jn 3:1-2.21-24

The passage, 1 John 3:1-3, expresses confidence in what we are and revelation of what we shall be. The Christian is a child of God, is born of God. The author expresses his amazement that this should be. And, even if we are God's children here and now, we, literally, 'have seen nothing yet'. In the world to come we shall clearly discern our resemblance to our Parent.

The message of 3:20-21 is that, whether Christians have sinned and repented or have not been conscious of sin, they can have confidence. This is because they realize that the God who judges is the God who loves sinners enough to call them his children (3:1; 4:9-10). To be truly children of God is to live, or to strive to live, accordingly. A gracious God will acknowledge our striving.

V. 23 brings together two leading and closely connected themes of the letter: faith in the Son, our brother, and love of his, and our, brothers and sisters.

V. 24 shows that the author does not take 'commandment' in any legalistic sense: he relates it to abiding in God, the closest form of intimate union.

Gospel Lk 2:41-52

The passage, concerning the twelve-year-old Jesus, is hardly an *infancy* narrative (though it is the conclusion of Luke's infancy gospel). Originally, the story seemed to situate the 'christological moment' – the moment when, in christological speculation, Jesus of Nazareth became Son of God – in Jesus' youth: here we have Jesus saying of himself what the heavenly voice will say at the baptism (Lk 3:22). Obviously, for Luke, the punchline is v. 49. Jesus declares that his vocation lies in the service of God who is his Father. Jesus' reply might be paraphrased: 'Where would you expect a child to be but in his father's house?' The significance of the reply is that Jesus declares that God is his Father (in contrast to his legal father, v. 48); he is conscious of his divine Sonship. It follows that the claims of this Father must override all other demands; his mission will break the natural ties of family (see Mk 3:31-35).

Though the episode ends with the Lucan notice of his obedience to

his earthly parents (2:51), his obedience as Son towards his heavenly Father transcends even that filial piety and obedience to Mary
and Joseph. His independent conduct here strikes a chord that will
be heard again in the Gospel proper, will offer a corrective that
reveals that Mary has progresed beyond the stage of misunderstanding attributed to her here (2:50) to one of those who hear the
word of God and keep it. In other words, for Luke Mary may be 'the
mother of the Lord' (1:43), but it is much more important that her
maternal ties yield to those of Jesus' heavenly Father. This is
foreshadowed here. (Fitzmyer, p. 438).

SOLEMNITY OF MARY, MOTHER OF GOD
OCTAVE OF CHRISTMAS

First Reading   Num 6:22-27

This is a priestly blessing, one of the most solemn, and arguably the
most beautiful, in the Old Testament. It is particularly apt on the first
day of the year. Three times the Lord is invoked. Firstly that he might
keep us continually in his protection. The second blessing is a prayer
that God might always be well disposed towards us, that he would let
his face shine on us. The climax is a prayer for peace, the highest gift
of God and the pure sign of his benevolence, when he uncovers his face
towards us. We pray God's blessing on our lives and on our work in
the year ahead; we ask especially for inner peace and for peace among
humankind.

Second Reading   Gal 4:4-7

God's saving plan has reached fruition: the sending forth of his Son
marks the fulness of time. This Son of God, 'born of woman,' shares
fully in our human condition. 'Born under the law', he like all his
people of Israel wore the yoke of the law. But he was able to dispel the
power of the law and free from its yoke all who, through him, would
enter into God's family. Paul had (3:24-25) declared that the law was
transitional; its role was that of *paidagógos*, 'custodian', 'disciplinarian', the slave who looked after the education of a minor until he came
of age. Those under the tutelage of the law would come of age only –
the whole letter makes clear – if they recognized and acknowledged
the Son. As freely-chosen sons and daughters of God they are heirs of
God's promise of salvation and blessedness.

Because their new status is well-nigh unbelievable, the Spirit of

God, sent into their hearts, will assure them of their filial relationship; for, indeed, the vivifying Spirit of the risen Lord is the dynamic principle of adoptive sonship (Rom 1:3; 8:15-17). Speaking to the heart of the Christian, the Spirit gives one the assurance of being a child of God. Sons and daughters of God emboldened by this Spirit will joyfully address their loving Parent as *Abba* – in the intimate manner of the Son their Brother. How sad that formal religiosity so readily shatters this filial trust and casts the Father as a stern judge. Let us be guided by Paul – and by Jesus.

Gospel   Lk 2:16-21

This reading coincides with the Gospel of the Dawn Mass on Christmas Day. Verse 21, however, an addition here, refers to the circumcision and naming of Jesus which is commemorated today. The earlier verses recall Mary's motherhood and her faith as she pondered the meaning of events still veiled – a faith which had won for her a blessing (see 1:45).

The law of circumcising a male child on the eighth day after birth comes from Leviticus 12:3. The description here (v. 21) is parallel to 1:59-63, the circumcision of the Baptist, and here, too, the emphasis is on the bestowal of the name. Born under the law (Gal 4:4) Jesus submitted to the observances of the law – the law which he was destined to bring to an end. It was the father's right to name his child (see Lk 1:62) and in this case, too, the heavenly Father had bestowed the name, indicated beforehand by the angel (1:31). The name of Jesus ('Yahweh saves') was not unknown; it had been borne by Joshua (it is the same) and by Jesus ben Sirach, author of Ecclesiasticus. But here is something new, a name that fits perfectly the character and achievement of that Saviour announced to the shepherds, he who is Christ the Lord (2:11).

SECOND SUNDAY AFTER CHRISTMAS

First Reading   Sir 24:1-2, 8-12

The poem in praise of wisdom (24:1-31) is one of those rich and evocative Old Testament Wisdom texts which laid the groundwork for the Johannine theology of Jesus as the *Logos*, the Word. In Proverbs 8:22-31 and Job 28:12-27 Wisdom is personified: it existed before the visible world and was present with God at creation. Later texts like Ecclesiasticus 24 and Wisdom 7:22-8:1 attribute an active role to

Wisdom in the creation of the world. The fact that Ecclesiasticus 24:23 explicitly identifies Wisdom with the *Torah*, God's 'instruction' to Israel helps us to understand today's reading which stresses the pre-existence of Wisdom ('from eternity, in the beginning, he created me') and its special presence in Israel ('make your dwelling in Jacob; I was established in Zion').

Because Wisdom (or the *Torah*) guided the lives of the people of Israel they were privileged above all peoples. God had clearly made his will known to them and had pointed out the way that would lead to salvation. In spite of the fact that the sages of Israel personified Wisdom and seem to refer to it as something outside God and operating independently of him, it would be quite wrong to think that they ever regarded Wisdom as a divine person distinct from Yahweh. Such an idea would be incompatible with their strict monotheism. If they personified Wisdom and spoke of its pre-existence they did so only to depict poetically and vividly God's plan for the whole created world. Such speculation did, however, prepare for the Christian doctrine of the pre-existence of Jesus (see Jn 1:1-18).

Second Reading   Eph 1:3-6.15-18

Our reading is formed of a blessing (1:3-14) and thanksgiving (1:15-16) leading into an intercession (1:17-2:22). The initial blessing is modelled on the Jewish *berakah*, a 'blessing' of God in response to his previous 'blessing.'

The blessing of Ephesians mentions the major themes of the letter and might be seen as a résumé of the letter. The God of Christians is the Father of our Lord Jesus Christ, the God who has revealed himself in Jesus. To acknowledge Jesus as Lord is to recognize God as Father (v. 3). God has chosen Christians for a purpose: to be holy and blameless before him – in simple words, to be like him (v. 4). We are predestined to be children of God, and we become God's children 'through Jesus Christ.' It is Jesus Christ who has revealed not only that God is Father but also how we are to realize our own divine sonship. If we Christians accept Jesus as 'Lord,' as the supreme influence in our lives, we must accept his view of God and acknowledge him as our Father.

In vv. 15-16 we have the writer's prayer of thanksgiving for his readers' faith and love, which runs, almost at once, into a prayer of intercession. He prays that his readers may really 'know' the 'hope' to which they have been called (vv. 17-18). He thus implies that, despite their faith and love, they still have to progress in their vocation. An understanding of the 'mystery' of God's plan of salvation is possible only as gift of God.

Gospel
Jn 1:1-18

Whatever may be said about the origins of the Prologue (most likely a pre-existing hymn) it now forms a fitting introduction to the Fourth Gospel since it tells us about the divine and eternal origins of him whose ministry is described in the following chapters. One cannot understand the unique significance of Jesus' message of salvation unless one is aware if his mysterious provenance.

The first words of John's gospel recall Genesis 1:1. In the Old Testament God's word manifested him: in creation, in deeds of power, in prophecy. John shows that Jesus Christ, the incarnate Word, is the ultimate revelation of God. The truth that all things were created through him is expressed first positively and then negatively. In vv. 6-8 John introduces the Baptist. He is the first in a file of witnesses who testify to the event of the incarnation. Witness is a fundamental idea in John. He designates as 'the world' those who refuse to accept Jesus and are hostile to him and to his disciples; they remain in darkness. Though his own people, on the whole, did reject him, those who had faith in the incarnate Word became children of God. To them he revealed his glory by his death, resurrection and ascension.

V. 14 is the climax of the hymn. By the incarnation God is present visibly and personally to humankind and has become man in the fullest sense. In the expression 'he pitched his tent among us' John recalls how Yahweh dwelt among the Israelites in the Tent of Meeting (Ex 33:7-11). 'Glory' (*kabod*) is another expression of God's presence (see Ex 40:34; 1 Kgs 8:11). In such terms John is expressing emphatically that, in Jesus, God is present among humankind.

The prologue depicts Jesus primarily as the one who manifests the Father to men and women. Since he alone was with God (v. 1) and since he alone had seen God (v. 18), he alone could reveal the full truth about God. Unlike the synoptists who presented Jesus as the Messiah who inaugurates the Kingdom of God, John will continue in the rest of the Gospel to present Jesus primarily as the Revealer of the Father and of the Father's plan of salvation.

EPIPHANY

First Reading   Is 60-1-6

The background to this reading is the period of restoration after the
first modest return from exile in Babylon soon after 538 B.C. It is a
time of sadness and gloom as the returned exiles survey the ruins of
their city. The prophet's message is one of hope and confidence in
these difficult times; he sees in vision the new, restored Jerusalem
shining like a beacon with the glory of the Lord summoning all people
to come and worship the true God. Its relevance to the feast of the
Epiphany is in the approach of the pagan peoples from Midian, Ephah
and Sheba – descendants of Abraham (Gen 25:1-4) now coming into
their heritage – with their gifts of gold and incense and singing the
praises of the Lord. The opening verses of the reading sound the
keynote of joy and give the passage a universal bearing with the
recurring reference to peoples and nations. Jerusalem when restored
will be the centre of a a new and greater Israel – the Church.

The theme of light, so prominent here, will be taken up in the New
Testament, e.g. 'a light for revelation to the Gentiles' (Lk 2:31). The
contrast between light and darkness points forward to John's Prologue. In sum the message is: the light of deliverance has dawned for
Israel, and all nations will benefit by its radiance (a figure of redemption). The exiles – now a great host, unlike the first pathetic group – are
pictured as gathering for return to Jerusalem, bringing with them the
wealth of the nations (a reversal of the captivity). The nations themselves will come from afar to pay tribute and to worship the Lord who
has made his home in Jerusalem. Though addressed to Jerusalem or to
Israel as God's chosen people now restored to their rightful place, the
prophecy will be fulfilled in Christ ('the light of the world') and in the
new Israel, the Church.

Second Reading   Eph 3:2-3.5-6

This reading effectively expresses the theological significance of the
feast of Epiphany: the fact that God invites all, Jew and Gentile, to
share on an equal footing in the new kingdom of his Son. This is the
mystery: God's plan of salvation, hidden in the past, now revealed in
Christ. It is difficult for us to share the sense of shocked bewilderment
that Jews felt at the fact that pagans were to be accepted on equal terms
with themselves; this is an aspect of the mystery that is particularly
stressed in the passage. The emphasis is on the perfect equality of all
men and women: in Christ all are part of the one body (the meaning of

'in Christ Jesus'). One can observe a definite shift with regard to Old Testament passages (like that of the First Reading) even when these, too, stress the universalilty of the new reign which would be established in Israel. The Magi of today's gospel are the first fruits of the Gentile world coming to receive their share in God's messianic blessings.

Gospel   Mt 2:1-12

In this narrative Matthew has cast back into the infancy of Jesus the reactions that, historically, greeted the proclamation of the risen Lord: some believed and paid homage; others rejected both the message and the preachers. In other words, christological revelation was followed by proclamation and by the twofold reaction of acceptance-homage and rejection-persecution. But this had been prepared for in the ministry of Jesus. The same pattern is presented in the infancy narrative. The negative reaction (of Herod and his advisers, the chief priests and scribes) turns the infancy narrative into a veritable gospel – for the gospel must have suffering and rejection as well as success.

There is little point in looking for the homeland of the Magi – whom Matthew seemingly would regard as astrologers of some sort. Nor is there any point in looking to a comet, a supernova, or a planetary conjunction to account for 'his star' (2:2). A star which rises, goes before, and comes to rest over a place is no natural phenomenon but a miraculous star – more precisely, a symbolic star. (The star may have been suggested by Balaam's oracle, especially in its Greek form: 'a star will arise from Jacob, and a man will stand forth from Israel', Num 24:17). More to the point is the fact that, for Matthew, the Magi represent the Gentiles, fittingly alerted not by an angel (as Luke's Jewish shepherds) but by a star.

The liturgical tradition of our feast of Epiphany has caught Matthew's intent. Note how all the details (the strange visitors from the east, the mysterious star, the gifts) lead up to the final gesture of homage and worship. The adoration of the child Jesus by the Magi fulfils Isaiah's prophecy (First Reading) of the homage to be paid by the nations to the true Israel in the person of the Messiah.

The adoration of the Magi has stirred the imagination of artists and poets down the centuries. There is a large element of mystery about these visitors from the east. Who were they? Where did they come from? They vanish from the gospel as swiftly as they appear. Later Christian tradition has filled in the details, giving them names, making them to be kings. The evangelist wants us to see the contrast between the faith of these pagan visitors and the unbelief of the Jewish leaders: the pagans have answered the call to faith in Christ while the chosen people have for the most part rejected it.

The Old Testament, and popular tradition based on it, form the basis of Matthew's magi story; its purpose is firmly christological. One may, however, find other interest in the characters of the story: in this respect the Magi. They are Gentiles, illustrating the universal breadth of the good news brought by the 'king of the Jews'. They are people of good will, open to God, ready to hear and follow the call of God. They are people prepared to follow a star, wherever it might lead. Open and starry-eyed, they are naive, guileless, easily taken-in by self-serving priests and a murderous king. They are romantic and lovable figures.

THE BAPTISM OF THE LORD
FIRST SUNDAY OF THE YEAR

First Reading   Is 42:1-4.6-7

This is the first of the four great Servant Songs of Second Isaiah. The anonymous prophet of the Exile paints a character portrait of a mysterious servant of God and describes the mission he is called by God to accomplish. The later Servant Songs (in chapters 45, 50 and 53) will fill in the picture with further details culminating in the great hymn of Isaiah 53 in which the redemptive death of the servant is described and his ultimate vindication and triumph. Jesus, in his person and mission, was to realise perfectly this prophetic role of the servant of the Lord, meek and humble of heart, totally dedicated to the will of the Father, accomplishing our salvation through his death and resurrection.

Point by point our passage speaks of: (1) the call or consecration of the servant to the task of bringing justice (that is, true religion, or knowledge of the true God); (2) the qualities of the servant: meekness, patience, mercy; (3) the mission of the servant: true justice or, equivalently, salvation; (4) the idea of 'covenant' suggesting the mediation of a new covenant between God and his people.

First Reading *ad libitum*   Is 40:1-5.9-11

This opening passage (40:1-11) strikes the note of the Book of Consolation (Is 40-55). The exuberant language serves a purpose. It is evident that, among the exiles, there was little yearning for a return.

This was, predominantly, a second generation doing quite nicely in Babylon. A devastated homeland of their ancestors did not beckon compellingly. The prophet had to drum up some enthusiasm. While, humanly speaking, there were no grounds for optimism, he can assure his people that God is ready once again to bring them out of captivity and into the promised land. This time Yahweh will lead them in solemn procession along a *via sacra*, a processional way hewn through mountain, valley and desert, all the way from Babylon to Jerusalem. God will manifest his glory (v. 3) through his saving deed on behalf of his people.

In his poetic vision the prophet hears the voice of God bid a crier run speedily to Jerusalem to carry the good news that the Lord leads his people to freedom. 'Good tidings': it is here that the New Testament writers found their 'gospel' – Good News. His message is to be: 'Here is your God.' The return from the exile fell far short of the glowing picture painted here. Yet, all is not poetic imagery, for the restoration is a sign of salvation; it is, in its measure, a redemption, a new creation. And the message could sometimes be reinterpreted in moral terms: the highway to be made straight was one's own life; the Kingdom was to be prepared for by repentance.

Second Reading   Acts 10:34-38

A significant milestone in Acts is the conversion of Cornelius – so important in fact that, like the conversion of Paul, Luke has narrated it three times (10:1-48; 11:1-18; 15:6-18). In our passage Peter begins his discourse in the house of Cornelius. He proclaims the good news: God has no favourites. He would bring salvation to all people in Jesus Christ. The 'message' that 'spread throughout Judea' refers to the preaching of the good news of 'peace through Jesus Christ' by the apostles, sent first to 'the people of Israel.' Peter's vision (10:9-16) was what made him realize that Christianity was a religion for all people, not a preserve of Jews.

For today's feast the relevant passage in the reading is the description of the baptism: it is the 'anointing' of Jesus of Nazareth 'with the Holy Spirit and with power.' Luke, who all through the Third Gospel and Acts stresses the role of the Spirit in the life of Christ and of the early Christians, thus characteristically describes Jesus' baptism. In the resumé of Jesus' ministry which he places on Peter's lips in the present text he wants to express the idea that God was present in him, in his preaching and in his work, manifesting the divine power to the world and offering salvation to all. This discourse of Peter (10:34-43) is an example of the early Christian preaching (*kerygma*) to non-Jewish converts.

Second Reading *ad libitum*   Tit 2:11-14; 3:4-7

V.11 echoes 1 Tim 2:3-4 – 'God our Saviour desires everyone to be saved.' V.11 insists that Christians live 'in the present age' – in the real world. God's grace permeates the human life of the Christian. It enables us to abandon what the wisdom of our time calls vice and to embrace what that wisdom calls virtue. We live in hope: the full revelation of our God and of our Saviour Jesus Christ. V. 14 echoes Mark 10:45 – 'The Son of Man also came not to be served but to serve, and to give his life a ransom for many.' He was one who 'went about doing good.' He gave himself that his people might, too, do good deeds in his world.

For 3:4-7 see above – Christmas Day: Dawn, p. 35.

Gospel   Lk 3:13-16.21-22

The reading gives a snatch of the Baptist's preaching and concludes with a brief account of the baptism of Jesus. The appearance of John – a prophet, when the spirit of prophecy had long been quenched – raised expectations: could it be that he was the Messiah? Luke has John deny that he is the Messiah. True, he is not as explicit as the fourth evangelist – 'He confessed, and did not deny it, but confessed, 'I am not the Messiah'' (Jn 1:20) but the implied disavowal is obvious enough. The Baptist looks to another whom he designates 'the coming one' and 'the more powerful one.' Not surprisingly, this other will baptize more efficaciously than John. The Baptist knew that his baptism was a preparation rite; it was bound up with a summons to repentance and with a confession of sins and it was simply a preparation for the coming messianic age. By saying that the baptism of the one who was to come would be a baptism 'with the Holy spirit and fire' John was indicating that it would have the purifying effect of fire and that it would give entry to the messianic community by bestowing the new Spirit promised for the end-time.

Luke tells us that Jesus joined the people who went to receive the baptism of John. He does not describe the baptism itself because he was more interested in the divine revelation and in the coming of the Spirit. The early Christians were conscious of the problem of Jesus joining the ranks of sinners who approached John (see Mt 3:14-15). Luke has shown that Jesus' acceptance of baptism was in keeping with his view of his messianic mission. He had come to minister to sinners and although he was sinless he would identify with them (see 2 Cor 5:21).

It is not surprising that Luke, with his interest in prayer, tells us that Jesus prayed at the baptism. Luke indeed gives the impression that it was in response to the prayer of Jesus that the Holy Spirit came upon him. And not impression only; it is Luke's intent that we should see it so. Later (11:13) we learn that the heavenly Father gives the Holy Spirit to those who ask. And Jesus' prayer was a plea to the Father that God would manifest himself, would declare their relationship. Unlike Mark and Matthew, Luke with his 'in bodily form' emphasizes that the event was a public event and not something that Jesus alone was conscious of. The figure of the dove at Jesus' baptism, likely, has reference to his mission. The dove was a symbol of the people of Israel (Ps 74:19) and a message of hope (Gen 8:8,12). Luke's baptism-story shows Jesus as a Spirit-filled Son and Servant, a messenger of God to his people.

Lent

Introduction to the Liturgical Season

The readings for Lent are best understood in relation to conversion and baptism. They put before us the contrast between life and death, light and darkness, grace and sin. They ask us to choose life. They assure us that the God who created the human race will never abandon it. They promise newness of life in Christ.

GOSPELS

For the first and second Sundays, the Gospels are those of the temptation and the transfiguration. For the third, fourth and fifth Sundays, the Gospels this year are on the theme of conversion and God's mercy: on the third and fourth Sundays they are from Luke, and contain the image of the fig tree which is given one more chance to bear fruit, and the parable of the prodigal son; on the fifth Sunday the Gospel is the possibly Lucan passage from John about the woman taken in adultery.

FIRST READINGS

The First Readings are chosen, as always, to harmonize with the Gospels. They are also meant to take us through some of the great moments in the history of salvation, as part of the catechesis which characterizes Lent. This year we see the creed of God's people, "My father was a wandering Aramaean", the covenant made with Abraham, the call of Moses, the celebration of Passover on arrival in the promised land, and the promise in Isaiah that the Lord will do a new deed and give his people to drink.

SECOND READINGS

The Second Readings harmonize with the First Readings and the Gospels, and try to provide a link between them. So, in Year C, they reflect on believing from the heart and confessing with the lips, the heavenly homeland, the warning contained in the history of God's people, reconciliation and new creation, and the newness that comes through faith in Christ.

Philip Gleeson OP

Lent

First Reading   Deut 26:4-10

The passage 26:1-11 is eminently suited for reading at Mass because
it describes a liturgical ceremony – with written-in rubrics. It is the
ceremony of the offering of the firstfruits. The firstfruits of the harvest
are to be placed in a basket and taken to the shrine of Yahweh. The
offerer will go to the priest on duty and declare: 'Today I declare to the
Lord your God that I have come into the land that the Lord swore to
our ancestors to give us' (v. 3). When the priest has taken the basket
and set it before the altar the offerer will recite his credo. That begins
with reference to Jacob (the 'wandering Aramean') and his descent
into Egypt. But Jacob is no longer an individual: he is Israel the nation.
(Note how v. 5 passes from the individual Jacob to the nation Israel).
This creed is really a summary of Israel's early history, from the
patriarchs to the possession of the land first promised to Abraham

The readings of the following Sundays will spell out individual
items in greater detail. We may note the concrete form this profession
of faith takes. It looks on God as the God who acts, whose fidelity to
the promises is seen in history. Noteworthy is the change from 'he' to
'we', 'us'; this shows the deep Hebrew feeling of participation in a
common historical heritage and tradition. Even more significantly it
expresses an awareness that the liturgy makes a saving event present
and brings the worshipper right into it.

Second Reading   Rom 10:8-13

Of its nature, faith is open to God's future intervention and thus issues
in hope. The tragedy of Israel in Jesus' day was that its faith was no
longer open in this sense. Having made of its own human traditions the
yardstick for the relevance of God's word, Israel was not prepared to
hear God speaking again to his people through Jesus. As Paul could say
of his own people in the passage immediately preceding today's
reading: 'I can testify that they have a zeal for God, but it is not
enlightened. For, being ignorant of the righteousness that comes from
God, and seeking to establish their own, they have not submitted to
God's righteousness' (10:2-3). God's way of righteousness was acceptance of redemption through faith in Christ.

This is what is implied in the Christian credo which in its simplest
form, given in today's reading, ran: 'Jesus is Lord'; that is, Jesus is the

risen Saviour, the one who died for our sins and was raised up for our justification. That this faith be genuine implies acceptance of what Christ's death and resurrection mean: death to sin and a life in accord with Christ's 'law' – paradoxically, a law of *freedom* (see Gal 5:1). It is a faith accessible to all who have heard the preaching of the gospel, without distinction of person, of Jew or non-Jew, of rich or poor.

Gospel
Lk 4:1-13

Luke's temptation narrative is very close to that of Matthew 4:1-11 except that he inverts the order of the last two temptations. Matthew's order is more logical and it can scarcely be doubted that Luke has deliberately changed the order so that the series may end at Jerusalem; this in keeping with his special theological interest in the holy city. The three scenes serve to correct a false understanding of Jesus' mission as Son. They depict him as the Son of God obedient to his Father's will, the faithful Son who will not be turned to using his power or authority for any reason other than that for which he had been sent.

In each of his three replies to Satan Jesus cites texts from Deuteronomy and these texts are the key to the meaning of each scene. (1) 'One does not live by bread alone' (Deut 8:3). Jesus had been challenged to seek food for himself, to use his power as Son apart from his Father's design. (2) 'Worship the Lord your God, and serve only him' (6:13). Jesus had been challenged to acknowledge someone other than the Father as Lord and master. If he is to have dominion he will have it from the Father alone. (3) 'Do not put the Lord your God to the test' (6:16). Again Jesus is challenged to use his power on his own behalf, this time to dazzle his contemporaries and conform to their idea of what a heaven-sent leader should be. Each time Jesus had vanquished Satan by 'the sword of the Spirit, which is the word of God' (Eph 6:17).

Jesus was 'tempted' in every respect as we, yet without sinning (Heb 4:15). He redeemed us as one of our race. God saw it fitting that the Son who leads men and women to salvation should be made perfect through suffering (2:10). Jesus learned from his sufferings what obedience to God's will means for humankind – 'and having been made perfect, he became the source of eternal salvation for all who obey him' (5:9). The temptations of Jesus are the temptations of Christians of all ages: the temptation to seek one's own glory even in religious matters; to seek the easy way and turn aside from suffering; the temptation to forget that the source of Christian life is to be found in the death and resurrection of Christ. Jesus redeemed humankind as the Suffering Servant, as Son of Man, by taking human nature on himself and uniting himself fully with his fellow men and women. We, in our turn, are redeemed by uniting ourselves with Christ, in his death and resurrection, by resisting sin and the temptations to it that assail us on many sides. It is these truths that the Church wishes to keep before our minds during the Lenten and Easter seasons.

SECOND SUNDAY OF LENT

First Reading   Gen 15:5-12.17-18

In this reading we learn of the solemn covenant between God and Abraham which is fundamental for an understanding of God's relationship with Israel. Abraham had already been promised innumerable descendants and possession of the land of Canaan through which he journeyed as a foreigner. Our passage presupposes an ancient rite of treaty- or covenant-making. To ratify a treaty or pact the contracting partners cut an animal (or animals) in two and walked between the divided parts, invoking the fate of the animals on themselves should they fail to observe the terms of the contract (see Jer 34:18). Since God's covenant with Abraham is unilateral only God (symbolized by the furnace and the torch) passes between the pieces.

This act is a divine pledge of fidelity. Because the covenant is sheer gift, Abram (as the 'man' in Genesis 2:21 when he receives the gift of woman) is smitten with the *tardemah*, a profound sleep: he is 'out cold'; the initiative is God's alone. The birds symbolize the forces hostile to Israel, forces that will be conquered through the faith of Abraham and by reason of God's covenant with him.

Thus, at the exodus (Ex 2:24), God recalls his covenant with Abraham and the patriarchs and in his faithfulness saves Israel. This covenant, then, leads to the exodus, the passover and the new covenant at Sinai. It also stands behind the possession of Canaan under the leadership of Joshua. In the course of time it would be made clear to Israel that more was included in the promise than possession of a given parcel of land. The concept 'land' would become spiritualized to mean the plenitude of messianic promises, the kingdom of heaven. It was in this spiritualized sense that Jesus, the true Joshua (Jesus is the Greek form of the name Joshua) would fulfil the promise made to Abraham. As leader of this new people he would lead them through the desert of this world to their eternal rest, to the real land of promise which is heaven.

Second Reading
Phil 3:17 4:1

Even the early Churches were not without fault, despite special graces. Christianity is indeed liberty, but it is freedom to live the Christian life, to come to know Christ and the power of his resurrection; it is the power to conquer sin and live in Christ which was given by the Spirit of the risen Saviour; it is the freedom to live a life in God's friendship which leads to the resurrection from the dead (Phil 3:10-11). The true Christian inheritance is described in 3:20-21. As important as their Roman citizenship was to the Philippians, their true city, their home or 'commonwealth' is heaven; Christians have a dual citizenship. As citizens of heaven they should perform their duties as citizens by a life worthy of the gospel (1:27), setting their minds on their real homeland. This does not mean withdrawal from one's duties as citizens of this world, as members of the human race. Humankind has the obligation of labouring for a better world, and this even by reason of the religion one professes. The believer, however, must see this world in perspective and so use temporal things so as not to lose things eternal. This outward and forward glance is, in fact, in the best interests of the earthly city. Looking on created realities as all that matter leads to sin and the ultimate disruption of the social order.

Gospel
Lk 9:28-36

At the baptism when Jesus was to begin his ministry the Father addressed him as his beloved Son in whom he was well pleased. Peter's confession at Caesarea Philippi marked a turning point in Jesus' life. From then on his gaze was turned towards Jerusalem, Calvary and the resurrection that would follow. At Caesarea Philippi, however, Jesus had corrected Peter's understanding of the messiahship by stressing his suffering and death (9:18-22). The transfiguration which followed on Peter's confession confirms the last part of the announcement 'and on the third day be raised.' Here, too, Peter had misunderstood. The three booths, one each for Jesus, Elijah, and Moses, would have put all three on an equal footing. Peter really 'did not know what he said.'

The voice from heaven will set the matter straight: 'This is my Son, my Chosen.' Jesus is not a Moses or an Elijah *redivivus* – he is God's Son and Chosen One. 'Listen to him': this Son is also the prophet-like-Moses whose teaching must be heeded (see Deut 18:15-19). Luke tells us that Moses and Elijah, representatives of the Old Testament, of the law and the prophets, had spoken with Jesus of his *exodos* (his exit, his passing, his departure) which he was to accomplish in Jerusalem. His 'exodus' was his death, his passing to the Father, which would be the new exodus of salvation for Christians. Furthermore, the three privileged disciples 'saw his glory': not yet a vision of the resurrection glory but, at least, a passing glimpse of it. The transfiguration episode took on significance when the disciples looked back on it in the light of resurrection. It helped them to realise that the glory of the risen Lord was hiddenly present in Jesus of Nazareth.

It is no longer possible to say what it was that transpired upon the mountain – Was it vision? Was it deep religious experience? We have been concerned with Luke's presentation of it; perhaps, behind his text, we can sense the original import. In the entire first part of Luke's narrative (9:28-32) Jesus holds the centre stage. He goes up on a mountain, the place of divine manifestation. He becomes absorbed in prayer and, in the immediacy of God's presence, his countenance is altered and his raiment shines with heavenly whiteness. Two angels ('two men,' v. 30), the biblical mediators of revelation, appear to him and speak of his 'exodus,' that is, his death. In other words, Jesus, in an ineffable mystical experience, receives a revelation that his fate is to suffer and die.

THIRD SUNDAY OF LENT

First Reading   Ex 3:1-8.13-15

On the occasion of the covenant with Abraham (first reading of the previous Sunday) God told the patriarch that his descendants would be slaves in a foreign country, Egypt. In that enslavement God remembered his covenant with Abraham, Isaac and Jacob (Ex 2:23-25) and intervened to rescue them. Moses, the one destined to be the deliverer, had fled for refuge to Sinai; he was received by the Midianite priest, Jethro, whose daughter he married. While there he had a vision of God at the sacred mountain of Sinai (also called Horeb) the 'vision of the burning bush.' There God revealed his name: Yahweh. The meaning of the name is given in v. 14 – literally, 'I am who am', but best translated as 'I am the Existing One'. Yahweh is the God whom Israel had to recognize as really existing.

The context is important. Just before the revelation of the divine name, God calls Israel his people (Ex 3:10) and tells Moses that it is this people that he must bring out of Egypt (3:11) and that he, God, will be with them for that task (v. 12). Yahweh is with Moses to save his people with whom he is united in a special way – Israel is his first-born son. Yahweh's care of his people is primary: he sends Moses to bring them out of Egypt and he commands the pharaoh to let them go. It is also for the benefit of the people that he reveals his name. The result is that Israel must recognize that Yahweh is, for Israel, the only Existing One and the only Saviour.

Second Reading
1 Cor 10:1-6,10-12

According to Exodus 13:21-22 a pillar of cloud went before the Israelites by day. In Psalm 105:39 it is said that 'he spread a cloud to cover them' and in Wisdom 19:7 the cloud 'overshadowed the camp.' In midrashic development the waters of Exodus 14:21-22 parted, to form something like a tunnel, to enable the Israelites to pass through. Exodus 17:6 describes how water gushed from the rock at Horeb when Moses had struck it. In rabbinic tradition this rock, with its spring of water, was said to accompany the Israelites in their desert wanderings.

It is against such a background that the otherwise hopelessly enigmatic Pauline passage may be understood. In passing through the sea, under Moses' leadership, the Israelites were delivered from bondage; and they were 'baptized into Moses,' united under him to form with him no longer a motley grouping of tribes but a people. So, too, the Apostle implies, Christians have been delivered by Christ and have been incorporated into him through baptism in water and the Holy Spirit. The 'spiritual (*pneumatikos*) food' is the manna (Ex 16:4, 14-18), spiritual because of its heavenly origin but, for Paul, more particularly because it is a type of the eucharistic bread. The water from the rock, too, as 'spiritual drink' also symbolizes the Eucharist. The food and drink of the Christian people of God was already anticipated in the heaven-given food and drink of the desert people of God. Christ becomes the rock which accompanied the wanderings of the Israelites; Moses becomes a type of the Messiah and, in some sort, anticipates baptism into Christ. The saving events of the journey through sea and wilderness are applied to Baptism and the Lord's Supper. We are dealing with a very early eucharistic theology.

Gospel
Lk 13:1-9

In popular religion of all times the misfortune befalling people can come to be looked on as divine chastisement for personal sins. It is after all but a short step from the belief that God punishes sin to a consideration of the accidents, mishaps, and so on that befall a person as penalties directly inflicted by God. Today's reading tells us how Jesus was once asked a question on the subject. Jesus' reply is that the mishaps that befall people are no indication at all that they are sinners. Yet it is equally true, he says, that sin calls for repentance. In declaring 'Unless you repent, you will all perish just as they did,' Jesus is primarily addressing the Jewish nation which was coming more and more to reject him. Unless they repent of this, he tells them, they will lose the promises; the kingdom will be taken from them and given to the Gentiles; the nation will end in revolt and Jerusalem in ruins.

The parable of the barren fig-tree teaches the same message. Luke, who has omitted the cursing of the fig tree (Mk 11:12-14), is alone in giving this parable. The tree had come to fruit-bearing age some three years before, and since it gave every sign of remaining unfruitful the owner of the vineyard felt it should be cut down. The vinedresser, however, pleaded for time; he would make a last desperate effort to save it – the putting on of manure was an unusual step. The fig tree symbolized Israel (see Hos 9:10; Jer 8:13) and, as in Jeremiah, a sterile Israel. Now the axe is laid to the root of the tree (Mt 3:10); this is the last chance. If, in the short moment left, Israel does not bring forth the fruits of repentance the time of grace will have run out. Throughout, the urgency of the hour is stressed and the warning is plain.

FOURTH SUNDAY OF LENT

First Reading   Josh 5:9-12

During the forty years Israel spent in the desert between the exodus from Egypt and its entry into Canaan, the promised land, its existence was semi-nomadic. A new era began when the people crossed the Jordan to take possession of the land of promise. Egypt and all it stood for in Israelite tradition (sin, darkness, bondage) lay behind. Israel could now face the future. The chain of events that led up to possession of the land began with the passover in Egypt. Now that they have reached the goal God's people celebrate anew the passover and the feast of unleavened bread that accompanied it. Possession of the land really became a reality when Israel ate of the produce of Canaan. Then the manna that fed them during the desert period ceased to be available to them. Like Israel the Church began with a passover and will end with the eternal passover of salvation. And during its earthly sojourn its spiritual food will be the Eucharist, the true food from heaven.

Second Reading   2 Cor 5:17-21

Possession of the land of Canaan was fulfilment, in a political and limited sense, of the promise made to the patriarchs. The nature of the blessings contained in this promise was richer and deeper than these early generations of Israelites dreamed of. The reality within the promise was a secret to be revealed only in the New Testament age. So great is the glory and splendour of the new dispensation that in comparison with it the Old Testament had no glory at all (2 Cor 3:10).

The work of Christ, in fact, takes one back beyond Abraham to the very beginnings of the world. It is nothing less than a new creation. It establishes again the friendship of God with humankind (see Gen 2). For, in Christ, God has reconciled the world to himself. 'God was in Christ, reconciling the world to himself' (v. 18). This is arguably the very best Christological statement, and it weds cristology with soteriology. Where Jesus is, there is God; and God is God *for us*. It was for our sake that God made him 'to be sin' (5:21); that is, God had sent his Son 'in the likeness of sinful flesh' (Rom 8:3), in order to become a sacrifice for sin. By dying in his flesh, the sensible sign of the sinful world, and by rising in a body made new, Christ himself and in him, virtually, all humanity passed from the carnal to the spiritual life. The Church has been commissioned to carry on his redeeming work, by exhorting people to repent and by imparting, through the sacraments, the effects of Christ's death and resurrection. It devotes the period of Lent to this exhortation.

Gospel   Lk 15:1-3.11-32

'There was a man who had two sons' – so opens the familiar parable of The Prodigal Son. Its Lucan setting would fix it, credibly, in the ministry of Jesus. The 'grumbling' of v. 2 speaks so much. The Pharisees had set the Torah as the way of righteousness and had found in the meticulous observance of it the achievement of righteousness. All who did not know the Law, or who did not keep it, were 'sinners,' strangers to the way of righteousness. 'But this crowd, which does not know the law – they are accursed' (Jn 7:49). Jesus staunchly refused to categorise people; to him no one is an outcast. The Pharisees could not bear that Jesus welcomes 'sinners' and sought them out. Worst of all, and there is a note of disgust, if not a note of horror, he 'eats with them'! It was axiomatic that one could not have communion with 'sinners'; contact with these outcasts rendered one ritually unclean. What right had Jesus to flout so basic a requirement of the broader Torah?

The story of the father and his two sons is allegory; the characters are God, the sinner and the righteous. Jesus' purpose was not only to depict God's gracious forgiveness. It was to hold the mirror up to his opponents. It was to challenge them to see themselves in the older son.

'So he set off and went' (v. 20). This was what the father had longed for. Not a word of reproof. Stirred only by loving compassion, he embraced and kissed the lost one. *All* is forgiven. The son's little speech is no longer a confession (as his rehearsed speech was meant to be); it is a spontaneous response to forgiveness. There are no strings to this forgiveness. Best robe, signet ring, shoes: the youth is reinstated. He is son as though he had never left, had never gone astray. Nor is this the end. It is a moment to be savoured, a time for joymaking. Such is *God's* forgiveness, Jesus says. God casts our sins behind his back; he buries them in the deeps of the sea. It is all too much for humankind as the second part of the parable brings out.

In contrast, the attitude of the elder brother was effective armour against the plea of vulnerability and the foolishness of love. He had never really known his father, and now he rejects his brother. The story ends with an invitation: the elder son is invited to acknowledge his brother and enter into the joy of homecoming. Only so will he know his father as *Father*.

On many counts this is a disturbing story for us Christians of today. Luke took it out of the ministry of Jesus and addressed it directly to the pharisees in his own Christian community. And, surely, we must look to ourselves, to our possible resentment towards God's graciousness to sinners. We can find comfort in the warm treatment of the younger son. Always, there is the father. He is the real challenge. Our gracious and forgiving God holds the stage.

This story persuasively shows God's loving concern for humankind and, in particular, his favouritism toward the outcast. It sets a question-mark against the theology of forgiveness reflected in much of our penitential practice. God's forgiveness seems too good to be true. Above all, there is the uncomfortable message that one really comes to understand this Father only by acknowledging the brother and sister as brother and sister – a lesson learned by the author of 1 John: 'Those who do not love a brother or sister whom they have seen cannot love the God whom they have not seen' (4:20).

FIFTH SUNDAY OF LENT

First Reading   Is 43:16-21

Second Isaiah addresses the Jews exiled in Babylon far from the promised land. His message to them is that there will be a new exodus, a redemption so glorious that the great events of the past need scarcely be remembered any longer. Their God is the redeemer who will gather together the scattered exiles and lead them back to their homeland. Today's reading begins by recalling that it was God who led Israel through the Red Sea at the exodus from Egypt. There 'Pharaoh's chariots and his army he cast into the sea; they went down into the depths like a stone' (Ex 15:4-5). The marvels of the exodus time will now be repeated, but this time in the desert between Babylon and Palestine. Israel can see the past being repeated in the present and look forward to a repetition of it in the future because its God is the God of the covenant.

Exodus and covenant could never merely be events of the past for the good reason that in each God's fidelity to his promise was involved. The first exodus fulfilled the promise made to Abraham and was at the same time a divine pledge that the divine plan of redemption would be perfected. And so Israel looked forward to a new exodus and a new covenant. These came along after the days of Second Isaiah – with the death and resurrection of Christ in fact. With this Old Testament reading the liturgy takes us to the threshold of the New, to the new and eternal covenant in the blood of Christ.

Second Reading
Phil 3:8-14

It is clear that the opening part (3:2-11) of the third chapter of Philippians is directed at Jews or judaizers. In referring to them as 'dogs' (v. 2), Paul turns back on them their own insulting estimate of Gentiles. He, Hebrew of Hebrews, a Pharisee by training, a flawless observer of the Law, is no less a Jew than any of them (vv. 4-6). In verses 7-10 Paul poignantly spells out the difference between his life as a Christian and his life as a Pharisee. He had, indeed, experienced a conversion – a radical change. But, to his eternal credit, he does not disparage his past, he makes no apologies. He had been granted a new vision in the light of which the past appeared in different guise. But he acknowledged the integrity of his former life.

Still, all of this which those others see as grounds of self-justifica-tion, he has sacrificed for Christ and for the justification that comes from God and for the hope of resurrection. Paul had learned that his zeal had to be channeled in another direction. The zeal that had made him a persecutor will now lead him into the role of victim. Henceforth, Paul's whole life becomes a radical critique of 'religion.' Christ has taken possession of Paul – but Paul is not complacent. Like a runner at the last stage of a race he keeps his eye on the winning tape and does not look back: the prize is yet to be won. Paul presses on, leaving behind him the privileges of his Jewish past, his blamelessness according to the law, the self-righteousness that flowed from it, and the painful memory of his persecution of the Church. He looks now only to 'the heavenly call of God in Christ Jesus.' With that goal in view nothing else at all matters.

Paul will not hesitate (v. 17) to propose himself to his disciples as a model to be imitated, for he is conscious of being a faithful imitator of Christ (see 1 Cor 11:1). The message of his life is that all Christian life is a living out of the paschal mystery of the dying and resurrection of Christ. By putting to death in themselves everything that is contrary to Christ, and by the trials and sufferings inherent in Christian living, believers share in Christ's death. In so doing, they experience the power of his resurrection. Through the power of the Holy Spirit they are changed into the image of Christ. This is the goal of all Christian life, for every believer as much as for the apostle of the Gentiles.

Gospel

Jn 8:1-11

This passage – The Woman Taken in Adultery – is not in context in the Fourth Gospel, while in form and style it closely resembles the synoptic tradition. It is quite in the style of Luke. It seems to have been inserted in John because of the reference of judgment according to the Law in John 7:51.

The purpose of the scribes and pharisees in bringing the adulteress to Jesus was to set a snare for him. If Jesus pardoned her, he could be accused of encouraging people to break the law of Moses which prescribed death by stoning for such conduct (Lev 20:10; Deut 13:9-10). In fact, as the wisdom literature makes clear, that grim prescription had long been a dead letter – but the law could still be invoked as a challenge to Jesus. And, if he would agree that she should be stoned to death, be would lose his name for mercy. Jesus deftly turned the challenge: let the woman's accusers look to their own sins! He will not be judge. Although the Father had given full authority to his Son to pass judgment (Jn 5:22) Jesus really judges no one (8:15). His message is of mercy and forgiveness.

The story ends with the quiet scene of reconciliation between Jesus and the woman and Jesus is left alone with her to proclaim God's mercy (vv. 1-11). Augustine comments: *relicti sunt duo – misera et misericordia*: two stood alone there – wretchedness and Mercy.

Passion Sunday and Sacred Triduum

Introduction to the Liturgical Season

Passion Sunday and the Sacred Triduum are the centre of the Church's liturgical year. They proclaim the suffering, death and resurrection of Jesus. They evoke the whole history of salvation. They recall the two great sacraments of Baptism and Eucharist. They call for conversion, and encourage us to bear witness to the risen Lord.

GOSPELS

The gospel readings take us through the Passion (Passion Sunday and Good Friday) and proclaim the Resurrection (Easter Vigil and Easter Sunday). If Mass is celebrated during the evening of Easter Sunday, the account of the road to Emmaus may be read. We also hear the account of the entry into Jerusalem (the procession on Passion Sunday). And, on Holy Thursday, there is the great symbol of Jesus' washing the feet of the disciples, a gesture which helps to show the meaning of the whole paschal mystery.

READINGS FROM THE OLD TESTAMENT

Again we read from the book of Isaiah, the third and fourth songs of the suffering servant (Passion Sunday and Good Friday). We are reminded of the institution of the Passover meal (Holy Thursday). The Easter Vigil is provided with seven readings from the Old Testament: the creation; the sacrifice of Abraham; the crossing of the Red Sea (never to be omitted); the passage from Isaiah about the everlasting love and faithfulness of the Lord, the creator and husband of his people; the invitation in Isaiah to come to the water; the passage in Baruch calling the people back to faithfulness; the passage in Ezekiel about the Lord pouring clean water over his people, and giving them a new heart.

READINGS FROM THE NEW TESTAMENT

Readings from the New Testament take up the theme of the passion, 'He was humbler yet ... ' (Philippians, Passion Sunday); 'He learnt to obey through suffering ... ' (Hebrews, Good Friday). They give us the tradition about the two great sacraments, the Eucharist (1 Corinthians, Holy Thursday) and Baptism (Romans, Easter Vigil). The Second Reading on Easter Sunday is a choice between Colossians on dying and rising with Christ, or 1 Corinthians, on Christ our Passover. And, on Easter Sunday, the first reading is from Acts, Peter's witness to the resurrection addressed to Cornelius and his household.

Philip Gleeson OP

Passion Sunday and Paschal Triduum

PASSION (PALM) SUNDAY

Processional Gospel
Lk 19:28-40

Apart from a few changes in detail, Luke has transcribed Mark 11:1-8. Clearly, the text of Zechariah 9:9-10 is in view: 'Rejoice greatly, O daughter Zion! Shout aloud, O daughter Jerusalem! Lo, your King comes to you; triumphant and victorious is he, humble and riding on a donkey, on a colt the foal of a donkey.' Yet, for all the similarity with Mark, Luke's introductory verse (28) sounds another note. Jesus 'went on ahead, going up to Jerusalem.' He went up to receive a kingdom – not any earthly kingdom, but kingdom of God. In v.38 Luke has clearly recast the acclamation (see Mk 11:9-10) on the model of the angels' canticle (Lk 2:14). The entry of Jesus into Jerusalem as messianic king is a sign that the peace, the salvation, decreed by God ('in heaven') is at hand; by that fact God glorifies his name, that is, manifests his power. The Pharisees obviously fear that the general enthusiasm may lead to a disturbance. But the moment is more significant than they suspect (vv.39-40). If people were silent, nature itself would proclaim this event (see Habakkuk 2:11). The acclamation of Jesus has taken place on the Mount of Olives – the symbolic 'mountain.' This episode is distinct from the entry, the purpose of which is that Jesus may take possession of the Temple (v.45).

First Reading
Is 50:4-7

In this extract from the third Servant Song (Is 50:4-9) the enigmatic figure is presented firmly as a teacher who has to learn before he can communicate his message to others (50:4-50). This message evidently meets with opposition and prompts the persecution of the Servant by the very people to whom he brings comfort (v. 6). But this is all part of the Servant's training. It is by suffering that his true mettle is proved and he is shown to be a faithful Servant. Through his confidence in Yahweh's unfailing support (v. 7) he testifies to Yahweh's power to draw victory out of apparent failure and to the ultimate triumph of his message. The problem of who precisely the Servant is does not obscure the central point that he is one in tune with God who hears God's message.

This is the challenge presented to us by the Servant whom we Christians, through the experience of salvation, know Jesus to be. We can see how perfectly well he was attuned to the will of the Father, knowing his word and bringing it to people.

Second Reading   Phil 2:6-11

It is widely accepted that this hymn is pre-Pauline. Paul has adopted it with some characteristic additions ('even death on a cross', 'in heaven and on earth and under the earth', 'to the glory of God the Father'). Christ Jesus, the subject of the poem, is in 'the form of God': the word 'form' designates the divine sphere in which God dwells. But Jesus did not snatch at and jealously guard the glorious condition that was his by right. Instead he 'emptied' himself; the nature of this *kenósis* ('emptying') is explained by the clauses that follow: he rendered himself powerless as a slave is powerless. Jesus, truly human, wished to share to the full the weakness of the human condition, except for sin (Gal 4:4; Rom 8:3; Heb 2:17). Like the slave he had chosen to become, he was obedient unto death; and the utter abasement of Jesus is emphasized by reference to the manner of his death, that of a common criminal. But from the depths plumbed by his self-renunciation, God has exalted his Servant to unparalleled heights by resurrection and ascension. And he has granted him the title of 'Lord.' The hymn reflects the words of Jesus himself: 'Was it not necessary that the Messiah should suffer … ?' (Lk 24:26).

But Paul cites the hymn not primarily for its christological depth but because it is a reminder to his readers of the 'mind' of Jesus, which should also be theirs (Phil 2:5). Jesus' career is not to be contemplated from afar, it is to the imitated. Christology is not just to be studied, it is to be lived. All Christians are to realize Jesus' career in their lives by 'emptying' themselves in the service of their fellows in humility and by finding God's will in the seemingly most hopeless circumstances. For nothing is more apparently hopeless than death. The whole purpose of Jesus' career is not that he should live, suffer, die and rise instead of us, but that we should be able to model our own lives on his. If Jesus is Saviour, his Church is Servant and will be properly successful only at the price of service and humiliation to the point of death.

The Passion   Lk 22:14 - 23:56

The four evangelists tell essentially the same story, but do so each in a distinctive manner. The Fourth Gospel obviously stands apart from the others. But, even among the Synoptics, differences are marked. This is so even in the area where all the evangelists meet most fully, in the Passion narratives. Because the Passion Narrative of Luke is read on Passion Sunday of Year C, it is appropriate to indicate here some of the distinctive features of Luke's text. I follow relevant lines of Raymond E. Brown's investigation (*The Death of the Messiah*, 2 vols, New York/London: Doubleday/Chapman 1994).

MARK AND LUKE

Mark's gospel is a *theologia crucis* – a theology of the cross. Understandably, this concern comes to a head in his Passion Narrative. It is evident in the Gethsemane episode (14:32-44) – 'he began to be distressed and agitated' (v 33): Jesus is shattered. He died with an anguished shout: 'My God, my God, why have you forsaken me?' (15:34). Mark has Jesus die in total isolation, without any relieving feature at all. It is only after death that Jesus is clearly recognized and acknowledged by any human in the awed confession of the centurion: 'Truly, this man was God's Son!' (15:39). Mark is making a theological point: salvation is never of oneself, not even for Jesus. That awful and awesome journey to the cross is comfort for all who have seen in Jesus of Nazareth the image of the invisible God. It is the consolation of all who have found in him the ultimate assurance that God is on our side. It is, above all, comfort for all who find it hard to bear the cross. It was not easy for the Master.

Luke has followed Mark's Passion Narrative, but has notably changed the tone of it. The Lucan Jesus is never distraught or agitated. The Lucan Jesus never experiences Godforsakenness. Instead, he is serenely in communion with his Father throughout, to the very end: 'Father, into your hands I commend my spirit' (23:46). Here is a positive aspect of the passion not found in Mark. And, in the Lucan gospel, it is not surprising to find stress on the healing and forgiving power of God mediated through Jesus, even in the passion. We turn to some special Lucan features in his Passion Narrative.

GETHSEMANE LK 22:39-46

Mark tells us that at Gethsesmane 'Jesus began to be distressed and agitated' and he said to his disciples: 'I am deeply grieved even unto death' (14:33-34). In contrast Luke has no portrait of Jesus in distress. The Lucan Jesus is so at peace with God that he cannot be distraught by suffering. There is, besides, a concern to have Jesus in his passion revealed as a model for Christian sufferers and martyrs. Proper to Luke are vv. 43-44 – 'Then an angel from heaven appeared to him and gave him strength. And being in agony, he prayed more earnestly, and his

sweat became like great drops of blood falling down on the ground.'
Assisting angels figure in stories of martyrs, Jewish and Christian. On
a wider showing, an angel can dramatize answer to prayer, as in the
Tobit story. Luke's angel gives striking expression to Hebrews 5:7 –
'he was heard because of his reverent submission.' The *agonia* of Lk
22:44 is not the distress and agitation of Mark 14:33. Rather, it refers
to anguished tension in face of entry into the great trial, the *peirasmos*
(v. 40). It is an athletic metaphor; see 1 Timothy 6:12; 2 Timothy 4:7,
'fighting the good fight' (*agón*).

> The Father cannot spare Jesus from drinking the cup, but the
> strengthening angel prepares Jesus so that he arises from prayer in
> tense readiness for the combat with the approaching power of
> darkness (Lk 22:53). The sweat that breaks forth and flows as freely
> as blood is the visible sign of that readiness for the cup and hints at
> martyrdom (Brown, *Death of the Messiah*, p. 190)

It should be acknowledged that the authenticity of these verses is
not quite sure: the manuscript witness is almost equally divided for and
against. On the whole, it is easier to explain omission rather than later
insertion. Christian scribes would have been embarrassed by the
portrait of a Jesus who needed angelic assistance.

ARREST   22:47-53

The question, 'Lord, should we strike with the sword?' (22:49) is a
Lucan addition echoing the Last Supper reference to possession of two
swords (v. 38). Distinctively Lucan is Jesus' healing of the servant
whose ear had been severed (v. 51). It is an instance of a recurring
motif: Jesus is healer and saviour throughout the Passion. Another
Lucan touch is 'the power of darkness' (v. 53). At the close of the
temptation story the devil departed from Jesus until 'an opportune
time' (4:13). One is reminded of the Fourth Gospel and the presence
of the devil in Judas (Jn 13:2, 27). The reference is, too, an echo of
Satan's demand to sift Simon (Lk 22:31).

PETER'S DENIALS   22:54-62

'The Lord turned and looked at Peter' (22:61). Only Luke has Jesus
together with Peter in the house of the high priest. It is this turning of
Jesus towards him and gazing upon him, rather than a cockcrow, that
brings Peter to recall 'the word of the Lord' (see v. 34). It was in
response to this gracious look that Peter 'went out and wept bitterly'
(v. 62). Satan has well and truly sifted Perter (v. 31); Jesus displays his

enduring care, already promised (22:32).

THE JEWISH INTERROGATION 22:66-71

In Mark 14:55-59 the Sanhedrists summoned witnesses who, it was hoped, would help to convict Jesus of threatening to destroy the Temple. Luke does not have these witnesses at Jesus' interrogation, but the accusation surfaces in the Stephen trial: 'They set up false witnesses who said ... "we have heard him say that this Jesus of Nazareth will destroy this place and will change the customs that Moses handed on to us" ' (Acts 6:13-14). (We must remind ourselves that Acts is the second part of the one Lucan work, Luke-Acts). In Mark the high priest, in view of unsatisfactory testimony, put, as a last resort, the challenging question directly to Jesus: 'Are you the Messiah, the Son of the Blessed One?' (Mk 14:61; see Matthew 26:63). Here, Luke has separated the titles: 'If you are the Messiah, tell us' (22:67); 'Are you, then, the Son of God?' (v. 70). Luke is thereby suggesting a distinction between 'Messiah' as understood by Jews and the Christian understanding of 'the Son of God.' The Fourth Gospel, also, has separate questions (Jn 10:24-25, 33-36) a link between Lucan and Johannine traditions. Jesus' response to the Son of God title – 'You (yourselves) say that I am' Lk 22:70) – is frequently taken to be an evasive answer, a qualified affirmative. In fact, it is a firm declaration.

The Lucan Jesus has turned the question of the Jewish authorities into an affirmation of the highest Christian title. In between the questions Jesus had declared: 'But from now on the Son of Man will be seated at the right hand of the power of God' (v. 69). It is in order, then, to add a word on the titles Messiah, Son of Man, Son of God.

TITLES

Messiah. It is quite unlikely that Jesus himself ever claimed to be the Messiah. It is very likely that some of his followers thought him to be the Messiah. It is also very likely that Jesus' opponents may have understood him or his followers to claim that he was the Messiah. On the other hand, after the resurrection, Jesus was, by his followers, regularly called the Messiah – Jesus *Christ* (Messiah).

Son of Man. The title goes back to Daniel 7 – the 'one like a son of man' – a heavenly symbolic figure to whom God had granted glory and dominion. There is some evidence that in first century A.D. apocalyptic circles Daniel 7 had given rise to the picture of a messianic figure glorified by God. In the Gospels 'Son of Man' occurs some eighty times and always (with two exceptions, Mk 2:10; Jn 12:34) as a self-designation of Jesus. Nevertheless, it has been doubted that Jesus could have referred to himself as the Son of Man. At most, it is maintained, he may have used 'son of man' in a neutral sense to refer to himself indirectly (a view which I had shared). Brown urges the distinct possibility that Jesus, reflecting on Daniel 7 and other OT passages, had seized on that 'one like a son of man' to whom God had given glory and dominion and had interpreted it as 'the Son of Man,' the specific human figure through whom God manifests his victory. He would have seen himself as this instrument of God's plan. Brown observes, pertinently: 'A Jesus who did not reflect on the OT and use the interpretative techniques of his time is an unrealistic projection who surely never existed' (*Death of the Messiah*, p. 513). Early Christians enmbraced and extended the use of the title and acknowledged it as a self-designation of Jesus.

Son of God. The Gospel evidence suggests that, unlike Messiah and Son of Man, the title Son of God was *not* applied to Jesus in his lifetime. Nor had he ever so designated himself (though it is likely that he thought and spoke of himself as 'the Son,' implying a special relationship to God). This being so, the high priest's question, 'Are you the Son of God?' (Lk 22:70) was not a formulation in a Jewish investigation of Jesus. In the New Testament, of course, Jesus is called 'the Son of God' – but this is a Christian title.

JESUS BEFORE HEROD   23:6-12

Proper to Luke is Pilate's sending Jesus to Herod Antipas. What is at issue is a preliminary investigation (*anakrisis*), a practice of Roman provincial officials. We find a similar situation in Acts 25 where the procurator Festus brings Paul before Agrippa. For Luke, the significance of the episode is that Herod emerges as an important witness to the innocence of Jesus – a point made explicitly by Pilate in 23:15. Early tradition had Herod hostile to Jesus (see 13:31). Here the same Herod 'treated him with contempt' in face of chief priests and scribes who stood 'vehemently accusing him' (23:10). He obviously did not set much store by their charges. Eminently Lucan is the observation: 'That same day Herod and Pilate became friends' (v. 11). This verse reflects Luke's theme of forgiveness and healing throughout the passion. Jesus was an occasion for the healing of the enmity of Pilate and Herod (v. 12).

JESUS BEFORE PILATE   23:1-25

Aside from Pilate's sending of Jesus to Herod, there are two other interesting features of Luke's Roman trial. In 23:2-5 there is marked conformity with trials of Paul in Acts. Compare Luke 23:2, 'We found this man perverting our nation, forbidding us to pay taxes to the emperor, and saying that he himself is the Messiah, a king' with Acts 24:1-2 where the high priest Ananias and elders accuse Paul to the governor Felix: 'We found this man ... an agitator among all the Jews throughout the world ... By examining him yourself you will be able to learn from him concerning everything of which we accuse him' (24:5,8). In other words, in Luke 23:2, Luke is reflecting a Jewish *versus* Christian polemic of the 70-80's.

Jesus is condemned to death

The second factor shows one of the two major links (the other being Lk 22:67,70; Jn 10:24-25, 33-36) with the Johannine tradition: Pilate's three 'not guilty' statements. These are: 'I find no basis for an accusation against this man' (Lk 23:4); 'You brought this man as one who was perverting the people; and here I have examined him in your presence and have not found this man guilty of any of your charges against him. Neither did Herod … Indeed, he has done nothing to deserve death' (23:14-15); 'Why, what evil has he done? I have found in him no ground for the sentence of death' (23:22). No ambiguity here. Compare John 18:38b, 19:4,6. After these firm declarations of

Simon of Cyrene helps Jesus

innocence, Pilate's abrupt capitulation is surprising in the storyline (Lk 23:23-25) – 'he handed over Jesus as they wished.' At this point Mark (15:15) has Jesus flogged – a flogging being a preliminary part of execution by crucifixion. The Lucan Jesus never is flogged or whipped. True, Pilate twice declares, 'I will therefore have him chastened (*paideuein*) and then release him' (23:16,22). The chastisement is a whipping, not a severe flogging or scourging. And, in Luke, it was not carried out.

JESUS LED TO THE CROSS   23:26-31

Verse 26 reads literally, 'they put on him the cross to bring behind Jesus.' The Lucan Simon of Cyrene is a positive figure. He smooths the way to the description of others not opposed to Jesus. Luke has a group of three parties favourable to Jesus before the crucifixion and a comparable group after Jesus' death. This is a significant structural modification of the Marcan narrative. *Before the crucifixion* (23:26-32). Here we have Simon of Cyrene (v. 26), women who bewailed Jesus (v. 27), two wrongdoers, one of whom will later proclaim the innocence of Jesus (v. 32). *After the death of Jesus* (23:47-49) – the centurion (v. 47), the crowds (v. 48), and the women (v. 49). These respective triads are sympathetic to Jesus.

> These triads fit Luke's theological outlook that while some opposed Jesus ... the lives of many others were positively affected by the passion. If for Mark the passion manifests human failure and evil with the overcoming power of God manifested chiefly after Jesus dies, for Luke God's love, forgiveness and healing are already present throughout the passion (Brown, *Death of the Messiah*, p. 931).

Luke has omitted the Marcan mockery of Jesus by the soldiers (Mk 15:16-20). Instead, after the reference to Simon of Cyrene he has introduced a passage peculiar to himself (Lk 23:27-31).

THE DAUGHTERS OF JERUSALEM

These women who followed Jesus 'beating their breasts and wailing for him' are surely sympathetic. Yet, his message to them is not one of compassion: it is word of woe. In 13:34-35 Jesus had directly addressed Jerusalem – the city that kills prophets and stones those sent to it. He warned, 'Behold, your house is forsaken.' Here the Daughters of Jerusalem represent the city; through them Jesus addresses the inhabitants of Jerusalem. His threat refers to the Roman destruction of the city when even innocent women and children would perish. The enigmatic sentence, 'For if they do this when the wood is green, what will happen when it is dry?' (23:31) seems to mean that if the Jewish leaders and people treat Jesus thus in a time of peace how much the worse will they fare when the Romans war on them. The oracle to the Daughters of Jerusalem as it stands reflects a widespread Christian interpretation of the Roman destruction of Jerusalem: they viewed it as divine judgment on those responsible for the death of God's Son, a punishment reaching to the next generation. It is the equivalent of Matthew's 'His blood be on us and on our children!' (Mt 27:25). There

Jesus with the daughters of Jerusalem

is an unhappy human propensity to envisage an angry, even a vengeful, God. Luke is, however, less harsh than Matthew.

The very fact that it is spoken to women who lament denies that the devastation will be deserved by all who live to see it. If the divine wrath cannot be diverted from Jerusalem because of its prolonged rejection of the prophets and Jesus, Luke shows that not all were hostile and leaves open the possibility that the God who touched the hearts of Simon, and of the wrongdoers, and of the centurion may in turn have been touched by the tears of those who lamented what was being done to Jesus (Brown, *Death of the Messiah*, p. 931f).

'FATHER, FORGIVE THEM' 23:34a

Crucified between two criminals, at the place called The Skull, Jesus, with typical graciousness, prayed: 'Father, forgive them; for they do not know what they are doing.' The 'they' includes both the Romans who crucified Jesus and the Jews who had brought him to death. Jesus attributes ignorance to the obdurate chief priests and their allies. Luke is suggesting that even perpetrators of evil never really appreciate God's goodness or the strange wisdom of his purpose.

Like 22:43-44, this verse is textually unsure. Though omitted from important manuscripts it is present in equally weighty ones. The style is Lucan. And there is Stephen's parallel prayer. 'Lord, do not hold this sin against them' (Acts 7:20) – surely best understood as an echo of Jesus' prayer. All in all, it is much more reasonable to posit omission than to propose later insertion. In that case one must ask how a copyist may have come to omit this striking verse. Two reasons come to mind. It may have been judged too favourable to Jews, and early Christians tended to regard Jews as relentless persecutors. And there is the moral problem: how can there be forgiveness without genuine repentance? We have an unhappy penchant for setting limits to divine forgiveness. Brown adverts to the irony that the most beautiful sentence in the Passion Narrative should be textually dubious and adds: 'Alas, too often not the absence of this prayer from the text, but the failure to incorporate it into one's heart has been the real problem' (*Death of the Messiah*, p. 980).

CRUCIFIXION 23:35-43

While in Mark reaction to Jesus on the cross is wholly negative, in Luke reaction is positive as well. His first observation is: 'And the people stood by, watching' – neutral bystanders. The 'people' in Mark

15:29 are the passersby who derided Jesus. In view of his different estimation of 'the people' (Lk 23:35) Luke, who preserves the series of three mockings found in Mark 15:29-32, had to find another category of mockers. Thus, in Mark the mockers are passersby, chief priests and scribes, and the co-crucified; in Luke they are the leaders, the soldiers, and one of the co-crucified. A challenge sounds through the three Lucan mockeries: that Jesus should save himself. Jesus will not save himself. Instead he will grant salvation to another.

SALVATION OF A WRONGDOER   23:40-43

The episode relates to Luke's theological purpose in two main regards: the 'other' wrongdoer (*kakourgos*) is a further impartial witness to Jesus' innocence, and he provides another instance of healing forgiveness during the passion. In rebuking his co-sufferer 'the other' acknowledges that both of them had been condemned deservedly – 'but this man has done nothing wrong' (23:41). He plays somewhat the same role as Pilate's wife in Matthew 27:19 who could affirm that a Jesus she had never met was 'a just man.' The wrongdoer addresses Jesus, 'Jesus, remember me when you come into your kingdom' (23:42). The direct address. 'Jesus', without qualification, is unique in the Gospels.

The idea conveyed by 'into your kingdom' is that of Jesus ascending into the kingdom from the cross. In dying Jesus had passed beyond time. The 'other' wrongdoer is asking to be remembered at the moment of Jesus' vindication. Typically, Jesus' response goes far beyond his expectation. 'Truly I tell you, today you will be with me in Paradise' (23:43). 'Today' means this very day; to be with Jesus in Paradise is to be with Christ in the full presence of God. Some commentators have baulked at this. A man who cannot have displayed *metanoia* (he had merely asked to be remembered) could not enjoy full salvation. In this view 'paradise' must mean some lesser form of closeness with God. Brown retorts tartly: 'A Jesus who was known as a friend of sinners (7:34), who received sinners and ate with them (15:2), may not have been squeamish about taking a sinner into the highest heaven once the sinner had asked to follow him' (*Death of teh Messiah*, p. 1010). Jesus is, indeed, concluding the pattern of mercy shown in the Passion Narrative. 'Frequently called the episode of "the good thief," this is rather another aspect of the good Jesus' (*Death of teh Messiah*, p. 1013).

DEATH 23:44-49

There are a number of interesting Lucan features in his account of the death of Jesus. 'The curtain of the temple was torn in two' (39:45). In Mark the rending of the curtain or veil occurred after the death of Jesus (15:38). Luke has it between the darkness over the whole earth and Jesus' final words. The reason for the shift is that in 23:47-49 Luke has three types of people who respond compassionately and so affirm the saving import of the death. The ominous sign of the rending of the veil would not be in place in this context; it is more akin to the ominous darkness.

'Father, into your hands I commend my spirit' (23:46). Contrast with the dying cry in Mark recalls the Gethsemane situation. There Luke had omitted the Marcan description of a distraught and troubled Jesus; now he omits the Marcan Jesus' desperate cry of abandonment (Mk 15:34). The reason is theological: the Lucan Jesus is always wholly at peace with God. Similarly, in Mark, from the 'Abba' in Gethsemane (14:36) to the 'my God' on the cross (15:34) there is a movement of alienation. In contrast, the Lucan Jesus prays 'Father' on the Mount of Olives (22:42) and 'Father' at the end, on the cross (23:34). And his prayer on each occassion is peculiar to Luke.

REACTIONS TO THE DEATH OF JESUS 23:47-49

We have noted that on the way to the cross there were three reactions: of Simon of Cyrene, of a large (sympathetic) crowd, and of women – the Daughters of Jerusalem. After the death the reactors are, similarly, an individual, the people, and women. Specifically, these are the centurion who, on the basis of what he witnessed, glorified God and declared: 'Certainly, this man was just' (23:47); all the crowd who, having seen what happened, returned home beating their breasts (23:48); Jesus' acquaintances and the women who had followed him from Galilee, observing from a distance (23:49). The order is Lucan, reflecting his more favourable attitude towards the Jewish people.

The reaction of the centurion is noteworthy. In Mark his is the climactic statement of that gospel, a full Christian profession of faith: 'Truly this man was God's Son' (15:39). Luke's version rings so differently: 'Certainly this man was just' (23:47). Luke's concern is not that of Mark. His designation of Jesus as 'just' (*dikaios*) was meant to fit the pattern of repeated insistence on the fact that Jesus was not guilty of the charges levelled against him. The centurion had witnesed Jesus serenely accept death with a prayer of total confidence. This was no criminal! He can speak with a conviction far beyond that of Pilate.

THE BURIAL   23:50-56

Of special interest here are Joseph of Arimathea and the women. Luke
joins Mark (15:43) in having Joseph a member of the Sahedrin – and
not a disciple as in Matthew and John. Luke however specifies beyond
Mark that Joseph 'had not agreed to the plan and action' of the other
Sanhedrists (23:51). As one 'waiting expectantly for the kingdom of
God' (v. 51) he takes his place with Zechariah, Elizabeth, Simeon,
Anna. The women in this Lucan passage have a prominent role: they
point to Easter and the discovery of the empty tomb. 'On the sabbath

The burial of Jesus

day they rested according to the commandment' (v. 56) – they are carefully law-observant.

Thus at the end of the Gospel the Lucan picture of the burial and resurrection of Jesus in Jerusalem features pious, law-observant characters of the same type as depicted at the beginning during Jesus' infancy and boyhood visit to Jerusalem (2:22-24, 25, 37, 41-42) (Brown, *Death of the Messiah*, p. 1287).

CONCLUSION

While Luke's Passion Narrative is based on Mark's version, it differs from Mark in structure and tone. Luke has some affinity with the Johannine tradition. Indeed, one might say that Luke's portrait of Jesus is halfway between the passion picture of Mark and John. His Jesus is not the anguished man of Mark's Gethsemane and cross. Nor is he yet the majestic Jesus who dominates the Johannine story. Luke's Jesus, though rejected and mocked and suffering, is ever in serene communion with the Father. He does not experience Godforsaskenness. His death is not with a lonely cry but with a tranquil prayer, 'Father, into your hnands I commend my spirit.' It is not chance that this prayer finds an echo in Stephen's death prayer, 'Lord, do not hold this sin against them' (Acts 7:20). This is not the only passion echo in Acts, as we have observed.

In Luke the disciples fare better than in Mark. Luke has no blunt, 'All of them deserted him and fled' (Mk 14:50), at the arrest of Jesus; they simply disappear from his story. If Peter does remain to deny his Lord, he experiences the look, surely full of tender understanding, of Jesus. And he will recall the comforting assurance, 'I have prayed for you' (22:31). The Jewish participants are shown in a less negative light. A multitude of people follow Jesus to Calvary, do not join in mocking him and, after his death, return home beating their breasts in a gesture of mourning. The Daughters of Jerusalem bewail him.

Perhaps the most distinctive, surely the most comforting, theme of Luke's Passion Narrative is his portrayal of the healing and forgiving power of God flowing from Jesus throughout the passion. Jesus heals the wound of one of those come to arrest him. He heals the enmity that had existed between his judges (Pilate and Herod). He looks upon a fallen Peter with deep compassion. He prays forgiveness on those who brought about his death, acknowledging that they did not really know what they had done. He promises to take with him into the presence of the Father a wrongdoer who simply asks to be remembered by him. In all of this Jesus is manifestly the Jesus who walks through the pages of Luke. But never more than in the passsion is Luke, in Dante's phrase, *scriba mansuetudinis Christi*, chronicler of God's foolish love manifest in Jesus.

We need Mark's stark story to remind us of the awfulness of the deed and to urge us to come to terms with the reality of the cross. We need Luke's gentler story to discern the forgiving love of God shine through the worst that humankind can wreak.

HOLY THURSDAY
MASS OF THE LORD'S SUPPER

Despite the well-known divergence between the Synoptic gospels and John on the precise date of the last Supper, its Passover setting remains clear. The first three gospels present the meal as a Passover meal. So, Lk 22:15 – 'I have eagerly desired to eat this Passover with you before I suffer.' John presents Jesus as the true Passover lamb: he died at the hour when the Passover lamb was slaughtered and, in his case, the prescription regarding the Passover lamb ('You shall not break any of its bones', Ex 12:46) was observed (Jn 19:36). The relationship between Eucharist and Passover is firmly embedded in the tradition.

First Reading   Ex 12:1-8, 11-14

This reading gives the account of the institution of the Passover as an established feast in Israel and indicates the prescribed ritual. The Passover was originally a simple feast of nomadic shepherds. The use of unleavened bread went back to a spring agricultural festival marking the early harvest and the offering of the first fruits. Our text represents a stage when both festivals were combined and firmly linked to the exodus event. The feast of Passover came to be regarded as a memorial, recalling God's fidelity to his covenant, and as an assurance that God would be faithful to his promises. At each Passover Israel looked backward to the first Passover and forward to the final deliverance which God had promised. In the Church the Eucharist is the memorial of the death and resurrection (of the Passover, see Jn 13:1) of Christ; at each Eucharist we look back to his death and forward to his coming again.

Second Reading   1 Cor 11:23-26

Paul begins by setting down the words used by Jesus to institute the Eucharist. These are introduced by the technical terms 'to receive' and 'to deliver' which place him as an intermediary in a chain of tradition. Paul's version of the words of institution is most closely related to that of Luke (22:15-20), and it has been plausibly suggested that it records the usage of the Church of Antioch. A distinctive feature of Paul's version is the twice repeated 'Do this in remembrance of me.' For Paul, authentic remembrance is concerned with the past only insofar as it is constitutive of the present and a summons to the future. What he desires to evoke is the active remembrance of total commitment to Christ which makes the past real in the present, thus releasing a power capable of shaping the future. The 'proclamation' takes place in and through the eating of the bread and the drinking of the cup.

The attitude of the participants is crucial. If their imitation of Christ (11:1) is non-existent or seriously defective, then, no matter how carefully the ritual gestures are performed 'it is not really the Lord's supper that you eat' (v. 20). Only if the participants have truly put on Christ (Gal 3:27), which is equivalent to putting on love (Col 3:14), is there effective 'proclamation' of the death of Christ in the Eucharist.

Gospel   Jn 13:1-15

Jesus knows that he is about to give the supreme manifestation (see 15:13) of his abiding love for his disciples. He himself brings out clearly the meaning of what he does, the act of humble service he now renders. The opening words (13:1) are a caption for all that is to come in chapters 13-19, the demonstration of Jesus' love for his own – a love to the end *(eis telos)* – without measure. He *lays aside* his garments (13:4,12) as he spoke of laying down his life (10:18). The disciples are to 'have share' with him (v. 8): the washing of the feet expresses symbolically that they are brought into communion of life with Jesus through his death, a supreme act of self-giving and humble service. It is necessary to be washed by Christ, giver of life, if one is to have part with him in eternal life – one must share in his death and resurrection.

'I have set you an example.' The disciples are not to look only to his ultimate gesture of love: humble service should characterise all the living of his followers. Here is a moving lesson in *diakonia*. Jesus is indeed Lord and Teacher; he has authority. But his style and exercise of authority is marked by *service*. And, bringing together the second reading and gospel, it follows that true union with Christ in the Eucharist, and consequently true communion among Christians, is possible only in this atmosphere of loving service.

The Mass is the celebration of the Christian Passover. The whole of Jesus' life, culminating in his death and resurrection, was a passage from 'this world' to the Father, from death to life, from sin to grace, *for us*. By faith we appropriate the Passover, we share in Christ's life, death and resurrection. The Eucharist, the meal at which we receive Christ as bread and wine, is the special sign, symbol, the 'sacrament' of this faith, But signs, symbols or 'sacraments' are effective only *as such*, that is, only if, and in so far as, they are received as expressions of the deeper reality which they convey. The reality which Christ gives to us in the Eucharist is himself as the 'man for others.' If we really receive him as such we must ourselves become 'people for others', servants of our fellows. Our Passover, of which the Jewish Passover is the model and Christ's Passover is the cause, is our continual 'passage' from selfishness to service.

GOOD FRIDAY

First Reading   Is 52:13-53:12

The fourth and finest of the songs of the suffering servant of Yahweh, Israel's deepest insight into the meaning of suffering, contemplates the fate of the man upon whom rests the hopes of Israel. Whatever may be said about the identification of the servant of this song, he surely stands forth sharply as an individual. Christians could not fail to discern in him the lineaments of their Lord.

The servant is innocent yet has suffered – in this respect he resembles Job. But there is something more: 'he was wounded for *our* transgressions, crushed for *our* iniquities.' The servant is innocent, gentle, humble. He is the one God has chosen to establish righteousness on earth. He achieves his goal through suffering as he bears the chastisement *we* had earned. His burden is the sin of others; his attitude in face of reproach and insult is silence; his sacrificial death, a gesture of love, counters human wickedness. The servant is truly the man for others, dying that others might live. His ultimate triumph and exaltation are glimpsed beyond present persecution, beyond rejection by his own people, beyond ignominious death.

The present passage has been called 'the fifth gospel' because it appears to anticipate so vividly Jesus' suffering, death and eventual triumph. The close correspondence between this Song and the Passion narratives is best explained by the recourse which the evangelists (along with other New Testament theologians) had to this passage. It provided a context in which to interpret what must have been one of the most severe challenges to faith in the person of Jesus. How could the all-powerful God permit his chosen servant to be subjected to the ignominy of death by crucifixion? The flow of the poem suggests that it was an offering of expiation leading to the ultimate vindication of the victim and opening up the possibility of life for his descendants. The Johannine Jesus could, in the spirit of the Servant, declare, 'I, when I am lifted up from the earth, will draw all people to myself' (Jn 12:32).

Second Reading
Heb 4:14-16; 5:7-9

A major theme of the letter to the Hebrews is the priesthood of Christ. The coming of the Son into our world is presented in cultic terms. It is almost as if he had come precisely to be our high priest who offers sacrifice for us (2:17; 8:1-6; 9:11-14; 10:1-18) and who intercedes for us. The fact that Jesus the high priest has entered the heavenly sanctuary (6:20; 7:26; 8:1; 9:11) is a motive for holding fast to the faith we confess (4:14-16).

Verse 15 is a reply to a latent objection: may not this surpassing greatness of the high priest imply an aloofness towards human misery. 'Sympathize' here means to enter into and share the suffering of others. We need have no fear. Our high priest can sympathize with us in our temptations; he can help us because he has experienced our trials and sufferings. Having such a high priest – now passed into the presence of God – Christians can advance with full confidence to present themselves before God. The 'throne of grace' is the throne of God's mercy. It is because it is now accessible to sinners that it is the throne of grace; the way of access is Christ the Priest, the link between God and humankind. Christians who approach the throne encounter the loving mercy of God who bestows on them his favours.

The passage 5:1-10 shows that Jesus has perfectly met the requirements of priesthood: he is a human person, officially constituted a mediator between God and humankind, who pleads the cause of men and women before God and who offers their gifts to God, especially sacrifice for sin. A true priest will be compassionate, greatly understanding of sinners; Jesus is eminently endowed with this quality.

Verses 7-10 show Jesus in prayer – Gethsemane is manifestly in mind. We are shown the means (suffering) by which the saving work of Jesus is effected (vv. 7-8), as well as the result for himself and those who trust in him (vv. 9-10). Through his obedience he gained an enriching experience, a practical understanding and appreciation of suffering which would enable him to sympathize fully with his brothers and sisters. He has entered heaven but he is joined to us still in his perfect understanding of our trials and difficulties. The distance between us, abolished by the incarnation, has not been broadened again by the ascension. He is always ready and able to help us because he is always our compassionate high priest.

The exhortation of the author of Hebrews brings encouragement to Christians in their experience of suffering. It underlines the humanity of Jesus; he shared in our human condition and he can identify with our sufferings since he suffered deeply himself. He gives us hope in suffering, for in and through his suffering he responded in loving obedience to his Father. In death as in life he bore witness to a loving God's limitless love of humankind.

The Passion   Jn 18:1-19:42

While one acknowledges that the portrait of Jesus in the Synoptic gospels is already, and inevitably, coloured by Easter faith, the Jesus of John is startlingly different. Contrast is sharpest between Mark and John.

One need but compare the two Passion Narratives (Mk 14:32-15:47; Jn 18-20), beginning with the arrest of Jesus (Mk 14:43-50; Jn 18:1-11), to see that the stories are, in several respects, historically incompatible. A look at the brief account of arrests will suffice to make the point.

THE ARREST OF JESUS Jn 18:1-11. See Mk 14:43-50.

Mark 14:43-50. The story-line: Jesus is 'still speaking' his closing words of the Gethsemane episode (14:32-42). Judas plays an essential role, leading the arresting crowd (sent by the Jewish authorities) to where Jesus was to be found and then, at night-time and in a group, identifying the right man. Jesus, quite passive, was at once arrested. The unnamed slave of the high priest was wounded by one of the bystanders; Mark gives the impression of a clumsy attempt to defend Jesus by someone other than a disciple. Jesus, now a prisoner, does protest at the manner and timing of his arrest: he is not a man of violence and there was no call for this show of strength. All the frightened disciples deserted him.

John 18:1-11. The story-line: Here reference to the 'words' of Jesus points not to Gethsemane (an episode absent from the Fourth Gospel) but to the solemn prayer of John 17. Judas guides not a 'crowd' but a Roman military detachment as well as Temple police. Jesus, fully aware of all that was to happen, takes the initiative and strides forward to accost the band of soldiers and police; there is no need for Judas to identify him, as is expressly noted. They are seeking 'Jesus of

Nazareth.' At the God-presence in him, manifest in his declaration 'I am' (*egó eimi*) they are rendered powerless – stricken to the ground. Jesus, completely in charge of the situation, lays down his terms: they may arrest him, on condition that they do not detain the disciples. These do not desert him, as in Mark; he protects them. It is 'Simon Peter' who strikes out and cuts off the right ear of 'Malchus' – the story has grown from its Marcan form. Jesus rebukes Peter (instead of protesting at the manner of his own arrest, as in Mark). Only now is Jesus arrested, and only because he permitted it to happen.

It is evidently the same incident, but how different the telling. The fact is: each version is completely at home in its proper setting; it just would not do to switch the accounts. This alerts one to the manner of proper understanding. There is little doubt that Mark's version is closer to what really happened. It would, however, be a mistake to think that Mark is primarily concerned with 'facts' and that, consequently, he does not propose a christology; or that, at best, he puts forward a low christology. It is one of the unfortunate results of such concentration on the Johannine picture that the christology of the other evangelists has been underrated. Indeed, the Marcan christology is not 'inferior' to the Johannine. It is notably different.

Fleeting reference above to Gethsemane suggests a further point of comparison. In Mark 14:32-36 we encounter a shattered Jesus, crushed to the point of death at the prospect of a gruesome death. He prayed, explicitly, that 'the hour might pass from him.' He needed to be assured that the path which opened before him was indeed the way that God would have him walk.

John, on the other hand, though clearly aware of the Gethsemane tradition, studiously avoids the Gethsemane episode. He has Jesus declare: 'Now my soul is troubled. And what should I say – "Father, save me from this hour?"' (Jn 12:27). So far, reminiscent of Mark. Then comes a distinctively Johannine twist: 'No, it is for this reason that I have come to this hour.' The Johannine Jesus explicitly refuses to pray the Gethsemane prayer. It is inconceivable that he could speak the words of Mark 14:36 because the Johannine Jesus 'knows all that was to happen to him' (Jn 18:4). There is a clash of christologies. For us, it is not a matter of choosing between them. It is, rather, a question of understanding both of them.

We could, usefully, examine the saying in John 18:5-6 – 'I am' (*egó eimi*). There are four absolute 'I am' sayings in the Gospel (8:24,28,58; 13:19) e.g. 'When you have lifted up the Son of man, then you will realise that I AM' (8:28). Each time there is an echo of the divine name of Exodus 3:14 or, more immediately, of Isaiah 43:10-11. Jesus declares: I am the bearer of God's name and power. The meaning in 18:5-6 is close to this: the name has the power to paralyse Jesus' enemies.

John presents the Passion as the triumph of the Son of God. The *dramatis personae* are sharply characterized. Despite appearances, *Jesus* is always in control. He is the Judge who judges his judge (Pilate) and his accusers ('the Jews'). He is the King who reigns, with the cross for a throne 'I, when I am lifted up from the earth, will draw all to myself.' *The Jews* are not the whole Jewish people but its leaders who see Jesus as a danger to them, the Establishment, and who are determined to destroy him.

Such are 'the Jews' in the story-line. For John and his contemporaries 'the Jews' are the leaders of a later Judaism vigorously opposed to the now distinctive Christian movement. *Pilate* recognizes, and three times acknowledges, the innocence of Jesus. He desperately tries to compromise but ends by yielding to political blackmail. He is a man who will not make a decision for or against Jesus – and finds himself trapped.

JESUS BEFORE THE JEWISH AUTHORITIES 18:12-24

Jesus was brought before Annas, a former high priest who had been deposed by the Romans but who still had considerable influence. This was not a formal trial but an interrogation. The episode throws light on the confrontation of the evangelist and his community with contemporary Judaism. Jesus becomes a defender of his followers against attacks of Judaism. Jesus was then sent to Caiaphas the actual high priest. In view of his cynical political decision (and unwitting prophecy), 'it is better for you to have one man die for the people' (11:50), Jesus cannot expect justice. As in the Synoptics John, too, has Peter's denials of Jesus (18:15-18, 25-27).

JESUS BEFORE PILATE 18:28-19:16a

The synoptic accounts of the trial before Pilate tell us little whereas John's dramatic reconstruction does bring out the significance of it. Only John makes clear why Jesus was brought to Pilate in the first place and why Pilate gave in to having him crucified. Only John shows the interplay of subtle (and not so subtle) political forces on Pilate and indicates how Pilate's original questioning of Jesus concerned a political charge against him. Yet Mark, we now realize, has given the key to the trial in the title 'King of the Jews' (15:2); thereafter he stresses that it is as king of the Jews (Messiah) that Jesus is rejected by the crowd and crucified.

There is a theological reason for John's stress on the Roman trial. We are to see Pilate in the light of the rest of the Fourth Gospel. He provides an example of an attitude to Jesus which purports to be neither faith nor rejection: the typical attitude of those who try to maintain a middle position in an all or nothing situation. Pilate's refusal to make a decision for or against the Light leads to disaster. Because Pilate will not face the challenge of deciding for the Truth in Jesus and against the Jews, he thinks he can persuade the Jews to accept a solution that will make it unnecessary for him to declare for Jesus. This is the Johannine view of the episodes of Barabbas, the scourging, and the delivery of Jesus to the Jews as 'your King.' For John this trial is our own tragic history of temporizing and indecision. Pilate, the would-be neutral man is frustrated by the pressure of others. He failed to listen to the truth and decide in its favour. He, and all who would follow him, inevitably end up enslaved to this world.

The Johannine presentation of the Roman trial is highly dramatic. It is structured, chiastically (a.b.c.d c'b'a'), in seven episodes or scenes. There are two settings or stages: the outside court of the praetorium where 'the Jews' are gathered; the inside room where Jesus is held prisoner. Pilate goes back and forth from one stage to the other. The atmosphere is notably different in either setting. Inside Jesus and Pilate engage in calm dialogue; outside is clamour as Pilate is pressurized to find Jesus guilty. Pilate's passing from one setting to the other is expressive of an internal struggle: while becoming increasingly convinced of Jesus' innocence he finds himself being forced to condemn him.

Scene 1. OUTSIDE. Jews Demand Death (18:28b-32).

The Jews who had brought Jesus to Pilate would not enter the Gentile praetorium. To do so would involve ritual defilement and prevent them from celebrating Passover. Pilate went out to them; they insisted that Jesus was a criminal deserving death. The execution would be according to Roman law: death by crucifixion. Jesus had already referred to his death as a 'lifting up' – on a cross! 'And I, when I am lifted up from the earth, will draw all people to myself' (12:32).

Scene 2. INSIDE. Pilate and Jesus on Kingship (18:33-38a).

Pilate questioned Jesus: 'Are you the King of the Jews?' Jesus wanted to know how he understood the title: in a political or in a religious sense? He himself proclaimed the otherworldly realm of truth; he separated his kingship from anything that could threaten

Pilate. His purpose was to bear witness to 'the way things really are' – the way God is, the way God is related to the world.

Pilate's response, 'What is truth?' is not to be understood as a profound philosophical question... Ironically it is a self-condemnation: his failure to recognize truth and hear Jesus' voice shows that he does not belong to God (Brown, *The Death of the Messiah*, p. 752f).

Scene 3 OUTSIDE. Pilate Finds Jesus Not Guilty (18:38b-40).

Pilate had shown that he was not on the side of truth. He had turned from the light. *He* was the one on trial. He went outside and declared that, having interrogated Jesus, he could find no case against him. V. 38a is the first of Pilate's three 'not guilty' statements (see 19: 4,6). He tried the ploy of the Passover amnesty: 'Do you want me to release for you the King of the Jews?' They shouted back: 'We want Barabbas' – a known bandit.

Scene 4. INSIDE. Soldiers Scourge Jesus (19:1-3).

Pilate, in failing to give Jesus justice, is forced to a travesty of justice. He ordered Jesus to be scourged. Scourged though he had already pronounced him innocent! His scourging of an innocent man proves that man's innocence! Pilate is getting more deeply embroiled. The soldiers twisted some thorn branches into a mock crown (diadem) and decked Jesus in a cast-off soldier's cloak. The saluted him: 'Hail, King of the Jews!' The kingship theme, already introduced in the dialogue with Pilate, would persist. Ironically, this mockery serves as a declaration of who Jesus is.

Scene 5. OUTSIDE. 'Behold the Man!' (19:4-8).

Pilate had Jesus presented to the crowd – all bloody as he was from the scourging and decked in the mock crown and robes: 'Here is the man!' He was showing them a pathetic human being who was no threat to either Rome or 'the Jews.' They howled for his death: 'Crucify him!' In exasperation Pilate retorted: 'Crucify him yourselves; I have no case against the man.' They shot back: 'According to our Law he ought to be put to death: he has claimed to be Son of God.'

By the end of the enquiry the divinity of Jesus as a threat to the unicity of God was emerging as the great issue between Jews and Christians, and John describes it as the factor beneath the surface in the Roman trial (Brown, *The Death of the Messiah*, p. 829f).

Scene 6. INSIDE. Pilate and Jesus on Power (19:9-11).

Pilate was now quite alarmed: the unbelieving politician is super-stitious. He came inside and asked Jesus: 'Where are you from?' Jesus was silent. When Pilate invoked his authority he was told, bluntly: 'You would have no authority over me if it had not been decreed so from above; but those who have handed me over to you are more guilty than you.' Pilate was now desperately anxious to release Jesus. He had been challenged by Truth – and had sought to compromise. He was hopelessly trapped. His next attempt to have the case dismissed was met with naked blackmail: 'If you set this man free you are not Caesar's friend; anyone who makes himself king is a challenge to Caesar.' Pilate was aware that his standing in Rome was, just then, not very secure; he could not risk a suggestion of disloyalty to the emperor. Time had run out on him. He could no longer evade a decision.

Scene 7. OUTSIDE. Jews Obtain Death (19:12-16a).

Pilate yielded to the Jewish demand for Jesus' crucifixion. John's account of the passing of the sentence of death is detailed, dramatic and theological; the only points of parallel with the synoptics are in the repeated call for crucifixion and the outcome of Jesus' being 'handed over.' The Old Testament background to this verb (*paradidómai*), used by all the evangelists, implies that Jesus was 'delivered up' to his enemies 'according to the definite plan and foreknowledge of God' (Acts 2:23); there was a mysterious divine purpose. The real trial was over when the Jews uttered the fateful words: 'We have no king but Caesar.' This is akin to the statement in Matthew's account: 'His blood be on us and on our children!' (Mt 27:25). Both evangelists are reflecting not history but apologetic theology. The tragedy of Jesus' death was viewed through the hostility between Church and syna-gogue in the late first century A.D. The audience at the trial is made to voice a Christian interpretation of the Jewish rejection of Jesus.

John also tells us that this was the hour when the Passover lambs were being sacrificed in the Temple. It is supreme Johannine irony: the Jews renounce the covenant at the very moment when the priests begin to prepare for the feast which annually recalled God's deliverance of his covenanted people. By the blood of a lamb in Egypt Yahweh had marked them off to be spared as his own. Now, they know no king but the emperor and they slay another Lamb. At that moment, just before the Passover, as Jesus set out for Golgotha to shed his saving blood, the trial of Jesus ends with the fulfilment of that proclamation at the beginning of the gospel: 'Here is the lamb of God who takes away the sin of the world!' (1:29).

THE CRUCIFIXION OF JESUS 19:16b-30

Jesus was led out, laden with the cross-beam and without human assistance, to Golgotha, the Place of the Skull. 'Carrying the cross by himself' – there is no Simon of Cyrene: John's christology has no room for Jesus' needing or accepting help. Jesus was crucified between two others. Pilate had ordered an inscription which was affixed to the cross: 'Jesus of Nazareth, the King of the Jews;' he had the notice written in Hebrew, Latin and Greek. The annoyed Jews protested: 'It should read, "this man *claims* to be king of the Jews."' Pilate retorted:

Jesus is stripped and his clothes are divided

'What I have written, I have written.' As representative of imperial Rome Pilate had made a heraldic proclamation, couched in the sacred and secular languages of the day – a worldwide proclamation of Jesus' Kingship. Supreme irony!

In 19:26-27 John has by the cross the mother of Jesus and the beloved disciple. The scene is surely symbolic as a new relationship is set up between the mother and the disciple. The disciple 'took her to his own.'

The crucifixion,
with Mary and the Beloved Disciple

What is peculiar to the beloved disciple, what is 'his own', is neither his house nor his spiritual space but the fact that he is the disciple *par excellence*. 'His own' is the special discipleship that Jesus loves. The fact that the mother of Jesus is now the disciple's mother and that he has taken her to his own is a symbolic way of describing how one related to Jesus by the flesh (his mother who is part of his natural family) becomes related to him by the Spirit (a member of the ideal discipleship). (Brown, *The Death of the Messiah*, p.1024).

JESUS' LAST WORDS 19:28-30

Jesus was conscious that his hour had drawn to its close; all had now been accomplished. In response to his call 'I am thirsty' John specifies that a sponge full of sour wine was raised to his lips 'on a bunch of hyssop' – a small plant that could not sustain a sponge. Significantly, in Exodus 12:22 it is specified that hyssop be used to sprinkle the blood of the paschal lamb on the doorposts of the Israelite homes. Plausibly, John introduced the unlikely hyssop here to suggest that Jesus is fulfilling the role of the paschal lamb. The last word of Jesus, 'It is finished!' is a cry of victory: now Jesus will draw all people to himself.

In *John* Jesus, who has come from God, has completed the commission that the Father has given him, so that his death becomes a deliberate decision that all is now finished, taken by one who is in control ... Accordingly his 'It is finished' refers both to the work the Father has given him to do and to the fulfilment of Scripture. As 'Lamb of God' he has taken away the world's sin, thus fulfilling and completing the role of the paschal lamb in OT theology. (Brown, *The Death of the Messiah*, p. 1078).

'Then he bowed his head and gave up his spirit' (v. 30b). In 7:37-39 Jesus promised that when he was glorified those who believed in him would receive the Spirit. His last breath was the outpouring of the life-giving Spirit – *his* Spirit.

REACTIONS AT THE CRUCIFIXION 19:31-37

The final episode, the *not* breaking of Jesus' legs and the flow of blood and water is the only part of John's crucifixion narrative which has no parallel in the synoptics. True Passover Lamb, not one bone of Jesus was broken (see Ex 12:46). The flow of blood and water is another proleptic reference to the giving of the Spirit – following on Jn 19:30. The risen Lord will give the Spirit on Easter day (20:22). Spirit-giving is multifaceted; but always the Spirit comes from Jesus because it is

Spirit of Jesus. The beloved disciple (surely the 'he' of v. 35) bears witness to the christological and salvific dimension of the death of Jesus. Note that blood and water flow from the *dead* Jesus. The drama of the cross does not end in death but in the flow of life that comes from death. The death of Jesus on the cross is the beginning of Christian life.

THE BURIAL OF JESUS 19:38-42

Joseph of Arimathea – a secret disciple of Jesus – got permission from Pilate to remove the body of Jesus. He and that other secret disciple, Nicodemus, gave Jesus a royal burial. They bound his body in linen cloths, sprinkling a lavish quantity of perfumed spices between the folds. Then they laid him in a new unused tomb in a nearby garden.

> Previously in John's Gospel believers who adhered to Jesus and were identified as his disciples have been contrasted with those who believed but were afraid to have it known that they were disciples. At this 'hour' of the death and burial of Jesus the beloved disciple in 19:31-37 is the example par excellence of the first group of believers. Hitherto Joseph and Nicodemus in 19:38-42 have belonged to the second group; but now they are presented as transformed through Jesus' victory on the cross. (Brown, *The Death of the Messiah*, p. 1267).

THE EASTER VIGIL

For the Easter Vigil there are seven Old Testament readings before the two New Testament readings of the Mass. These Old Testament readings may be reduced to three and, in special circumstances, even to two, with the proviso that the third, the narrative of the crossing of the Red Sea (Ex 14:15-15:10) must be read. Where a selection needs to be made it is preferable to choose those readings which have a more direct bearing on the paschal theme and carry a message for Christians today. If three readings are to be selected, one would suggest the first, third and seventh.

A. Old Testament Readings

First Reading   Gen 1:1-2:2

Few passages of Scripture are more at home in a liturgical setting because this, in its present form, is assuredly already a liturgical text.

At its close one has the over-powering impression that indeed God *is* the Creator of all that exists – that all he has made is *very good* And one should have grasped the deeper and more comforting truth that *humankind* is the pride of God's creation: his image, his representative.

'Let us make humankind in our image, after our likeness' (1:26). This is the high moment of the story of Genesis 1-11. The earth had been shaped, and the sky with its lights; the waters had been gathered into their place. Grasses and cereal plants and fruit trees flourished. Birds and fishes teemed; cattle, wild beasts and creeping things roamed the earth. The world was riotously alive. All was good. God looked, complacently, on the works of his word. The world pulsed with life. Yet, there was an emptiness, a silence. There was wanting the crowning glory, the masterpiece. There remained the desire of God, his need of a counterpart. 'Let us make human beings in our image.' God will not remain alone. He set to creating a creature that would correspond, one with whom he can speak and who would listen. In God's creation human beings are unique in that they are God's counterpart; their *raison d'être* is their relationship to God. With humans alone, in all creation, can God have dialogue. Because he is a loving God, that dialogue will be free. His counterpart will respond to him in freedom – or not at all. Humankind is God's image: his representative to administer the earth in his name.

'Have dominion': the commission reflects the relationship of God to creation. Humankind is ever God's representative, with a dominion that carries heavy responsibility. The earth has been entrusted to humankind, but it remains God's property: 'The earth is the Lord's and all it contains' (Ps 24:1). Humans have been granted no licence to exploit – in a destructive sense – nature, to despoil the earth. Humankind's special obligation, as image of God, is a call to respect for the natural world. God has concern for *all* of his creation, not only for humankind. Human dominion over the earth is meant to be a wise and benevolent rule so that it may be, in its measure, the sign of God's lordship over his creation.

In Genesis 1, a refrain runs through the litany of creation: 'God saw that it was good' – leading to the climactic declaration: 'God saw everything that he had made, and indeed, it was very good' (1:31). The Creator alone can say this of his creation because the Creator alone can see the whole of it. *We* cannot look upon our world and declare, with truth: 'It is very good.' We cannot blind ourselves to so much that is, to our eyes, far from good. Job understood this. When he sketched the facile authority of the Creator over chaos and the heavens and the great waters (Job 26:5-13), he exclaimed, in awe: 'These are indeed but the outskirts of his ways; and how small a whisper do we hear of him!' (26:14).

Second Reading   Gen 22:1-18

The restoration of creation as God had willed it began with God's call to Abraham. The new relationship with God is based on total faith in him, symbolized here by Abraham's readiness to give up his only son Isaac. A poignant story indeed. The man who had, without hesitation, at the Lord's bidding, set out from his homeland (Gen 12:1), now, without question, sets out to do this awful deed. He obeyed with a heavy heart, a heart pierced to the quick by Isaac's unsuspecting question: 'Father, the fire and the wood are here, but where is the lamb for a burnt offering?' The tragic dignity of Abraham and his sad readiness to give his son stirred a Christian sentiment. The deed of Abraham has surely coloured the telling of a greater love: 'He did not withhold his own Son, but gave him up for all of us' (Rom 8:32); 'God so loved the world that he gave his only Son' (Jn 3:16). Abraham had put his faith in God, a seemingly capricious and callous God. For, Abraham saw, what Paul and John were to recognize, that his God is always a foolish God – a God who loves with divine abandon. He can make outrageous demands because he will always be faithful.

Third Reading   Ex 14:15-15:1

The reading describes the final act in the drama of the Hebrews' liberation from Egyptian slavery. It marked the decisive confrontation between God's protection of his people and the obduracy of Pharaoh. The crossing of the Sea of Reeds and the defeat of the Egyptians became the great symbol of God's saving actions in history. Here in Exodus (and in the Vigil liturgy) it flows into the song of victory of Ex 15. Later, the author of Revelation will have the conquerors of the Beast sing, beside the heavenly sea, 'the song of Moses, the servant of God, and the song of the Lamb' (Rev 15:2-4). When Israel saw what God had achieved 'they believed in the Lord and in his servant Moses' (Ex 14:31). We, too, contemplating the mighty work of God in our Exodus, believe in God and his holy Servant Jesus (see Acts 4:30).

Fourth Reading   Is 54:5-14

Already in the eighth century B.C. the prophet Hosea had introduced the daring figure of Yahweh as the husband of his people (Hos 1-3). Two centuries later, the unknown prophet of the Exile takes up that image to comfort a shattered people. God seemed far away and Israel a wife forsaken. Israel receives the promise that the Lord, the Holy One, will take her back into his love and that their renewed relationship would abide – 'with everlasting love I will have compassion on you.' The Church, the Bride of Christ, is heir of this promise.

Fifth Reading   Is 55:1-11

The previous reading sang of Yahweh's enduring love; this reading, virtually its continuation, sings of his eternal covenant. It is an appeal to the exiles to turn from the ineffective things of this world to the word of God which alone achieves its purpose and can satisfy human longing. We Christians can be encouraged by the assurance of 'an everlasting covenant, my steadfast, sure love for David' – an assurance in the improbable setting of the ruins of the house of David! Why? Because the thoughts and ways of the Lord are not subject to human limitations (vv. 8-9) and the word of the Lord *will* accomplish its purpose (vv. 10-11). We, disciples of the Word, have no grounds for pessimism nor any excuse for discouragement.

Sixth Reading   Bar 3:9-15; 32-4:4

Part of the great wisdom poem of Baruch (3:9-4:4). It is a call to return to God, source of true wisdom. Israel is privileged to be recipient of this wisdom; if Israel lives by it, it will have life and peace. Wisdom is to be sought and found in Torah, the law of Moses. From a Christian perspective this wisdom is embodied in Christ. An exhortation to seek wisdom is all the more poignant on the Easter night when Christ crucified, the wisdom and power of God (1 Cor 1:24), triumphs over death.

Seventh Reading   Ezek 36:16-28

The capture and destruction of Jerusalem and exile of the people had not only convinced the nations of the powerlessness of Yahweh but had led Israel to doubt his might and his protection. Ezekiel reminds the exiles that the disasters had not come because of God's impotence but were caused by their sins. He assures them that their God will act – because he owes it to himself to vindicate his honour. He will gather his people, cleanse them from their sins and put a new spirit within them. Thus he would show himself to be their God and they would once again be truly his people. The hauntingly beautiful passage 36:24-28 is very like Jer 31:31-34. God will cleanse his people of their sin, giving them the new heart and spirit which will render them capable of fidelity to the Lord. For the Christian, this cleansing is to be understood in the new life celebrated in baptism.

B. New Testament Readings

First Reading
Rom 6:3-11

This reading takes us to the very heart of Christianity. The death and resurrection of Jesus are his 'Passover' to the Father. They are likewise the Passover of Christians, the new exodus to salvation. On Calvary Jesus died to this order of things, to the 'flesh' in its weakness and mortal nature; at his resurrection he entered into a new order of being, into a life glorious and immortal.

Baptism incorporates one into this Passover of Christ and into all that his Passover symbolizes and achieves. The Christian, in baptism, has shared in the death of Christ. Therefore, as far as sin is concerned, the baptized one is dead to its power. Sin no longer has absolute rule over us (v. 6) Having been buried with Christ in baptism (vv. 4a,5a,8a) we are now to regard ourselves as in fact dead, as far as the power of sin is concerned (v. 11a). This is, of course, only half the story. By dying Christ conquered sin (he 'died to sin', that is, he died rather than sin); and by rising he conquered death. If by baptism we shared in that death, do we not also share in that overcoming of death? We do but not yet! While our participation in Christ's death is described in the past tense, our participation in the resurrection is described exclusively in the future tense. It is an instance of Paul's constant insistence on the fact that our share in the glorified life of the Lord belongs to the future. Jesus is Lord not because he transports us out of this world but because he enables us to serve him in the confines of this world.

But, if we do not yet share the glory of Christ's resurrection, this share in his glory is enough for now: For the first time, we can choose not to sin. For the first time, it is possible that exhortations to good can be followed. By it Christians are crucified, die, with Christ to a purely earthly order of things. They die to weak human nature which is prey to sin and death. They die to it in the sense that now another power is present in them, the power of the risen Christ which gives them the means of triumphing over sin and eternal death. In baptism, too, they rise with Christ to the new life which he now enjoys because, through his resurrection, Christ is the life-giving Spirit. All this is the paschal mystery which is operative in Christian life: death to sin and life to grace. This conviction of Christians is hope and challenge: we should live by the Christ-life we have received.

Gospel   Lk 24:1-12

It is clear, from the New Testament, that Christians were, from the first, convinced that the crucified Jesus was not held by death. In Jewish faith and prayer, God is he who 'makes the dead live'. Jewish faith and hope looked to a resurrection of the righteous at the end of time. What the first Christians asserted was that, in the person of Jesus of Nazareth, this divine act had taken place. Jewish expectation was eschatological: resurrection was an event of the End-time. Christians asserted that an eschatological event had taken place in time. If one can put it so, the resurrection of Jesus is an event at once eschatological and historical. In essence it is a spiritual event, beyond our world of time, and it has impinged on our world of time.

The passage Luke 24:1-12 (based on Mark 16:1-8) breaks fresh ground. Luke explicitly records failure to find the body of Jesus. The women (v.10) had come, as in Mark, to anoint the body. While they puzzled over the absence of the body of 'the Lord Jesus' (v.3), 'two men in dazzling clothes stood beside them' (v.4) – a fascinating development of Mark's 'young man' and Matthew's 'angel of the Lord' (Mt 28:2). The 'two men' challenge the women's concern with the tomb: why are you seeking the living one in this place of the dead? (v.5). In vv. 6-8 we have a striking example of Luke's editorial freedom. Since, in his theological plan, the climax of his gospel must be in Jerusalem he cannot, without bringing about an anticlimax, record apparitions in Galilee. So he rewrites Mark 16:7 and changes the promise of an appearance in Galilee into a prophecy made by Jesus 'while he was still in Galilee'. Again, unlike the women of Mark 'who said nothing to anyone' (Mk 16:8), the women in Luke 'told all this to the eleven and to all the rest' (Lk 24:9). The 'apostles', however, set no store by this 'idle table' (v.11). Verse 12 offers one of the many contacts with the Johannine tradition in Luke's passion and resurrection narrative. It tells that Peter went hastily to the tomb, saw the linen clothes (which had wrapped the body of Jesus) lying there, and came away, quite puzzled.

Eastertide

Introduction to the Liturgical Season

The readings for the Easter season evoke the presence of the risen Lord in the Church, and they speak about the life and worship and witness of the Christian community, animated by the Holy Spirit.

GOSPELS

The gospel of the second Sunday of the Easter season is from John, the appearances of Jesus to the apostles on the first day and on the eighth day. The Gospel of the third Sunday gives John's account of the appearance by the sea of Tiberias. The gospels for the fourth Sunday show Jesus as the Good Shepherd. Those for the fifth, sixth and seventh Sundays are taken from John, the discourse and prayer of Jesus at the Last Supper, about life and love and Spirit and unity.

FIRST READINGS

The First Readings are from the Acts of the Apostles, arranged in 'a three-year cycle of parallel and progressive selections'. They give a picture of the early Church's way of life, its witness to the resurrection, and its growth. They include material about prayer, breaking bread, baptism, laying on of hands, and church order, which remind us that this is a time of reflection on the life of the Church, including its liturgy.

SECOND READINGS

For Year C, Second Readings are all from the Apocalypse. These readings are chosen to express 'the spirit of joyous faith and sure hope proper to this season'.

Ascension Day: The Easter season includes Ascension Day, on which the Gospel is from one or other of the synoptics, and the First Reading is Acts' account of the ascension. The Second Reading is from Ephesians, about God raising Christ from the dead and making him sit at his right hand. An *ad libitum* Second Reading for Years C is one from Hebrews reflecting on how Christ has entered, not a man-made sanctuary, but heaven itself.

Pentecost: The Easter season ends with Pentecost Sunday. The Gospels are passages from John about fountains of living water, symbolizing the Spirit (vigil Mass), and about Jesus breathing on the disciples and saying "Receive the Holy Spirit" (Pentecost Sunday). An *ad libitum* Gospel for Year C is a passage from John about the promise of the Spirit.

An interesting choice of First Readings is given for the vigil Mass of Pentecost: the Tower of Babel, the theophany on Mount Sinai, Ezekiel on the dry bones being brought to life, or Joel on the pouring out of the spirit on all humankind.

The Second Readings are Romans on the Spirit who pleads for us (vigil Mass); First Corinthians on the variety of gifts and the one Spirit (Pentecost Sunday); and Romans on the Spirit who gives life and makes us children of God (Year C *ad libitum*).

The First Reading for Mass during the day is Acts' description of Pentecost, with all its implications for the life of the Church.

Philip Gleeson OP

Eastertide

First Reading
Acts 10:34.37-43

From now until Pentecost Sunday inclusive, first readings are drawn from Acts of the Apostles. Since Acts is the second volume of one work (the third gospel being the first) it should be understood for what it is; more correctly a sequel to Luke's gospel than a history of the early Church. Given this close relationship, we are not surprised to find that the structure of gospel and Acts runs along parallel lines. The narrative of the ministry of Jesus is formed of two more or less equal parts: the first, covering the preaching in Galilee, centres in the Twelve and ends with the mission confided to the Twelve; the other part, the journey to Jerusalem, begins with the mission charge to the Seventy, and has material not found in Mark and Matthew. Similarly, Acts has two parts: one in which Peter has a leading role and which looks to Jerusalem (1:1-15:35); the second, centred in Paul, breaks out of this geographical framework and turns towards Rome (15:36-28:31).

In Acts Luke is concerned with showing the progress of the Good News throughout the whole world (1:8). He is especially interested in the passing of the preaching from Jews to Gentiles and in the progress of the Gentile mission. Behind the continuous spread of the Gospel throughout the provinces of the Empire he sees the power of the Holy Spirit. Luke was aware that the Gentile mission had been set on foot before Paul had begun to play his part and he knew that Paul was not the only architect of the Gentile Church. But since his purpose was to portray the spread of the Church, he could not have chosen a more dramatic and effective way of doing so. For it is true that Paul the missionary and Paul the theologian has set his stamp on Christianity.

Our reading is part of Peter's speech in the home of the Roman centurion, Cornelius. The discourse gives an outline of the ministry of Jesus, ending with the narrative of his resurrection. Noteworthy is the emphasis on the fact that Peter and his companions were eyewitnesses of the resurrection – more precisely, that they had encountered the risen Lord. They are witnesses so that they can be sent to preach redemption, the forgiveness of sin.

The risen Saviour continued to be with his Church after the resurrection. And it was because Jesus had risen again from the dead that the apostles could preach the reality of redemption, of the forgiveness of sin. Because God was with him, Jesus during his ministry went about doing good. God is present in a special way with his people in the person of the risen Christ. In him the fullness of God dwells, an overflowing plenitude of divine power and goodness, bringing new divine life to all who believe in Christ. This is the power of Christ's resurrection of which Paul speaks in Philippians (Phil 3:10).

Each successive generation of Christians can proclaim, and must proclaim, the reality and the significance of the resurrection as confidently as Peter did. The Church does so unceasingly, but does so in a special manner at Easter. And down the ages the opening words of the Easter Mass have brought us Christ's reassuring message: 'I have risen and am with you still, alleluia.' The passage of years has made no difference. The risen Lord is the same yesterday, today and forever.

Second Reading   Col 3:1-4

According to the author, baptism is a participation in Christ's death and resurrection, symbolized by the ritual of being 'plunged' into water (2:12). This real sharing in Christ's death and resurrection has profound and far-reaching repercussions in the Christian's present moral life. It entails the rejection of all that is 'earthly' (3:2-5), that is, all that is opposed to God. It calls for the pursuit of the 'good life' – not by the world's standards but as the good life has been lived by Jesus. Here we have the reality of *Christian* freedom. Though by one's sacramental death in baptism the Christian is liberated from past constraints, one is, nevertheless, bound to lead a new life in conformity with the gospel.

Alternative Second Reading   1 Cor 5:6-8

Paul is concerned in 5:1-13 with a case of incest in the Corinthian community. He argues that this 'immoral' person, like yeast within a lump of dough, affects the whole community. The historical context does not exhaust the meaning of the image. We today cannot expect to share fully in the newness of Christ's sacrifice if we cling to the evil and wickedness of our life without Christ.

Gospel   Jn 20:1-9

John has preserved two versions of the women's visit to the tomb – 20:1-3 and 11-13. Underlying the first of them (vv 1-2) would seem to be the earliest form of an empty tomb narrative in any gospel. John has introduced the Beloved Disciple and has, for his own dramatic purpose, reduced the original group of women to Mary Magdalene – preparing the way for the later Christophany to her (vv. 14-18). It is this christophany, and not an angelic spokesman, which explains the meaning of the empty tomb (vv 12-13). But the tradition which was thus rewritten is early indeed.

Thoroughly Johannine is 20:1-10. At Mary Magdalene's disturbing news (v. 2) Peter and 'the other disciple' hurry to the tomb. In the tradition, Peter's companion was unnamed. John has introduced him as the Beloved Disciple so that his coming to faith might interpret the significance of the empty tomb. The burial cloths and, more unexpectedly, their arrangement, are a sign that Mary's interpretation of the empty tomb ('they have taken the Lord out of the tomb', 20:2) is not the correct one. Jesus has not been 'taken' anywhere. Rather, he has left mortality behind him. Only the Beloved Disciple (vv. 2,8) seeing the sign, believes – 'he saw and believed' (v. 8). Manifestly, he believed, even *before* any appearance of the risen Lord, in the risen Christ himself. The fact of the matter is that while the 'beloved disciple' is a real person and the source of John's tradition, he also represents the Christian disciple who is sensitive, in faith and love, to the presence of the risen Jesus. With this one exception – theological exception – of the Beloved Disciple who saw with eyes of faith, the 'empty tomb' is never regarded as a reason for faith. The conviction that Jesus can no longer be found in the tomb because he is risen Lord (and not for any other reason) follows on encounter with the risen Lord.

What is the *significance* of the resurrection of Jesus? The confession: 'God raised Jesus from the dead' implies more, much more, than the deed of raising from the dead. It implies that the kingdom of God – the rule of God – is indeed come in Jesus. The resurrection should not be regarded as an isolated fact. In declaring 'Christ is risen' one is acknowledging that God's saving promises have been accomplished in Jesus. Jesus had seen his whole life and his whole mission in relation to the fulfilment of such promises: 'We had hoped that he was the one to redeem Israel' (Lk 24:21). It was because of their former hope in him that the disciples were able to interpret the resurrection as God's confirmation of all that Jesus stood for. Because he was raised from the dead, Jesus holds decisive significance for us. Because of the fact of his resurrection we know that meaningless death – and meaningless life – now have meaning. Jesus had died with the cry on his lips: 'My God, my God, why have you forsaken me?' (Mk 15:34). The sequel was to show that God had never abandoned Jesus. We have the assurance that he will not abandon us.

If the life of Jesus showed the meaning of his death, the life-and-death of Jesus showed the meaning of his resurrection. As Jesus' lifestyle, his praxis of the kingdom of God, had prepared for his death, his resurrection was the vindication of all he stood for. This involves more than the authentication of his message. Resurrection, for one thing, underlies the reality of Jesus' Abba-consciousness, his communion with God, which death could not interrupt. The resurrection of Jesus demonstrates that God is indeed the God of humankind who holds out, to all of us, the promise of life beyond death. In other words, the resurrection of Jesus is not only something that happened to him; it reaches to us. And not only as it concerns our future resurrection. Already, as risen Lord, Jesus himself is present to us and with us in our striving to give substance to the Kingdom. He is Emmanuel – God-with-us.

SECOND SUNDAY OF EASTER

First Reading   Acts 5:12-16

This is the last of the three summaries in Acts which describe the life and activities of the earliest Christian community (2:42-47; 4:32-35). Since it is clear that Luke considers this earliest community at Jerusalem to be a model for all Christian communities, these passages have a special importance as a sort of blueprint making up the picture of the Christian community as it ideally should be. The third summary concentrates upon Christians' external relations, their good repute – a point often noted also about individuals by Luke who is much concerned about one's good name – and the miracles they work.

In Luke's gospel the working of miracles often occurs especially in connection with Jesus' authority so that his power in word and deed is seen to be a single manifestation of the presence in him of the Spirit and of the advent of the kingdom of God. So also in Acts the miracles of the apostles serve particularly to give weight and authority to their message. The New Testament writers look on miracles chiefly from the point of view of fulfilment: the time of the Messiah was to be a time when all evil, sickness and unhappiness were to give way to an era of peace, prosperity and joy. The healing miracles, then, are signs that this age has arrived and continues to spread in the apostolic age.

Second Reading
Rev 1:9-13.17-19

Revelation does not figure largely in the liturgical prayer of the contemporary Church. In the lectionary it provides the second reading for Sundays 2-7 of Easter in Year C.

THE BOOK OF REVELATION

Bewilderment – that, in all likelihood, is the reaction of one who comes, for the first time, to the Book of Revelation. Those scrolls and plagues, those elders and living creatures, the dragon and the beasts – what can it be about? Is it any wonder that the book has become a happy-hunting ground of fundamentalists and of others who are mesmerized by prospect of the End? Is there any sense to be made of it? In truth, Revelation is a thoroughly Christian writing which, despite first impression, carries a message of startling hope.

In Greek the word for revelation is *apocalypsis*, from which we get the word 'apocalypse'. What is apocalypse? It is a literary form with its own technique and conventions. An apocalyptic seer claims to have been let into the secrets of the heavenly realm. He has had access to heavenly secrets either by means of vision or audition (hearing the heavenly word), or through other-worldly journey – in effect, a guided tour of heaven. A constant element is the presence of an an angel as interpreter or guide – an *angelus interpres*. This is to underline the fact that revelation alone is not enough; supernatural aid is required if one is to understand. The seer puts his message across in the language of imagery and symbol.

Literary Form

This literature flourished in Judaism from the second century B.C. and was adopted by early Christians. Because of unfamiliarity with the form, apocalypse is, for us, strange, disturbing – when it is not wholly incomprehensible. We must remember, in the case of Revelation, that for John and his readers it would have been part of their culture. They would have understood its literary conventions and have heard its message. An apocalyptic writer is usually addressing what he perceives as a crisis situation. He is most anxious that his word be heard. He does not go out of his way to invent a bizarre form that would pass over the heads of his readers. Apocalypse was not at all as strange to those to whom it was first addressed as it has become for us.

'Apocalypse', then, is the literary form in which apocalytpic views are expressed. An apocalyptic group sets up its own system of thought within which it can live its life. Usually, it does so in protest against the dominant society with which it is in conflict. The group has a painful experience of alienation. That may be due to a quarrel with the power group within its own society. Or, it may be a nation, or section of it, in protest against a system imposed by a foreign power. In either case there is the experience of powerlessness. Apocalyptists reject the dominant culture which they regard as irremediable. The current world is inherently, inescapably, evil. Hope lies in a divine intervention which will destroy the present evil age – and vindicate the alienated suffering ones. A favoured manner of giving vent to the frustration and the hope was in writing; and we have the literary form apocalypse.

Dualism

It is taken for granted that a supernatural world stands above our earthly world. That heavenly world is the 'real' world. There is, indeed, a twofold dualism – vertical: the world above and our world; horizontal: our age and the Age to come. In short, the presumption is of an other-worldly reality which dictates the fate of our world. There is a looking to life beyond death, a life very different from the life of our experience. In that future the apocalyptic group will be finally vindicated and come into their blessed home. There is always a definitive eschatological judgment: the final clash between Good and Evil, issuing in the total victory of God and the end of Evil.

The Book

Revelation addresses a group of seven Christian communities in the late first-century Roman province of Asia (the western part of modern Turkey). The author, John, knew these Churches thoroughly. In his estimation all was not well. He had perceived a radical incompatibility between the Roman world of his day and the Gospel message. In his view the perennial conflict between good and evil was being played out in terms of Rome and Church. There were Christians who did not share his assessment, those who sought accommodation. In his radical view there was no place for compromise.

God and Lamb

Two figures dominate Revelation: the Almighty One on the heavenly throne (God), and the Lamb (Christ). The One on the throne displays his power in and through the Lamb who was slain. In his way John makes the same point as Paul: 'We proclaim Christ crucified ... Christ the power of God and the wisdom of God' (1 Cor 1:23-24).

Encouragement

In light of his challenge to his readers, with its call on their 'patient endurance', a marked feature of John's work is encouragement and comfort. His encouragement is paradoxical. His model is the Lamb *who was slain*. The Lamb has pointed the way to victory: the Victor is the Victim. The Christian communities of John's concern were small groups, quite helpless before the might of Rome. There will be suffering and death. There will be victims. His encouragement was the assurance that those who are faithful unto death already rejoice, now and forever, with their Lord: 'Blessed are the dead who die in the Lord henceforth' (14:13). Furthermore, one may discern, threading through the book, the theme of universal salvation. Or, better expressed, that God's final word is positive: salvation only. The message of Revelation is more than word of encouragement to those who suffer tribulation. It is promise of a wider hope.

Liturgy

Revelation is a letter that carries an explicit direction for its reading in liturgical assembly (1:3). It was designed to be *heard*. Somewhat as with radio-drama, the listener assimilates its words imaginatively. Spangled with heavenly liturgies, it sustains a liturgical dimension throughout. John's heavenly liturgies are, surely, echoes of community celebrations of his Churches. Not surprisingly, there is an echo of eucharistic celebration.

Challenge

John wrote his letter to specific communities of his day. He addressed their situation – not ours. Still, he has a message for us. His radical stance challenges us to look more critically at the standards of our world. We must ask ourselves if we may not have, too readily, come to terms with the prevailing culture. He challenges our complacency. We do not need to be quite as uncompromising as John (who rejected wholly the Roman world of his day). But if we have the courage to look at our Christian situation through the prism of the Gospel, we may observe more shadow than we are eager to acknowledge. Beyond the shadow shines steadfast hope. We may glimpse the New Jerusalem, the ultimate Rule of God – where God will be all in all. We may see the God of Justice – who wills the salvation of all. *Our* God is manifest in the Lamb. Our prayer is *Marana-tha* – 'Come, Lord Jesus!'

John is not addressing an abstract 'Church.' He speaks, directly, to communities of men and women – communities good, bad, and indifferent. The messages (chapters 2-3) peg Revelation firmly to our world. It is word of hope to people who need hope, people who may falter. This realism – and we find it throughout Scripture – brings us comfort and encouragement. There never has been a perfect Christian community. Christians have been faithful and heroic, and Christians have been frail and vacillating. It is not enough for us to find solace in the word to Philadelphia (3:7-13); we must also hearken to the word to Laodicea (3:14-22).

Relevance

If Revelation is seen only as crisis literature, written in the stress of active persecution, it is not easy to see that it can have much to say to our western Churches. We do not live in an atmosphere of apocalyptic crisis. We certainly do not experience, or envisage, violent persecution. But, if we regard Revelation as a reflection of John's assessment of his world, we may see how and where it does address us. John was not coping with a situation of actual persecution. If there were to be 'tribulation ' on a grand scale, it would be in response to a radical Christian rejection of the *status quo* – which had not happened but which he was inviting. Revelation does have something to say to our world – if we interpret its symbols in relation to our situation.

The challenge of the Way remains. There is an incompatibility between wholehearted following of Christ and the standards of a world unenlightened by the gospel. There is the danger that Christians can settle, too readily, for a 'reasonable' accommodation. It is the charism of a prophet to see to the heart of things. Only the starkest words can match his uncomplicated vision. The genuine prophet will speak a message of comfort, based on the faithfulnesss of God, but it will never be a comfortable message. John's prophetic messages to the Churches (chapters 2 to 3) urge us to look to ourselves, to our contemporary Ephesus and Philadelphia and Laodicea. The Beast in our world – in our western world at least – is not as openly oppressive as the Beast of John's world. It may be all the more dangerous, because more insidious.

Perhaps the relentless John is right after all: there is no compromise! More to the point, from these messages we can draw a comfort that comes from a better grasp of the overall New Testament situation. We learn that our first brothers and sisters in the faith were no different from ourselves. They, as we, had, in human frailty, to live out their faith in an unsympathetic, often hostile, world. They, as we, had their doubts and their fears. They, as we, had to hear the warning: 'in the world you have tribulation.' And, despite every appearance to the contrary, had to cling, in hope, to the assurance: 'Take courage; I have conquered the world!' (Jn 16:33).

Commentary on Revelation 1:9-13,17-19

A brief prologue (1:1-3) introduces Revelation as a letter of the prophet John, a letter meant to be read at the liturgical assembly. John is conscious of being spokesperson of the supreme pastor of the Church: Christ. John is 'brother' of those to whom he writes. Like them he is incorporated into Jesus as he shares fully their destiny of suffering and glory. And he shares fully 'patient endurance'. This term occurs seven times in Revelation (1:9; 2:2,3,19; 3:10; 13:10; 14:12); it is the characteristic virtue of the persecuted. It is grounded on faith in Jesus, the Lord who comes; it is inspired by the certainty of his love; it is marked by strength of soul which enables one to endure, and it finds expression in the bearing of trials in steadfastness under tribulation.

It is a matter of first importance that John's opening statement about the 'one in human form' (literally, 'like a son of man'), his introduction of Christ, is that he saw him among the 'lamps' (or 'lamp-stands'), that is, among the Churches (the seven Churches, symbolized by lamps, to which the message of John is addressed). The risen and ascended Lord is no absentee landlord. He is present in his earthly communities; he knows their 'works'. It is in his name that John speaks his prophetic messages. The overall effect of the vision is one of terrifying majesty; John's reaction is that of Daniel (Dan 10:8-9). Yet, this majestic figure remains the Jesus of the gospel, and John hears again his comforting, 'Do not be afraid' (see Mk 6:50; Mt 28:10).

The first characteristic of Christ revealed by John is that he is present among the earthly congregations of his people. The details of the vision of the Son of Man (vv. 14-15, omitted in the lectionary reading) have symbolical value and refer to the eternity, divine knowledge, stability and authority of Christ. John is overawed by the terrifying majesty of the vision; but the Son of Man is 'the first and the last'. He is the Living One: though he had died, by the resurrection he had entered upon a new, victorious life in which death was forever conquered, death can no longer frighten Christians (v. 17).

This inaugural vision effectively brings out the oracular character of the first part of Revelation, for it is closely parallel to the inaugural visions of the Old Testament prophets (Is 6; Jer 1; Ezek 1-3). But where they proceeded to speak in the name of Yahweh ('thus says Yahweh'), John will make known the 'revelation of Jesus Christ'. And, since in his eyes, the symbolic seven reaches beyond the communities he addresses immediately, his message – the message of the Lord – has meaning for the Church until the end of time.

Gospel   Jn 20:19-31

The risen Christ appears to his disciples only to entrust them with a mission. The mission is nothing more or less than the one he has received from the Father and, indeed, accomplished by his death and resurrection: the reconciliation of men and women with their Father (the forgiveness of sins). He greeted his disciples with the common Jewish salutation 'peace be with you.' Jesus considered peace a gift that comes from God, which established a relation of harmony and friendship not only between the Israelite and his neighbour but also between the Israelite and his God. Jesus had declared during his lifetime that the world cannot give true peace and that he had come to bestow it (Jn 14:27). Now as glorified Lord he communicates his peace to his disciples and thus binds them to himself and to one another in a union of love and harmony.

To carry out their mission they are enlivened and inspired by the Holy Spirit – which is Christ's Spirit, making them one with him. They are to be Christ's body in the world. One of the effects of the gift of the Spirit was that they could forgive sins. John did not tell us who could exercise this power or how it should be exercised. It would be blatantly anachronistic to read back into this text the later sacrament of penance. What one can confidently say is that the Church's use of the sacrament of reconciliation is one valid and legitimate way of exercising the power over sin given by the risen Jesus to his disciples.

The episode of Thomas (vv. 24-29) is of great importance for the fourth evangelist and is, indeed, climactic in his gospel. (Chapter 20 is the close of the gospel proper, chapter 21 being an appendix). The disciple, Thomas, passes from unbelief to belief. The last word of a disciple in the gospel is a full-blooded christological profession of faith.

Thomas refuses to accept the word of the other disciples and insists on having concrete proof of the reality of the resurrection of Jesus (vv. 24-25). In the event, he comes to belief without a need for the crude verification he seemed to demand (20:25,27-28). It is enough to have seen (v. 29, see vv. 20,25). It is unfortunate that Thomas has been remembered for his stubbornness – 'doubting Thomas.' He ought to have been remembered for the most forthright confession of faith in the gospels: 'My Lord and my God.' It is the supreme christological conviction: Jesus may, by Christians, be addressed by the same terms in which Israel had addressed Yahweh. Thomas' confession is an acknowledgment of the God revealed in Jesus. It is, most likely, a confessional formula of the evangelist's Church.

Thomas has made the last utterance of a disciple of Jesus. The evangelist adds a comment that is crucial for all disciples of the risen Lord – those of us who live in 'that day': 'Have you believed because you have seen me? Blessed are those who have not seen and yet have come to believe' (20:29). The evangelist is writing for a generation that has not 'seen' the Lord. He would insist that Thomas and the later disciples are equal, sharing the same blessedness through their common faith in the Lord, though he be not visible. It is the tranquil assurance of union with him.

THIRD SUNDAY OF EASTER

First Reading   Acts 5:27-32.40-41

Luke instances a constant Christian paradox; faith brings joy, thanksgiving, praise of God for his wonderful works – and opposition and persecution serve to enhance this joy, thanksgiving and praise. The effectiveness of Christ's mission is demonstrated even in opposition to it; it is the effectiveness which counts. Persecution had not taken the apostles by surprise – Jesus had spoken of it beforehand: 'They will arrest you and persecute you; they will hand you over to synagogues and prisons, and you will be brought before kings and governors because of my name. This will give you an opportunity to testify' (Lk 21:12-13).

This prophecy is fulfilled to the letter: here they have been brought before Jewish meetings and have undergone imprisonment; a Paul will be brought before 'kings and governors', and on each occasion they bear witness to the power of the Spirit (see Acts 16:25-34). The central point of Peter's witness, on this occasion as always, is the resurrection of Jesus. The Jews had killed 'the Author of life' (3:15) but God has raised him from the dead to be 'Leader and Saviour'. God's purpose was to bring Israel to conversion – precondition of forgiveness of sins. The apostles are witnesses of the resurrection, but they do not stand alone; beside them is the powerful witness of the Holy Spirit, 'given to those who obey him'. Peter and John had already insisted, before the Jewish authorities, on their determination to listen to God rather than to men (4:19). Now, rejoicing is their privilege of suffering for 'the

Name', they are going to ignore the Sanhedrin's solemn prohibition to preach (5:40-41).

> Peter speaks up, establishing the guiding principle for all authentic religion – the pursuit of God's will. For decades Peter had believed God's will was discovered primarily through the guidance of the religious leaders of his nation. Like devout believers of every generation, he needs to accept responsibility for his decisions and life. While respecting religious leaders, he cannot hide behind a belief that these leaders are always right. They had put Jesus to death to preserve the status quo, and Peter denounces their infidelity and failure to give authentic leadership. (Doohan, p. 181)

Second Reading   Rev 5:11-14

Chapter 5 of Apocalypse depicts a transfer of power: God handed over to the Lamb (the crucified and risen Christ) a sealed scroll, since the Lamb alone has been found worthy to open that sealed book. The reading gives the close of the chapter, part of the first of the heavenly liturgies so frequent in the book. Of particular interest to us is that these are either early Christian hymns or have been modelled on such hymns. The 'One seated on the throne' is named frequently throughout: God as king and judge. The 'living creatures' are, in Jewish tradition, the four angels who direct the physical world; therefore they symbolize the created universe. (The identification of the 'living creatures' with the evangelists, apparently originating with Irenaeus, is wholly fanciful.) The elders, twenty-four in number (4:4) are the heavenly representatives of the earthly Church. The living creatures and the elders had sung a hymn to the Lamb (5:9-10); now a new feature is introduced: the praise of the countless host of angels (see Dan 7:10). The first four words of the doxology concern the Lamb's dominion; the other three express the adoration of the angels (5:12). Finally (5:13-14) the whole of creation joins in the great canticle of praise (5:13-14). John *hears* the voice of the great acclamation; to it the four living creatures, heavenly representatives of the created universe, give their 'Amen' – and the elders worship.

> The Almighty God has his plan and purpose for his world. In his dealing with a the human world, he will not proceed without the co-operation of humankind. He sought his agent, he found him in the Lamb. This Messiah, scion of David, is the Lamb who was slain. Our Almighty God manifests his power in the Cross. In the Cross, in the blood of the Lamb, he offers forgiveness and holds out

salvation to all. The Lamb, as the manifestation, as the very presence, of our gracious God, is worthy of our honour and worship. He is worthy precisely as the slain Lamb, as the crucified One. Like Paul and Mark, John, too, in his manner, proposes a *theologia crucis*. That comforting – if challenging – theme threads through his work. (Harrington, p. 87f)

Gospel   Jn 21:1-19

The gospel proper has ended with 20:31; this chapter is an appendix. After an introductory listing of the disciples concerned (1-3), we have an appearance of Jesus by the lakeside, Peter's reaction, and the miraculous draught of fish (4-8); then Peter's hauling the net ashore, followed by breakfast with Jesus (9-14); and finally the commissioning of Peter and the prophecy of his death (15-19). The chapter is built around Peter and the Beloved Disciple. In a fishing scene and at a meal Jesus reveals himself to his disciples; he invites them to faith. The ease and intimacy of his meeting with them is reminiscent of his first meeting with them (1:37-39). But the disciples again have difficulty in recognising him (21:4,12). This is a constant feature of the resurrection narratives: the Lord is not at once recognized; it required some word or familiar gesture to make him known. This is an effective way of making the point that Jesus had not returned to life as before but had passed, beyond death, to *new* life with God. He is Jesus – and yet he is different. Though Peter has the more important role (vv. 2,3,7,11) it is the Beloved Disciple who is sensitive in faith to the presence of the risen Jesus and recognizes him (v. 7).

The miraculous catch of fish, with its symbolical reference to 'fishers of people' (Lk 5:10) is a summons to an apostolic mission. The great haul of fish suggests a universal and abundant mission. At the lakeside breakfast Jesus 'took the bread and gave it to them'. His gesture answers the question how Jesus remains present to his disciples: he is present among them as they share the eucharistic meal. Peter, who had failed his Master (18:15-27) is now reinstated and is entrusted with a special pastoral mission. Peter's story is one of calling, falling and recalling. It is noteworthy that he is entrusted by the Lord with '*my* lambs, *my* sheep'. The Lord is, and remains, 'the chief Shepherd' (1 Pet 5:4)

FOURTH SUNDAY OF EASTER

First Reading   Acts 13:14.43-52

In chapter 13 of Acts a clear pattern emerges. Paul preaches first to
Jews, the chosen people. They reject him; he turns to the Gentiles. The
pattern is repeated in chapters 18 and 28. Indeed the turn to the Gentiles
is the final result of Paul's missionary activity (28:26-28). Each time
we are reminded by a scriptural text or allusion that this had been
foreseen in the will of God. We should not imagine that Paul's words
in vv. 46-48 declare Jewish unbelief to be the primary cause of the
Gentile mission; the place of Jews in the work of salvation has already
been established (2:39; 3:25-26). The point being made is that the
inexplicable refusal of many still falls into place in God's plan. It is a
rather tortuous answer to the question: Why is it that the Jewish people,
by and large, did not acknowledge their Messiah? The simple answer:
God knows! Paul's own missionary work fulfils God's words concerning the Suffering Servant (vv. 47-48) – he is bringing salvation 'to
the ends of the earth'.

> The call to change one's way of life is a joyful and liberating
> invitation for some. For others it implies letting go of past values,
> which they feel implies abandonment and failure, and they fight
> against such change. (Doohan, p. 182)

Second Reading   Rev 7:9.14-17

This 'great multitude' is not a group distinct from the 144,000 (itself
a 'great multitude') of 7:4-8; it is the same group viewed under a
different aspect: it is the Church triumphant in heaven. More particularly, for John, these are the Christian martyrs. In keeping with his
consistent outlook they are presented as happy here and now; they
stand before God and the Lamb, celebrating a heavenly Feast of
Tabernacles (Tabernacles was the most joyous of Hebrew feasts).

As martyrs sharing in Christ's victorious death, they have immediately received their white robes of victory (6:11); palm branches are a
symbol of triumph and joy. But the martyrs stand for all faithful
Christians and in their priestly role (1:6) they serve God, adding their
necessary human voice to the prayer of creation (4:8). In their
heavenly Feast of Tabernacles there is no need for the martyrs to
construct their own booths (Lev 23:323-36); God himself will be their
tabernacle, their tent (*skene*) – there is a probable reference to the
shekinah, the immediate presence of God in the Temple (see Rev

21:3). The texts of Isaiah (49:10; 52:8), which refer to the happy return from the Babylonian exile, find their fulfilment in the shepherding of the Lamb who leads his own sheep to the unfailing fountains of life (Rev 7:16-17). For, in startling and beautiful paradox, the Lamb has become a shepherd. In the Fourth Gospel the Lamb of God (Jn 1:29,36) is also the Good Shepherd (10:14-16).

> 'Was it not necessary that the Christ should suffer these things and then enter into his glory?' (Lk 24:26) is the rebuke of the risen Lord to the uncomprehending Emmaus disciples. John pictures the glory of the victors beyond their tribulation. They have triumphed, but not on their own. Victory is theirs because, and only because, the Lamb had first conquered. It is a conviction shared by the fourth evangelist – 'apart from me you can do nothing' (Jn 15:5) – and by Paul – 'I can do all things in him who strengthens me' (Phil 4:13). It is a lesson we need to take to heart. A glorious destiny awaits us, yes; but precisely as faithful followers of the Lamb. If we cannot share John's expectation of imminent eschatological tribulation, we may well be failing to discern a more insidious and pervasive challenge. John saw through the empire of his day, discerned its distorted standard of values. We have become so much part of our contemporary empire, the lifestyle of the Western world, that we may no longer be stirred, excited, by prospect of heavenly joy. (Harrington, p. 102)

Gospel
Jn 10:27-30

The passage 10:22-39, in the setting of the feast of Dedication, presents Jesus as Messiah and Son of God. The opposite question is raised in v. 24 – 'If you are the Christ, tell us plainly'. Jesus begins his answer to the question about messiahship by recalling the works he is doing (v. 25). Vv. 26-27 recall 10:1-21; the faithful sheep know the voice of their shepherd (v. 3). V. 28 recalls the thought of the wolves who snatch the sheep when the hireling guards (rather, fails to guard) the flock (v. 12). Jesus is the true shepherd and no one will snatch from his care the sheep that the Father has given him. Note the correspondence of vv. 28 and 29: 'no one will snatch them out of my hand'; 'no one can snatch them out of the Father's hand'. What comfort for the sheep! Securely shepherded by Father and Son, what have they to fear? And, if Father and Son are one (v. 30), they bind men and women to themselves as one (17:11).

Christianity is a submission of faith: 'My sheep hear my voice'. It is a superior knowledge, a transcendent awareness: 'I know my own and my own know me' (v. 14: see v. 27) It is a discipline: 'My sheep follow me'. And it is the only absolute security humanity can have: 'I give them eternal life, and they will never perish. No one will snatch them out of my hand'. Fundamentally, it is the security of the steadfast God, because 'the Father and I are one'.

FIFTH SUNDAY OF EASTER

First Reading   Acts 14:21-27

This passage is the conclusion of what is commonly called 'the first missionary journey' (Acts 13:14). Paul and Barnabas retrace their steps encouraging the little communities they had founded. They leave them under no illusion: they will have to prepare for persecution. Of special interest is the appointment of elders 'in each Church'; the presumption is of a generally accepted institution. Paul may sometimes have appointed local community leaders, but his own authority remained paramount (1 Cor 7:17;2 2 Cor 11:28). Luke's statement is, very likely, anachronistic. The appointment here takes place only after prayer and fasting. Luke, in Gospel and Acts, stresses the importance of prayer in Christian life.

Second Reading   Rev 21:1-5

The closing part of Revelation opens with the vision of a new heaven and a new earth, the setting of the new Jerusalem. The former creation has passed away (20:11) and all evil has been destroyed; now is the first phase of God's plan. The structure of Revelation 21:1-2 is modelled on Isaiah 65:17-19: the appearance of a new world, the disappearance of the former things, and the manifestation of a new Jerusalem. The new Jerusalem is a city of heavenly origin, a city 'whose builder and maker is God' (Heb 11:10; 12:22; Gal 4:26). Jerusalem was an accepted figure of the people of Israel, the people of God; it was a tangible sign of the covenant, the focus of Jewish faith and hope. To present a new Jerusalem was, in the concrete language of imagery, to proclaim the election of a new people and the sealing of a new covenant. The twofold image of 'city' and 'bride' is traditional; in this chapter John combines the images, slipping abruptly from one to the other.

In the new Jerusalem sorrow and pain will have no place; the positive defeat of the satanic forces, graphically described in 19:11-20:10, has brought to an end all that made up a world of sin. Now is fulfilled the promise of the most intimate sharing of life between God and his people – a constant theme in Jewish Scripture. Then God speaks. He speaks the creative word which calls the new world into being; it is the process of re-creation by which the old is transformed into the new. God is at the beginning and at the end. He is at the origin of all and at the end of all. All things have tended toward God, and now all things are found in him.

> What is eternal life with God? We, in our earthly existence, creatures of time and space, must perforce picture heavenly reality in terms of time and space. Here, John has two central images. There will be a new heaven and a new earth. The dragon once had his place in the old heaven; he had ravaged the old earth. A creation that is, at last, utterly free of evil can only be new. Humankind was the summit of God's creation, his pride and joy (Gen 1:26-31). His destined home for humankind was the garden of delights (2:15). There will a new home for humankind in the new creation: a city, the city of God, the new Jerusalem. It is a heavenly city, yet a habitat of men and women. (Harrington, p. 211)

Gospel
Jn 13:31-35

This passage is towards the close of chapter 13 of John, after the washing of the disciples' feet, the instruction on discipleship, and the prophecy of the betrayal. After Judas' departure Jesus is alone with his own. The general context is that of the Eucharist which, though never explicitly mentioned, is implied throughout. 'Now the Son of Man has been glorified'. The 'now' is the hour of decision and consummation, belonging in time, yet decisive for eternity. *Now*, by going forward to the cross, by being 'lifted up' he is about to return to glory. Already he had told the Jews, 'where I am you cannot come' (7:34; 8:21-22); but the reason on that occasion was their 'sin'. Here it is the separation from his disciples occasioned by his death. But, while they cannot come to him, *he* will come to them. In the meantime they will live by his 'new commandment'. The 'newness' here is the newness of the new covenant founded and perpetuated in the Eucharist. What is new in this covenanat is love 'as I have loved you'. Even if Jesus departs and they cannot now follow him to the Father, they can still be 'followers' of Jesus here and now and they can keep his spirit alive among themselves (vv. 34-35). As long as they keep true to the 'new commandment', as long as Christian love is in the world, the world still encounters Jesus.

The essential idea in the first part of the scene (vv. 31-35) is that when Jesus looks at his death and beyond it, he sees that his human life, far from being a meaningless God-denying absurdity, something which chills the heart into fear-filled immobility or devouring self-indulgence, is instead a place of unprecedented divine generosity and regeneration, a place in which God shines forth and in which God's shining reveals Jesus' own glorious self. And he sees that this mystery-filled generosity – like gentle sunshine which invites children to come out and play – invites people to discover another rejuvenated self and to throw themselves into its spirit of love. In other words, God's glorious presence so lights up life that it invites people to love.

> But love is not easy. One cannot love as Jesus has loved, one cannot give oneself as Peter proposes to do, without outside help. There are barricades which make love inaccessible, and so, before speaking of it, before issuing the invitation, Jesus refers to his own going away (v. 33), to what is, in fact, a mission to overleap the barricades. Through his departure in death he will release a stream of spiritual life which, while sweeping away all obstacles, will impart a new life, a new power of loving. (Brodie, p. 454)

SIXTH SUNDAY OF EASTER

First Reading   Acts 15:1-2.22-29

This Jerusalem meeting (*ca* 49 AD) was a decisive moment for the history of Christianity. Palestinian Jewish Christians had been upset by the reception of Gentiles (Cornelius and his household) into what, until then, had been an exclusively Jewish movement. Now, at the news (from Antioch) that Paul and Barnabas had gone out, vigorously, into the Gentile world and with notable success, some of them feel that the time has come to take a stand. These Gentile converts must be made to become good Jews: 'It is necessary for them to be circumcised and ordered to keep the law of Moses' (v. 5; see vv. 1-2). If this view had prevailed, Christianity could never be more than a Jewish sect. The fateful decision at Jerusalem determined that it would be a universal religion. Acts 15 is Luke's version of the episode; we have Paul's account in Galatians 2.

The two accounts do not agree in detail – which is not surprising. Paul wrote an *apologia*, defending his apostolate; Luke had no such concern. Paul wrote from personal recollection and his statements have unique importance; Luke was obliged to compile details from different sources.

Shortly after Paul and Barnabas had returned to Antioch from their journey in Asia Minor (45-49 A.D.) certain brethren came from Jerusalem and proclaimed that circumcision and Mosaic observance were necessary for salvation (Acts 15:1; Gal 2:4). The Church at Antioch decided to send Paul and Barnabas, with some of their own number, to Jerusalem (Acts 15:2; Gal 2:1). In Jerusalem they were received by the community and by the apostles and elders (Acts 15:4); but some converts from pharisaism demanded that Gentile converts should be subjected to circumcision (15:5). Peter brought forward the case of Cornelius: it would be 'putting God to the test' to impose any burdens on the converts since he had manifested his will so clearly. It was by the grace of the Lord Jesus alone that Jews and Gentiles were saved (15:7-11). James, arguing from the Old Testament for the call of the Gentiles, agreed fully with Peter on the question of circumcision.

However, he added the 'James-clause': the Gentile Christians were to abstain from meat sacrificed to idols, from marriage within the forbidden degrees of kindred (*porneia*), from eating the meat of strangled animals, and from blood (15:13-21): this would enable Jewish and Gentile Christians to associate and have eucharistic table-fellowship. It is very likely that the 'decision' formulated by James was a compromise following on the conflict on table-fellowship at Antioch (the row between Paul and Peter – Gal 2:11-14). Luke made it part of the earlier Jerusalem agenda. As he has it, a formal letter was duly drawn up addressed to 'the believers of Gentile origins' in Antioch and Syria and Cilicia.' It was sent with Paul and Barnabas, who were accompanied by two distinguished members of the Jerusalem Church, Judas and Silas (15:22-29). Thus was the authority of the mother-Church invoked to settle a problem that had troubled the great missionary Church of Antioch and had imperilled the future of Christianity. Jerusalem had approved the 'gospel' of Paul; and Paul himself was officially acknowledged as Apostle of the Gentiles (Gal 2:7-9). It would be quite wrong to imagine that Paul had received his apostolate from the Jerusalem Church. What Jerusalem did was to recognize the *independent* authority of Paul. He had his call directly from the Lord Jesus himself.

Second Reading   Rev 21:10-14.22-23

Revelation closes with a majestic view of the new Jerusalem, the heavenly Church of the future, the true kingdom of God. John's model for his presentation of the new Jerusalem is Ezekiel's vision of the messianic kingdom (Ezek 40-48). The prophet was carried, in vision, from Babylon to Israel and was set upon a very high mountain. There he saw, opposite him, 'a structure like a city': the temple of the future. Fittingly, the heavenly city of Revelation has heavenly gatekeepers, and the gates of the new Jerusalem bear the names of the tribes of Israel (Rev 21:12). When he goes on to tell us that the names of the twelve apostles are inscribed on the wall's foundations (v. 14), John asserts the continuity of the Christian Church with Israel. A city which is built on the foundation of the apostles is built on the apostolic tradition, the revelation of God of which the apostles were eyewitnesses and guarantors.

We might expect John's glowing description of the city (21:15-21) to be followed by a particularly striking description of its temple (the temple was the glory of the earthly Jerusalem). Instead – a brilliant touch – we learn that there is no temple, nor any need of one: God himself dwells there with the Lamb (vv. 22-23) Now, indeed, 'the dwelling of God is with mortals' (v. 3), and the glory of his presence pervades the whole city (vv. 11,18), making the new Jerusalem one vast temple. This is reminiscent of 7:15 where God himself is the tent of the heavenly feast of Tabernacles, for the liturgy of that feast appears to be present to the seer throughout our passage. A nightly ceremony with bright lights and rejoicing was a feature of Tabernacles. In the new city the Lamb will give light by night and God will replace the sun. God is not hidden as he was in the temple of old.

Gospel   Jn 14:23-29

The farewell discourse is dominated by the thought of the forthcoming departure of Jesus. He is concerned to assure his disciples that he will not leave them orphans. Despite his going away he and they will not be apart: they will be drawn into the love of the Father and Son. To love Jesus is to 'keep his word', that is, to respond in all their life to the challenge of Jesus. If this be the case, then 'my Father will love them, and we will come to them and will make our home with them.' This is a personal coming of the Father in the Son. Besides, the *word* of Jesus – his revelation – also abides with them. There is another sense in which they will not be alone: the Holy Spirit will take Jesus' place and carry on his work (vv. 25-26). In union with Jesus ('in my name') he will teach. But his teaching will have reference to the words of Jesus, leading the disciples into a fuller understanding of what Jesus revealed and taught; he is the interpreter of Jesus to his disciples (see 16:13-14). Only through the power of the Spirit can we come to understand the real meaning of Jesus' person and mission of salvation. But the Spirit, who knows the depths of God, teaches us and enables us to say 'Jesus is Lord.' As the Spirit of God moulds us into the image of Christ, makes us into the Body of Christ, we know then that we are a community gathered together in his name.

Verse 28 gives the basis for our unshakable peace and joy and confidence ' I am going to the Father, because the Father is greater than I.' The confidence of Jesus rests on his subordination to the Father. Our confidence rests on our subordination to Jesus. God reaches down through the Son, through the Spirit, to lift us up through the Spirit, through the Son, to God.

THE ASCENSION OF THE LORD

First Reading
Acts 1:1-11

Luke follows contemporary practice when at the beginning of his second volume (Acts) he echoes the close of his gospel. The introduction to Acts passes from a brief recapitulation of the gospel (vv. 1-2) to a summary of the conversation of Jesus with his apostles after his resurrection (vv. 3-80, and a description of the Ascension (vv. 9-11).

In 1:6-8 the question of the apostles and the answer of the risen Jesus provide an answer to questions that had been asked many times before Luke wrote. Just as the conception of Jesus, 'Son of the Most High,' was due to the coming of the Holy Spirit on Mary (Lk 1:35), so the inception of the mission of the Church is brought about by a coming of the Holy Spirit on the apostles. In v. 8 Luke offers the programme his story is to follow. The phrase 'to the ends of the earth' harks back to Isaiah 49:6, a prophecy of universal salvation. Rome, where the story will end (28:30-31), while not the end of the earth, is the centre of the Empire from which all roads lead to the end of the earth. In vv. 9-11 Luke describes the departure of Jesus. The cloud is the vehicle which transports Jesus into the presence of God. The cloud of ascension will be the vehicle on which he will come at his parousia (v. 11). In the Gospel (24:50-51) the ascension is placed at the close of one Easter day of appearances; it comes as a solemn finale. In Acts the ascension comes at the end of forty days and has something of the flavour of a farewell. (It goes without saying that we must avoid any impression that our feast of Ascension is, or ever was, meant to mark a first return of the risen One to his Father). The ascension marks the close of an era. Jesus' journey to God has been completed by his 'being taken up' into heaven. It likewise signals the beginning of a new era, that of the mission of the Church which is about to be inaugurated.

Luke sets out to show how Jesus continues to act and teach after his resurrection through the Holy Spirit and through the followers of Jesus who will be his 'witnesses' to the ends of the earth. They are the nucleus of his Church which is the continuation of his presence and power. They no longer experience Jesus among them in the same way as before when they walked and talked with him during his earthly ministry. He is no longer earthbound; yet, while sharing in the glory of his Father, he continues to guide and direct his community. His followers receive a promise and a mission. The same Jesus, now in the glorious presence of his Father, will continue to be with them through the Spirit – a power enabling them to become Christ's 'witnesses.' Through them the message of Jesus would reach out in ever-widening circles.

Second Reading   Eph 1:17-23

Here ascension is viewed as the logical conclusion and completion of the resurrection. The passage must be viewed against the background of the letter as a whole. The letter was occasioned by controversy over the cosmic role of Christ. There were some who claimed that he should be classed among a host of beings, intermediaries between God and humankind (v. 21). The author formulated his own view in contrast. The meaning of the resurrection-ascension event is that God has raised Jesus above those nebulous powers to his due position as crown of creation. First-born of all creation by nature, and first to be born form the dead by resurrection, he is first in every way (see Col 1:15-18). But what interests the author is the consequences of this for Christians. The Father's exaltation of Christ is evidence of 'his power for us who believe.' If Christians are baptized into Christ, they have risen with him, and with him have been exalted into heaven, and with him glorified (Rom 8:30). In another sense the transformation into the glorious Christ is still to come; at least it is yet to be revealed (Col 3:4). The basis of the Christian hope in the ascension is that by it the Christ in whom we already abide is raised to the right hand of the Father and his power is at work in the Church.

Second Reading *ad libitum*   Heb 9:24-28; 10:19-23

The Christiasn High Priest does not officiate in an earthly sanctuary; his rightful place is in heaven itself. There he appears, now and forever, before God on our behalf. Hebrews uses three images to express the work of Christ in the heavenly sanctuary: (1) ritual of the Day of Atonement, which reconciles God and people (v. 23); (2) appearance in the presence of God (vv. 25-26); and (3) 'intercession' (v. 25). All three images are combined in v. 24.

In 10:19-23 the 'sanctuary' is heaven, the focal point of union between God and humankind, and the goal of our pilgrimage toward salvation (12:22). The 'blood of Jesus' is a theological symbol of his saving work and its fruits (9:12, 22; 12:24). The 'curtain' which separated the Holy of Holies from the outer sanctuary (9:3) is here, as in 6:19, a symbol of the barrier which separates heaven from what is without. 'Through his flesh' is to be attached to 'way': it is precisely because he has taken on our flesh and blood that Christ has been enabled to become the way that leads his brothers and sisters into heaven. V. 22 gives the qualification for drawing near to God: a sinless heart and fulness of faith. 'Sprinkled' and 'washed' offer an allusion to baptism. There are two exhortations: 'let us approach'; 'let us hold fast'. The first follows on the fact of being enabled to approach (v.19). The holding fast is based on firm hope in God's faithful promise.

Gospel Lk 24:46-53

At the close of his gospel, Luke (24:44-49) summarizes the last commission of Jesus to his disciples and repeats it the beginning of Acts. More pointedly, the outline and words of this passage echo the apostolic kerygma of Acts. Jesus first (v 44) recalls the occasions on which he had warned them that he, in fulfilment of the will of God enshrined in the Scriptures, would have to suffer, die, and rise again. 'While I was still with you': his relations with the disciples are not what they were before his glorification.

Then (vv. 45-48) he proceeds to give them a new understanding of the Old Testament, an insight that will enable them to see how and where it 'bears witness to him' (see John 5:39). The reinterpretation of the Old Testament is a basic element of the primitive kerygma: the dawning of the age of fulfilment (v. 44; see Acts 2:16; 3:18; 3:24); the suffering of the Messiah and his resurrection on the third day (Acts 2:23-24; 3:13-15; 4:10). The kerygma always includes the proclamation of repentance and forgiveness of sins, a proclamation to humankind – the universalist note is very much at home in Luke (Acts 2:38-39; 3:19-20; 4:12). These are the points which Paul developed in his discourse at Antioch of Pisidia (Acts 13:26-41). The message of salvation will go forth from Jerusalem, preached by the apostles who are witnesses of the fulfilment of the prophecies (see Acts 1:8), men who had seen the risen Christ and who can attest that this Lord is the same Jesus with whom they had lived (Acts 1:21; 2:32; 3:15; 5:32; 10:39-42; 13:31). The disciples are convincing witnesses and efficacious missionaries because they have seen the Lord and have believed in him; all who would, effectively, bear witness to Christ must have encountered him in personal and living faith.

Today, when the call of the apostolate is urgent and the role of witness is seen as the obligation of every Christian, we are more keenly aware that religion is not the acceptance of a body of doctrine or the adherence to a code of law, but attachment to a Person. Knowledge of Christ, in the biblical sense of acceptance and commitment, is the essence of Christian life; it is obviously the first requirement of an apostle.

Luke has undoubtedly given the impression that all the events of chapter 24 had taken place on Easter day (see vv. 1, 13, 22, 29, 44, 40). This arrangement is editorial and the passage vv. 44-53 is a telescoped version of Acts 1:3-14. Though it is true that Jesus did ascend to his Father on Easter day (see John 20:17), it is clear that the Ascension in question here is the same as that of Acts – the final, visible departure of Christ forty days (Acts 1:3) after the resurrection. 'As far as Bethany' (v. 50): in Acts the place of ascension is 'the mount called Olivet' (Acts 1:12) – Bethany lies on the eastern slope of the Mount of Olives. With his hands raised in blessing (see Lev 9:22; Sir 50:22) Jesus parted from them (Acts 1:9). The joy of the disciples (v. 52) at the moment of parting, though at first sight surprising, is explained by their realization that 'the Lord has risen indeed' (v. 34). And they have his assurance that, very soon, they will be 'clothed with power from on high' (v. 49). Their minds have been opened to understand the Scriptures: now they have grasped the plan of God and they realize that Christ, their Lord, has triumphed. Thankfully, they hasten to glorify God in his temple. Luke has closed his gospel as he began it, in the Temple; yet all is changed, changed utterly! He has shown the 'time of Israel' yielding to the 'time of Christ.' And now, about to begin his account of the word of salvation going forth from Jerusalem to 'the end of the earth' (Acts 1:8), he leaves us at the beginning of a new age, the 'time of the Church.'

SEVENTH SUNDAY OF EASTER

First Reading   Acts 7:55-60

The most striking feature of Stephen's martyrdom is its similarity to
the passion of Jesus in Luke's version. Jesus is tried before the
Sanhedrin and the decisive element of his trial is his statement about
the Son of man at the right hand of God (Lk 22: 69). He was then led
out of the city to be killed, while he forgave his killers and commended
his soul to the Father (23:26, 34, 46). Stephen, too, was haled before
the council (Acts 6:12) and dragged out of the city to be stoned to death
(7:58). He forgave his killers (7:60). There is the significant difference
that where Jesus had committed his spirit to his Father, Stephen
prayed; 'Lord Jesus, receive my spirit'. Luke's lesson is clear: the
death of the martyr mirrors and repeats the death of Jesus. Stephen had
taken up his cross after Jesus.

The statement of Stephen which sparked off the hostile reaction –
'I see the heavens opened, and the Son of man standing at the right
hand of God!' – is an echo of that made by Jesus at his trial (Lk 22:69).
The Sanhedrin are being reminded of the former occasion. Stephen is
a witness of resurrection, a witness to the fact that the prophesied
glorification of Jesus has already occurred. Forgiveness is a typically
Lucan concern. He alone carries the saying of Jesus (Lk 23:34) to
which Stephen's cry here corresponds (Acts 7:60).

Second Reading   Rev 22:12-14.16-17.20

Like the Fourth Gospel and the first epistle of John, Revelation also
closes with an appendix or epilogue, giving the last words of the angel,
the seer and the Lord (22:6-21). The lectionary reading is content with
the words of the Lord. The time has come for 'rewarding God's
servants'. Christ comes exercising a divine prerogative; he comes
'bringing his reward with him'. It is perfectly natural that the earthly
paradise of Genesis 2 should become a symbol of heavenly blessedness. The tree of life is within the city, so one must pass through the
gates to reach it; the beatitude (v. 14) makes eternal life accessible to
all but only through the blood of the Lamb, the cross of Christ.

The whole of Revelation is 'the revelation of Jesus Christ,' his
'testimony', made known through an angel to John (1:1); it is a
message for the whole Church (1:4). At the close (22:16) Jesus sets the
seal of approval on the fidelity of his prophet. The final verses (22:17-
21) have an unmistakable liturgical ring. The Spirit inspires the
Church (the earthly Church) to respond with eager joy to the Lord's

announcement of his coming. While the hearer welcomes the coming of Christ, 'the one who is thirsty' is invited to come to Christ. And Christ, who bears his own solemn testimony to the contents of the book, assures his Church that he is coming soon (v. 20). It is a response to the earnest prayer of the Church (v. 17) and a link with the promise at the beginning of the book: 'Look, he is coming with the clouds' (1:7). But this time the promise stands in the liturgical setting of the Eucharist. 'Come Lord Jesus' is a rendering of the Aramaic *marana tha* ('Our Lord, Come!', see 1 Corinthians 16:22) of the liturgy. There is an intimate link between the Eucharist and the coming of Christ: 'For as often as you eat this bread and drink the cup you proclaim the Lord's death until he comes' (1 Cor 11:26).

> Perhaps it is in our Eucharistic celebration that Revelation might challenge us. It was on the night when he was delivered up that the Lord took, gave thanks, and broke bread: 'This is my body which is for you.' He is the Lamb who was slain. His death is victory for all. The victim is the victor. That is the 'remembrance' of the Eucharist. That is the message of Revelation. Behind the surreal vision of the plagues is the Lamb. And with the Lamb is the One on the throne – the Father of our Lord Jesus Christ. 'The grace of the Lord Jesus be with all'. This 'revelation of Jesus Christ' is a word of grace. 'Blessed is the one who hears' for these words are trustworthy and true. (Harrington, p. 226f)

Gospel   Jn 17:20-26

The most solemn prayer of Jesus in the gospels is the great prayer of John 17 – the priestly and royal prayer. This prayer is, in its way, a commentary on the passion of Jesus which reflects the drift of the fourth gospel's emphasis: the coming of Jesus, revealer of the Father, into this world (17:1-12), then the return of Jesus to the Father (vv. 13-26). Structurally, though, the prayer falls into three parts, as Jesus prays for himself (1-5), for his disciples (6-19), and for the community of the future who will 'believe through their word' (20-26). Our reading takes up his third part.

The mission of the disciples (vv. 6-19) will be efficacious, made so by the prayer of Jesus. The power of his prayer reaches out to those others, those who will come to 'believe into him' – that is the force of the Greek; for faith means a personal relationship with Jesus, union with him. And Jesus prays for the unity of the community. Unity follows on the communion of the Christian with Father and Son. The missionary role is not lost to sight: 'that the world may believe.' Those

W

• In the spirit of *Sint Unum*, therefore, we invite you to pray for one
another this coming year, thanking
God for the wonderful gift of life,
and asking for the grace to be faith-

ful to our call to holiness, to be renewed in mind and heart and to be reconciled with one another and with our world in a spirit of compassion, healing and peace. To give this prayer a unifying focus, we suggest that on one specified day each week, we pray especially for our own menbers, associates, families and friends in one particular province or region e.g.

Sunday	Brazil
Monday	England
Tuesday	France
Wednesday	Ghana
Thursday	Ireland
Friday	Nigeria + Benin
Saturday	U.S.A.

And as we too need prayer, perhaps you might include the four of us in our regions of origin.

later disciples, like the initial group, are sent, as the Master was, 'to testify to the truth' (18:37). 'Glory' will be theirs as, in their turn and measure, they make Father and Son known. But they can have this 'glory', this revealing role, only if they are one with Father and Son and with one another. Only so will their witness have force. Only so will it be witness to a God who is love.

If Jesus had prayed that his disciples should be taken out of the world (17:15) that was in view of their task of carrying on his work. As he had come into the world to do the saving will of the Father and, that task accomplished (19:30), to return, in glory, to that beloved Father, so he wills and prays that his disciples, when they have accomplished their task, will enjoy unending blessedness with him. Then, for them too, the message they had preached will be wholly clear. They will see, and share in, the perfect union of Father and Son and glow in their love. All will be achieved in and through their being with Jesus, fully and forever. It is because the Father had given them to the Son, and because they had been joined with him on earth, as branches of the Vine, that they will be united with him forever. They are those who have known Father and Son – and that is what eternal life is all about (17:3).

The closing words of the prayer brings us back to earth. Jesus will make the Father more deeply known. But that will be at the cost of love. It is only in a loving community that the love of Father and Son can be experienced, that Father and Son can be truly known. Only in loving one another can the disciples be one with Jesus; only so will he dwell among them and be in them. It is the earnest prayer of Jesus that this be so: 'I pray for them' (17:20).

PENTECOST SUNDAY

First Reading
Acts 2:1-11

The story of the coming of the Spirit at Pentecost is not naive description, but is packed with theological significance. Basically, what happened is seen as repeating, and transcending, what, in Jewish tradition, occurred at the giving of the Law at Sinai. It was believed that at the giving of the Torah there came a might sound which turned to fire from which issued a voice proclaiming the Law. The fire acts as the vehicle for what was constitutive of the people of God (the Law) as now it is the vehicle of the Spirit which is the life-principle of the Church. In another form of the tradition, the fire split into seventy tongues of fire, corresponding to the seventy nations of the world (by Jewish reckoning). Thus, there is already built into the Jewish tradition the missionary dimension which is given in Luke's narrative by reference to the different peoples.

The incident takes specifically Christian colouring in terms of the fire and the speaking in tongues. Jesus declared that he had come 'to bring fire on the earth' and desired that it may be kindled (Lk 12:49). This is perhaps the occasion on which it is kindled, the baptism 'with the Holy Spirit and fire' of which the Baptist had spoken (Mt 3:11). Speaking in tongues is a sign of the presence of the Spirit and of the Spirit's transcendence of human limitations. Usually in the New Testament this teaching in tongues is enigmatic speech in praise of God which needs to be interpreted by one who has a corresponding interpretative gift of the Spirit (1 Cor 14:27-28). Here the speech is intelligible to those whose native languages are varied. Luke links this spontaneous praise of God in the Spirit with the first missionary effort of the nascent Church. Luke's message, in this passage, is that on this day the last age begins, the time of the Church which, today, receives its life-principle, the Spirit. Present are witnesses from that whole world into which the Church is destined to spread; they see the irresistible power of God at work.

Second Reading   1 Cor 12:3-7.12-13

Paul is in the midst of his treatment of the varied gifts of the Spirit at Corinth, diverse ways in which the influence of the Spirit expressed itself in the young and enthusiastic community there. The diversity of these gifts and the extraordinary character of some of them (prophesying and speaking in tongues) were causes of some dissension in the community. This moves Paul to stress the unity in diversity which should be a mark of the Church. To explain his point, he makes use of the image of the body. This image was already widely used in the ancient world to express the working of many elements in different ways towards a common end. But for Paul the meaning is far deeper: the image of the body is reality, not metaphor. How real, for him, is the incorporation of the Christian into Christ's body is shown by two other passages in the same letter: if a Christian beds with a prostitute he is taking Christ's body and joining it with her (6:15-16); through sharing in the body and blood of Christ believers are united with him and with one another (10:16-17). In using this terminology of the body Paul means to imply that our union with Christ is real and total, a union of whole person, not just a 'spiritual' union. It is the presence of Christ's

Spirit in us which achieves this union; it means that we act by his power and in his person.

Alternative Second Reading   Rom 8:8-17

The passage 8:1-17 centres on the contrast between 'flesh' and 'Spirit,' between two ways of living. Life pursued according to the flesh is life influenced by rebellion, life without Christ, and, therefore, doomed to frustration and death. Life in the Spirit, on the other hand, is life in Christ, a life set free from bondage to self and sin. 'Flesh' means not exclusively, or even primarily, our physical bodies but rather an orientation to our world which is dominated by rebellion and sin. What Paul means by 'flesh' and 'spirit' is splendidly spelt out in Galatians 5:19-23 which reflects on two diametrically opposed life-styles dominated, respectively, by 'works of the flesh' and 'fruit of the Spirit.'

Paul names the 'Spirit', the 'Spirit of God' and the 'Spirit of Christ,' and eventually changes his ground to assert that *Christ* himself is 'in you.' In itself *spirit* is a vague notion and is essentially relative. We can only understand a spirit when we know that of which or of whom it is a spirit. For Paul, the 'Spirit' is the Spirit *of Christ*, that is, what made Christ live. We cannot see Christ's Spirit; we can only see its effects in his manner of living. The 'Spirit of Christ' is the way Christ lived. And to have Christ's Spirit is to live with his life, to live as he lived. In v.11 we find one of the most forceful of Paul's expressions of Christian hope. We may put this complex sentence more simply in three propositions: (1) God has given you the same spirit which he gave to Christ; (2) God the Father raised Christ from the dead; (3) you can be absolutely certain that the Father has assigned to you the same destiny of glorious resurrection because the same spirit dwells in you.

By the gift of the Spirit, Christians are made children of God. This is the reason why they can address their Parent with the intimate title used by Jesus himself: *Abba* (8:14-16). Now the undreamt-of effect of God's gift of his Spirit emerges: it is our adoption as God's children, our participation in the sonship of Christ. The Spirit who animates and activates Christians, who is the source of our new life, makes us children of God.

The 'Spirit' of God (or of Christ) is not a 'spirit' of slavery, a slave-mentality - a play on the word *pneuma*. It is the Spirit who brings women and men into union with Christ and establishes them in a special filial relationship to the Parent. The God who had adopted us as his children awakens in us an awareness of that fact, and then gently helps us in our wondering acknowledgment of that fact: Abba! The close of v. 17 brings us firmly down to earth. True, we are indeed children of God and fellow heirs with Christ - 'if, in fact, we suffer with him.' That is his way: 'Was it not necessary that the Christ should suffer these things and then enter into his glory?' (Lk 24:26). There is no *Christian* way to glory other than his.

Gospel   Jn 20:19-23

This gospel reading represents John's version of the birth of the Church as the first reading does that of Luke. The disciples are to continue Jesus' mission from his Father and this mission will, as his, involve judgment. His mission was to bring humankind to the light and to the Father. By their reaction to him, by their acceptance or rejection of his message, men and women are themselves judged. In the fourth gospel there is a continuous process of confrontation with Jesus, and of self-judgement. The differing attitudes of humankind to Jesus will continue in the reactions to his presence in the Church.

It is significant that in John the Church is founded by the risen Lord. When Jesus breathes upon the disciples it shows that a new creation is taking place. Just as God made 'the man' into a living being by breathing life into him, and as in Ezekiel 37 the dead bones of Israel are stirred to life by the breath of God, so the life of the Church comes from the breath of the Spirit of Jesus. This is the new or eternal life which Jesus came to brnig, which plays such a major part in John's gospel. In this sense everything is already accomplished when Jesus breathes life into his disciples.

Alternative Gospel   Jn 14:15-16.23-26

In John 14:1-11 Jesus had described his own closeness to God; now (vv. 12-13) he goes on to indicate how others are brought into a similar closeness. Loving Jesus means listening to his word and putting it into action. To obey is to love. Jesus 'comes' to all who respond in this way to his word. He comes through the Spirit. Here (v. 16), for the first time in the Gospel, the Holy spirit is called 'Paraclete'. Paraclete means assistant or advocate. Jesus had been a paraclete to his disciples, helping them as their teacher, assisting them in their faith. Now, risen and with the Father, he will be present to them in another manner. The purpose of the Spirit being 'in', or being 'with' the disciples is to make Jesus present to them.

The farewell discourse is dominated by the thought of the forth-coming departure of Jesus. He is concerned to assure his disciples that he will not leave them orphans. Despite his going away, he and they will not be apart; they will be drawn into the love of the Father and Son. To love Jesus is to 'keep his word', that is, to respond in all their life to the challenge of Jesus. If this be the case, then 'my Father will love them and we will come to them and will make our home with them'. This is a personal coming of the Father in the Son. Besides, the word of Jesus – his revelation – also abides with them.

There is another sense in which they will not be alone: the Holy Spirit will take Jesus' place and carry on his work (vv. 22-26). The former togetherness is over (v. 25). Instead there is another form of togetherness: the Holy Spirit will bring to mind – and at a deeper level of understanding – what Jesus had said (v. 26), and will bring them into 'peace' (*shalom*).

The Solemnities of the Lord

THE MOST HOLY TRINITY
SUNDAY AFTER PENTECOST

First Reading
Prov 8:22-31

The passage is taken from the latest part of the book of Proverbs (chapters 1-9), written well after the return from the exile in Babylon, when Israel had come to understand more deeply the concept of wisdom. In the first thoughts of Israel about wisdom the sages had taken over many of the notions of neighbouring peoples of the Near East for whom wisdom was largely a practical matter, a series of counsels about how to succeed in life or, at worst, how to become reconciled to lack of success, to suffering, and to loss. But Israel realized that such qualities were the gift of God and could come only from him. The next step was to realize that these qualities are in God to a supreme degree until finally wisdom came to be understood as the power by which God acts in the world, and so as an offshoot of God himself.

Quite regularly, wisdom came to be personified. In our passage (reminiscent of Genesis 1 and Psalm 104) we look to the role of Lady Wisdom in creation. Wisdom's claim is that the Lord 'created' her she is his first-born child. Though herself created, wisdom is closely associated with God's creative activity. She delights in the presence of God and is at home in the company of the human race. Through wisdom, God's deed of creation becomes an act of communication; through her he 'delights in the children of men.' By her intimacy with God and association with humankind, Wisdom reveals to humankind the key to the ultimate meaning of life.

Second Reading
Rom 5:1-5

In the previous chapters of Romans, Paul had discussed the human condition without Christ and the act of justification by faith in Jesus Christ. Now he shows how what he has said can be developed into a rich theology of salvation. The first consequence of justification by faith is 'peace with God' – proper relationship with God and the enjoyment of divine blessings. The hostility and alienation described in the preceding chapters are now overcome. And this is possible 'through our Lord Jesus Christ' – Paul feels a compulsion to refer to Christ's role in any saving action or effect. The 'grace' of v. 2 is the possession of divine fellowship which, in turn, gives rise to the hope of sharing God's glory. The hope is not illusory. It is so firm that we can 'boast' of sufferings, because suffering reminds us of our reliance on God. That awareness will enable us to endure, to continue despite the odds; endurance can produce character or the power to resist evil, and character breeds hope. The whole salvation process rests on God's certain love. The central place of the Spirit in Christian life firmly emerges. The affirmation that 'God's love has been poured into our hearts through the Holy Spirit which has been given to us' (v. 5), asserts not only that the Spirit is gift but stands as a witness to the outpouring of divine love. In the Spirit we can recognize God's love for us.

Gospel   Jn 16:1-16

In the farewell discourses of the Fourth Gospel (chapters 14-16) we have five passages in which the Holy Spirit appears as 'the Paraclete' or, in the last of them (our reading), under the synonymous title of 'the Spirit of Truth.' The Spirit of truth carries on in the church the work of Christ after Christ himself has departed to the Father. He differs from Jesus in not being corporeally visible; his presence is by indwelling in the disciples (14:16-17). In 16:13-14 (as in 14:25-26) the Spirit is teacher of the disciples. Jesus had told them: 'I still have many things to say to you, but you cannot bear them now' (16:12). Only after his glorification could there be an understanding of what was said and done during the ministry. Then, after the resurrection, the Paraclete will guide them into the full meaning of what Jesus has said. If he will lead them into *all* the truth, he will still not speak on his own. There is new revelation because there cannot be new revelation: Jesus is *the* revelation of the Father, the Word of God. But what does it mean that 'he will declare to you the things that are to come'? Rather than any fresh revelation this means a spelling out to successive generations of the contemporary significance of what Jesus has said and done.

CORPUS CHRISTI
THURSDAY AFTER HOLY TRINITY

First Reading   Gen 14:18-20

The whole passage Genesis 14:1-24 is an intriguing episode, appearing abruptly in the Genesis narrative. Our passage – Abraham and Melchizedek – has, it seems, been inserted into the narrative of Abraham's encounter with the king of Sodom. It is probably this

Melchizedek incident which explains the importance of the whole passage (14:1-24) in the mind of the compiler, and the reason why it was included in the story of Abraham. The only other place in the Old Testament where Melchizedek is mentioned is the royal psalm 110. Both Psalm 110 and the present passage may be seen as underpinning the political and religious status of David. By linking Abraham with the future capital of David, the text is justifying Israel's ancient connection with Jerusalem and the right which the king and the priesthood held over Israel. The biblical author of Genesis 14 had no trouble with the fact that Melchizedek was a heathen king. For him there was only one God Most High and Jerusalem was his holy city.

The midrashic development of Hebrews 7:1-10 exploits the priesthood of Melchizedek in christological terms: it is a type of the perfect priesthood of Christ. Though the author of Hebrews makes no capital of the bread and wine which Melchizedek 'brought out' as food for Abraham and his men, in Christian tradition that bread and wine were taken to prefigure the Eucharist.

Second Reading   1 Cor 11:23-26

The striking point in this passage is that Paul does not think of the Eucharist and Christ's presence through it in a static way as might be suggested by the formulas, 'This is … ' Instead, the account is full of dynamic expressions. It is no mere making present of Christ's body and blood but it is a proclamation, and memorial, of his death, of an event. Similarly, the cup is 'the covenant in my blood', that is, an event, the making of a covenant which has lasting and definitive consequences for the life of the people who are included in the covenant.

This is emphasised still more by two further phrases: 'in remembrance of me' and 'until he comes.' The first recalls the prayer of the Jewish passover meal that God may remember the Messiah, that his kingdom may come. The 'memorial' is not only something in the past but is a memorial of what is to happen in the future. The first phrase links up with the other 'until he comes'. Prominent then is the idea that the Eucharist not only looks to the past but looks forward to the fulfilment of the kingdom.

Gospel   Lk 9:11-17

The eucharistic significance of the multiplication of loaves is brought out, cleverly and economically, by the use of familiar liturgical language: Jesus 'took … blessed … broke … gave.' Besides, this is a meal of the Messiah with his own: by acting as host at the extraordinary meal in the desert, Jesus does suggest that he would preside over the great Messianic Banquet and would bring salvation to his people. For a fuller appreciation of the significance of the feeding episode one needs to understand the background references: Yahweh already had provided bread for his people in the desert. The narrative is modelled on 2 Kings 4:42-44, where Elisha, in similar fashion, miraculously distributed bread among his followers. Jesus thus stands in the prophetic tradition; but he works a more striking miracle. We may note, too, that Luke (v. 11), observes that Jesus was teaching the crowd and healing them. In the Eucharist the Church continues the teaching and healing mission of Jesus and offers salvation to its members.

THE MOST SACRED HEART OF JESUS
FRIDAY AFTER SECOND SUNDAY AFTER PENTECOST

First Reading   Ezek 34:11-16

Chapter 34 is one of the most striking in Ezekiel. The lead-up to today's reading (vv. 1-10) is not only an indictment of the unworthy 'shepherds' of Israel (kings, priests and prophets); it is an abiding warning to the leaders and guides of the people of God. There is something frightening in the assertion that God will *rescue* his flock from its shepherds! (v. 10) But that assurance is hope and promise for the 'sheep'. Jesus had this chapter in mind when he presented himself as the good shepherd (Jn 10:1-8).

Ezekiel wrote against a background of despair and disillusionment when the bottom seemed to have fallen out of the Israelite's world. Ezekiel's hearers are exiles in Babylon convinced that all their hopes in God's protection and of eventual rehabilitation are vain. To them Ezekiel brings the promise of renewed hope. Though their rulers had failed, the ultimate shepherd, God himself, does not abandon them. It is the same promise as that of the second part of Isaiah. God will re-unite his scattered people in the promised land, and bring them healing for their ills. In this promise there is a significant ambiguity: the prophecy also announces, 'I will set over them one shepherd, my servant David, and he shall feed them' (v. 23), Is the shepherd God himself? Or is it David who stands for the perfect messianic king who is to come? The answer is given in John, 'I am the good shepherd', where Jesus is both messianic shepherd and divine Son.

Second Reading   Rom 5:5-11

Chapter 5 brings us to the central section of Romans. We have learned that people are justified freely by God (chapters 1-4); henceforth (chapters 5-11), we shall see that the Christian, justified through faith, finds in the love of God and the gift of the Spirit the guarantee of salvation. Christ has won for us entry into the friendship of God; the love of God for us bears the hallmark of divine love: it is while we were sinners that Christ died for us (5:1-11). With his theme of 'justification' Paul's argument in Romans has something of a forensic colouring, a smack of the law-court. This factor gives a striking dimension to Paul's statement. What God does is to reconcile to himself his 'enemies', to justify us 'while we were yet sinners.' We speak glibly of the *justice* of God. We speak of God as a *just* God. Well it is for us that our God is *unjust*! We find our hope in the *injustice* of our God! If God be Judge he is the Judge who acquits the guilty – those who enter a plea of 'guilty' – while we are yet sinners. It is not a matter of handing down a suspended sentence or a lenient sentence. No, he simply accepts the plea of 'guilty' – and dismisses the case! Such conduct is an affront to our idea of justice. But God is doing it all the time (see Mt 18:24-27). We should rejoice in the *injustice* of our God. *We* have a problem in our striving to reconcile God's mercy with his justice. Let us not sleep over it: *God* has no problem.

Gospel   Lk 15:3-7

In 15:1-2, Luke has given a credible setting for the little parable of The Lost Sheep. The tax collectors and sinners (outcasts by pharisaic standards) were flocking to Jesus and listening to him; the pharisees and scribes were scandalised by these goings-on: 'So he told them this parable.' Jesus defends his conduct. He consorts with sinners precisely because he knows that God is a loving Father who welcomes the repentant sinner. God does not regard sinners as outcasts but follows them with love and receives them tenderly when they come back to him.

Jesus tells of the shepherd who went in search of a sheep that was lost and of his joy when he had found the stray. The solicitude of the man is such that he leaves the ninety-nine in the desert, that is, in the scanty pasture of the Judaean hill-country, while he searches for the other. And his joy at finding the lost sheep is so great that he must tell his neighbours of it. The moral of the story is stated in emphatic terms: God will rejoice ('joy in heaven' is a circumlocution) that, together with the just, he can also welcome home the repentant sinner. Or we might render v. 7: 'Thus God, at the Judgment, will rejoice more over one sinner who has repented, than over ninety-nine respectable persons, who have not committed any gross sin.' That is why Jesus seeks out sinners, while the scribes and Pharisees, by cavilling at his conduct, are criticizing the divine goodness. (See Twenty-Fourth Sunday of the Year, pp. 202-203 *infra*).

Ordinary Time

Introduction to the Liturgical Season

GOSPELS

For the second Sunday in ordinary time, the Gospel every year is from John and continues the theme of revelation or manifestation which ran through the Christmas season. This year we have the passage about the wedding at Cana, with Mary saying, 'Do whatever he tells you', and Jesus working the first sign.

Then, beginning with the third Sunday in ordinary time, there is the semi-continuous reading of one of the synoptic gospels each year. The readings run from the beginning of the public ministry of Jesus to the eschatological passages which precede the accounts of the Passion. The aim is to enable us to appreciate the different perspectives found in each gospel. The English lectionary (Vol. I, pp. xlviii-xlix) includes useful tables which show how the texts in the lectionary are related to the overall structure of each gospel. These tables let us see how the lectionary takes account of the combination of narrative passages and discourses in Matthew's Gospel of the Kingdom; the gradual revelation of the mystery of the Son of Man in Mark; the journey towards Jerusalem in Luke.

FIRST READINGS

The First Readings are taken from the Old Testament, and are chosen to harmonize with the gospels. They provide quite an amount of material, and are an invitation to become more familiar with the Old Testament.

SECOND READINGS

The second readings (the readings 'from an apostle') are semi-continuous, beginning on the second Sunday. They are from Paul, James, and Hebrews; Peter and John are read during Eastertide and Christmastide. The first letter to the Corinthians is divided up between the three years. Hebrews is divided between Years B and C.

SOLEMNITIES

The solemnities of Trinity, Corpus Christi, and the Sacred Heart are provided with suitable readings.

The last Sunday of the year celebrates Christ the Universal King.

The three sets of readings present quite a striking juxtaposition of texts. In the Gospel assigned for this year, we meet the Crucified One who promises a share in his kingdom to the repentant thief who suffers with him (from Luke). The First Reading presents the figure of King David (Second Samuel). It is the second readings especially which give voice to the joy and thanksgiving of the Church – the Father has created for us a place in the kingdom of the Son, and wants all things to be reconciled through him and for him (Colossians).

Philip Gleeson OP

Sundays of the Year

SECOND SUNDAY OF THE YEAR

First Reading
Is 62:1-5

The destruction of Jerusalem and its temple by the Babylonians in 587 B.C. was a shattering blow for Jews. They had need of encouragement. It came from an anonymous disciple of Isaiah. His message is found in Isaiah 40-55. Some time later another anonymous poet-prophet composed, in Jerusalem, the poems we find in Isaiah 56-66. When the poet of our passage wrote, the holy city was still in ruins. The city's plight reflected that of God's people: once God's spouse, she was now rejected (Hos 2:1-13), a barren wife, or a widow bereft of her children (Is 54:1-9). But her husband, the Lord, was faithful to his promises and would again rejoice over his bride. He was the God of the covenant, faithful and forgiving. Inspired by such faith, the poet must sing of Zion, the new Jerusalem, and her future glory, a new city to bear a new name. The new names 'My Delight in Her', 'The Married', will express the new joyful relationship. There will be another wedding-feast for God and Zion. This was to come about through Christ and is symbolized by the miracle of Cana (Gospel reading). He is the bridegroom who will change the water of Jewish religion into wine.

Second Reading
1 Cor 12:4-11

The partly consecutive reading of 1 Corinthians begins in Year A (chapters 1-4), continues in Year B (chapters 6-10), and is carried on in Year C (chapters 12-15; Sundays 2-8).

In chapters 12-14 Paul treats of the final question raised in the Corinthians' letter to him, one concerning the 'charisms' or spiritual gifts granted to the community. The whole section 12:4-14:40 is devoted to the relative merits of the spiritual gifts. The significant and – no doubt, for his readers, disturbing – point of his analysis is his insistence that not only is there a variety of gifts, but that there is a variety of *service*; that the gifts are, essentially, gifts of service. It is not likely that the Corinthians had regarded them in this light. Paul (12:4-11) begins by pointing out that the gifts of the Spirit are far more varied than the Corinthians had imagined. The Corinthians are assured that their profession of faith, 'Jesus is Lord' comes from God's Spirit and only from that source (12:3).

The same Spirit, too, is the source of all spiritual gifts. The charisms are designated 'gifts,' 'services,' and 'works' (vv. 4-6). As gifts they

are attributed to the Spirit, who is *the* gift, sent by the Lord Jesus and
the Father; as services or ministries they are attributed to the Lord
Jesus who came among us not to be served but to serve; as works they
are attributed to the Father, the source of all being and activity. In the
last analysis the charisms are, firmly, the gift of God, imparted through
the Spirit; and the Spirit is none other than the risen Lord considered
as present and at work in the community.

It becomes abundantly clear, in chapters 12-14, that Christian
endowments are truly such only if they edify, build up. Behind these
specifically Christian gifts stand Spirit, Lord, and God; the gifts are,
impressively, of divine provenance. The divine activity is never
dissipated but is necessarily unified. There is, then, unity in the
diversity of charisms, for all come from the same Holy Spirit, and are
destined for the building up, the edification, of the community.

Gospel   Jn 2:1-12

The narrative of the miracle of Cana links this Sunday with the feast
of Epiphany and with Jesus' baptism – all are manifestations (epiphanies) of Christ's glory. Here the miracle of Cana is solemnly described
as 'the first of his signs'; by that fact we are sufficiently warned not to
take it at face value. The water ('for the Jewish rites of purification'),
turned into wine, symbolizes the old order which yields place to the
new. For the evangelist the narrative is the symbol of something that
occurs throughout the whole of Jesus' ministry – the revelation of the
'glory' of Jesus. Revelation in John is the self-revelation of Jesus; all
the rest stems from this. The significance of the wine is that it is Jesus'
gift, a sign which comes from him and points to him. As a gift of Jesus
the wine is, significantly, given at the end; so precious and copious, it
is the eschatological gift of the Messiah. The evangelist is not referring
to any particular gift (such as the Eucharist) but to Jesus himself as the
Revealer. Noteworthy is Jesus' initial refusal of the request that he
should perform a miracle because his 'hour has not yet come' – the
hour of the passion, which is the hour of the glorification of Jesus. The
lesson is that the event of revelation is independent of human desire or
manipulation. It comes to pass where and how God wills – and then it
surpasses all human expectation.

Jesus had said to his mother, in answer to her request: 'Woman,
what concern is that to you and to me? My hour has not yet come.' The
'hour' cannot be advanced and yet the 'sign' in response to Mary's
request already symbolizes it: 'Jesus did this, the first of his signs, in
Cana of Galilee, and revealed his *glory*.' Standing thus at the begin-

ning of his work, Mary is associated with the whole of it.

Within the gospel as a whole the wedding at Cana represents a considerable development. It indicates, more clearly than any of the preceding episodes, that the ministry of Jesus has become quite public. It also indicates explicitly that his disciples have come to believe in him. Thus it represents a dramatic advance in the narrative.

At the same time it gives an idealized summary of God's gift to the world and of life to the Church. It is a Church which is sensitive to need and ready to take initiative, but it is also a Church which, in its directives and in its service, draws upon Jesus' decisive hour and listens eagerly to his word. As a result there flows through it and through its servants, like a rich and abundant wine, a sense of union with Jesus and, through Jesus, with God. Here there is no dichotomy between spiritual depth and external service. Rather it is spiritual depth – attentiveness to the Word – which fuels external service. (Brodie, p. 175)

THIRD SUNDAY OF THE YEAR

First Reading
Neh 8:2-6.8-10

Return to Judah followed a half-century of Babylonian exile; the Jewish nation had to be rebuilt. Reconstruction was the work of two men. The political reorganization was carried out by Nehemiah, appointed by the Persian overlords as governor of the tiny province of Judah. The Persians entrusted Ezra with the task of reconstituting the Jewish religion – he was 'Minister of State for Jewish Affairs'. Perhaps we today would be inclined to follow ben Sirach who eulogized Nehemiah ('The memory of Nehemiah also is lasting; he raised for us our fallen walls', Sir 49:13) but did not mention Ezra; for it does seem that Ezra's contribution would not have been possible without the long and careful preparation of the other. But we can be sure that the Chronicler (author of 1,2 Chronicles, Ezra, Nehemiah) would not have shared our view. For him Ezra is the father of Judaism; and his judgment has the support of later Jewish tradition which witnesses to a continual growth in the stature of Ezra.

Ezra brought with him from Babylon 'the book of the law of Moses' (Neh 8:1). It seems certain that the title designates the Pentateuch in its final form, or in something very nearly its final form. This 'book of law' was accepted by the people as the law of the community, and

Ezra, by his cultic and moral reforms, brought the life of the community into conformity with this norm. From this time the life and religion of Jews was directed and moulded by the Torah, and Judaism assured its distinctive characteristic of strict adherence and fidelity to the Law.

Second Reading   1 Cor 12:12-30

Paul's lists of charismatic gifts do not presume to be exhaustive. Some of the gifts he lists are a constant feature of the life of the Church, while others are conditioned by particular circumstances at a given time. For the most part, the charisms take the form of services within the Christian communities. Paul's fullest classification of charisms is in 1 Cor 12:4-11. He has a supplementary list of charisms in 12:28 in which he enumerates further services: apostles, prophets, teachers, miracle-workers, healers, helpers, administrators, speakers in tongues (see Rom 12:6-8). Charisms are adapted to the needs and tendencies of different Churches. And they are adapted to the way of life of the individual Christian. Paul insists that Christian marriage, quite as much as the choice of celibacy, is a charism: 'each has a particular gift (*charisma*) from God, one having one kind, and another a different kind' (1 Cor 7:7).

In 12:12-26 Paul introduces the analogy of the body with its members. The human body is one, yet it is composed of many members. The Apostle would suggest that the body with its various parts may be compared to the body of the Church with its many and varied Spirit-inspired ministries. We are not really dealing with metaphor or image: because Christians have been baptized, by the one Spirit into one body (12:13), this body is the body of Christ, it is Christ himself. Each individual Christian is a member of the body of Christ and each has his or her part to play within the body (vv. 27-31). Paul ranks apostles, prophets and teachers in the first three places. The lengthy list would suggest that he is making the point that no single person can perform all the needed functions. The need of variety within the community abides; a Christian community cannot expect to speak with a single common-denominator voice. The voice of the prophet, at least, ought to ring out challengingly, disturbingly.

Gospel   Lk 1:1-4; 4:14-21

From today until the thirty-fourth Sunday inclusive, Gospel readings are from the gospel of Luke.

THE GOSPEL OF LUKE

It is unfortunate that an understandable desire to group the four gospels meant the separation of Acts of the Apostles from the gospel of Luke. The fact is, Luke and Acts belong together as two parts of a single work, and each can be properly assessed only in relation to the other. The gospel begins in Jerusalem, more specifically in the temple, with the message of an angel to Zechariah; it closes with the disciples of Jesus at prayer in the temple (Lk 24:53).

Luke follows closely the order of Mark. He breaks with Mark in what are known as the 'great omission' – the dropping of Mark 6:45-8:26 – and the 'interpolations' (insertion of material not found din Mark): Luke 6:20-8:3 and 9:51-18:14. The latter, the 'great interpolation,' witnesses to his skill and his literary independence. Mark did have a rather hurried journey of Jesus to Jerusalem; Luke turned it into a leisured stroll during which his Jesus had ample time to fit in varied teaching and a host of parables, most of them proper to Luke. It does seem that the first draft of the gospel began with the present chapter 3 – 3:1-3 has all the appearance of a formal opening. The prologue, the infancy narrative (chapters 1-2), was Luke's brilliant afterthought.

Luke was a second-generation Christian who wrote about 80-85 A.D. Though a Gentile convert (for such, it appears, he was) he was concerned with Israel and acknowledged the place of Israel in God's salvation history. He did not look to an imminent parousia; his two-volume work was written for Christians who lived in the post-apostolic age. 'Today', 'now' is the time of salvation; now life is poured out in the Holy Spirit. But now, too, is the period of *ecclesia pressa*, a Church under stress. Luke has shown what may be made of Jesus' deeds and words in a time after the era of Jesus. For us in the twentieth century, conscious of a gap of two millennia between the first proclamation of the Christian message and our own striving to assimilate that message, Luke's form of the kerygma, the preaching of the Good News, may be more congenial than others.

The Lucan Jesus does not set out to found a 'new' or different covenant. But he is the covenant prophet with an authentic word of God. As a saving figure for Jews and Gentiles alike, he is the legitimate covenant leader. Two distinctive Lucan titles for Jesus are Prophet and Saviour. As prophet Jesus speaks God's authorised word and does mighty deeds. As prophet he is critical of sin; as prophet he was rejected. Jesus is Saviour of the world – a Saviour-Benefactor, ruler of God's universal covenant people.

Luke's attitude to our world is twofold. On the one hand he affirms the world; on the other hand, he challenges it. He views the world as God's good creation: 'God saw everything that he had made, and indeed, it was very good' (Gen 1:31). He was sure that God acts in and through our world. Salvation comes from a real human being – through human causality. Luke, however, is painfully aware that all is not well in the world of humankind. God has created a good world. He created humankind with freedom, and human freedom frequently distorts creation. In the line of Old Testament prophets, Luke challenged conventions of religious piety (e.g. the parable of the pharisee and the tax-collector, 18:9-14) and announced a reversal of human standards (e.g. the poor and the rich, 6:20-26). Response to God and his goodness is in faith; and faith demands expression in prayer. It is not surprising that prayer figures largely throughout Luke-Acts.

For Luke the word of God was made flesh in Jesus but in another manner than for John. It is not the Johannine pre-existent Word but the word of God formerly addressed to the prophets that has taken flesh in Jesus (Acts 10:36-37). One may equally well say that in Jesus the flesh becomes word; the messenger becomes the message. In their turn the apostles carry on the incarnation of the word as they become the human and suffering bearers of God's message. They carry the word differently from Jesus – in his name, not in their own.

Dante named Luke *scriba mansuetudinis Christi* – the writer who had caught and portrayed the sensitivity of Jesus. His Jesus had found in Isaiah 61:1-2 the programme of his mission. In his Nazareth synagogue Jesus opened the scroll of Isaiah and read out:

> The Spirit of the Lord is upon me,
> because he has anointed me to bring good news to the poor.
> He has sent me to proclaim release to the captives
> and recovery of sight to the blind,
> to let the oppressed go free,
> to proclaim the year of the Lord's favour.

Then he declared: 'Today this scripture has been fulfilled in your hearing' (Lk 4:18-19, 21). The Lucan Jesus displays gracious concern for the 'little ones.' Instances leap to mind: the raising of a poor widow's son (7:11-17), welcome of the 'lost son' (15:11-24), healing of a crippled woman (13:10-17). Most eloquent, perhaps, is the graciousness that sparked the extravagant and brave response of a woman who had experienced the forgiving love of Jesus (7:36-50). Throughout the gospel there is an unmistakable apprehension before the threat of affluence and a corresponding sensitivity to the plight of the poor. While there is no need to imagine that this attitude, so evident in the Lucan gospel, does not, in the long run, go back to the teaching of Jesus, it is clear that Luke had made it his own and saw it as an imperative need of the Christian community for which he wrote. There is great gentleness, but there is nothing soft or easy-going about this Jesus of Luke. Indeed, there is something almost shocking about the call for total renunciation, his invitation to give up all one has.

Luke's spirituality is firmly inspired by his commitment to Jesus – that much is obvious. What matters is his commitment to a Jesus he *recognized*. And here is where Dante's observation is perceptively true. The Jesus of Luke is – though the title occurs only once (2:11) – the Saviour. God's 'preferential option for the poor' might seem to be a new-fangled invention of liberation theology. In fact, it is a belated rediscovery of an option that was there from the first. The Lucan Jesus does indeed reflect the God who is, disconcertingly, God of sinners. Apart from the so-called judgment-scene of Matthew 25:31-46, there is no passage more subversive of Christian 'orthodoxy' than Luke 15:11-32. A 'sinner' is welcomed back into the house of his Father, welcomed without strings, welcomed at the word: 'I will arise and go.' The Father-God had yearned for an opening – he needed no more. The Lucan Jesus, who truly knows the Father, is wholly in the business of lifting the burden of sin – not of adding to it. That is why Jesus is Saviour.

Commentary on Lk 1:1-4; 4:14-21

In the manner of the Greek writers of his day, Luke dedicates his book to a patron, at the same time setting out the occasion, method and purpose of his work. He does so in an elegant Greek which contrasts sharply with the style of the following chapters. It is probable that this prologue was meant to introduce both parts of Luke's work and the brief reference in Acts 1:1 marks the link between both volumes and suggests the continuity of the whole. Luke had decided to write a gospel and has done thorough preparatory research: he has carefully studied these things 'from the beginning,' which meant going beyond the starting point of the apostolic catechesis, the baptism of Jesus, to the infancy of Jesus and of his precursor. His work will be 'orderly,' with a theological rather than chronological order. Theophilus, addressed as 'Most Excellent,' is a man of some social standing who will help to promote the work. He himself can learn from this gospel an appreciation of the solid historical foundation of the teaching he had received.

Jesus knew it to be his vocation to proclaim the true God – the Father. He knew that in faithfulness to his task he was making the kingdom present – in other words, he was proclaiming the coming of God as salvation for humankind. How he saw his task is vividly portrayed in Luke's introduction to Jesus' ministry (4:16-21). Jesus stood before his people in that Nazareth synagogue and read aloud the passage in which the prophet acknowledged himself to be Spirit-appointed to his task, his mission of preaching to the poor, healing the blind, releasing victims of oppression (Is 61:1-2). Jesus then declared that these words of their Scripture were being fulfilled in and by himself. That Nazareth audience did not grasp the import of his proclamation. No more do we, perhaps. We tend to hear only words and miss their startling implication. Jesus was pointing to the recipients of the good news: captives, blind, oppressed – all who are weakest and powerless. They are 'the poor.'

The 'poor' are not only those with few or no possessions, not only those whose poverty is 'spiritual.' In the biblical context the poor are the 'little people' who are incapable of defending themselves and hence, by reason of their dependent need and sorry state are God's protected ones. The designation 'poor' (as in the beatitudes, for instance) is not idealisation: the poor really do need help, the hungry stand in need of nourishment, the mourning are visibly sorrowing. All cry out for compassion. The 'poor' to whom Jesus announced the good news of the kingdom and whom he pronounced 'blessed' are not those whom he proposes as models of virtue but are persons literally 'down and out.' The kingdom of God, the consolation of the new age, is granted to the weak and despised – to those who suffer, who weep, who sorrow.

FOURTH SUNDAY OF THE YEAR

First Reading   Jer 1:4-5.17-19

Jeremiah is better known to us as an individual than any of the other prophets, for his book contains many passages of personal confession and autobiography as well as lengthy sections of biography. He stands out as a lonely, tragic figure whose mission seemed to have failed utterly. Yet, that 'failure' was his triumph as later ages were to recognize. Our reading is an excerpt from the narrative of the call and commission of the prophet (chapter 1).

Jeremiah came from Anathoth, a village four miles north-east of Jerusalem. His father Hilkiah was a priest. His prophetic call came in 626 (Jer 1:2) while he was still quite a young man, and his mission stretched from Josiah (640-609) to Zedekiah (597-587) and outlasted the reign of the latter, that is to say, he lived through the days, full of promise, of the young reformer king, Josiah, and through the aftermath, the tragic years that led to the destruction of the nation.

It is possible to trace the spiritual progress of Jeremiah and to see in him the purifying and strengthening effect of suffering, for the most impressive message of the prophet was his own life. He was a man of rare sensitivity with an exceptional capacity for affection – and his mission was 'to pluck up and to pull down, to destroy and to overthrow' (1:10). Jeremiah had never really wanted to be a prophet (1:6) and he continued to discuss the trials of his office with Yahweh throughout his life. He felt overwhelmed by the sheer burden, the humanly impossible elements of his task; his prayer is the prayer of Gethsemane.

Jeremiah has particular relevance for our day. His predecessors, as far as we know, accepted their prophetic mission with submission – Isaiah indeed with eagerness (Is 6:9). But Jeremiah had to question and to understand. And he was not at all satisfied to accept, uncritically, traditional theological positions. But, mostly, it was his own prophetic office that was his burden and it was indeed a burden far heavier and more painful than that of any other prophet. He needed, all the more, the support of his God. His obedience was so much the greater because of his questioning, because he felt its yoke, because it led to a feeling of being abandoned. Jeremiah is the supreme example – until Jesus Christ – of the triumph of failure.

Second Reading
1 Cor 12:31-13:13

The Corinthians' question to Paul had been: which is the highest gift? More precisely, it seems to have been whether prophecy or tongue-speaking is the higher gift. Paul is not content to settle the matter on this level, to set off one against the other. There is 'the still more excellent way' (12:31) of love, in the light of which all other gifts may be evaluated. At first sight chapter 13 of first Corinthians seems an intrusion, interrupting the natural flow of chapter 12 into chapter 14. These two chapters are concerned with gifts of the Spirit, the charisms; it might seem that chapter 13, on *agapé*, is a digression. In fact the treatment of *agapé* is vital to Paul's argument and is meant to help us to see all the charismatic gifts in proper perspective. This chapter, then, enables us to evaluate correctly the Pauline assessment of the charisms.

The chapter falls naturally into three parts or strophes:
1. Charity is the Christian way *par excellence* (13:1-3). Paul's

worry over the Corinthian preoccupation over tongues is manifest: 'If I speak in tongues of men and of angels ....' But here his concern (as it will be in chapter 14) is not that tongues should be, in some sense, articulate; it is, rather, that they might be meaningless. Gong and cymbal by themselves are without melody and simply make noise. So, too, speaking in tongues, without love, is devoid of meaning. The sacrifice of one's goods, the sacrifice even of one's life, may be motivated by other factors than love. They could be a gauntlet flung down, a fierce gesture of independence. Paul makes the uncompromising and frightening statement that, without love, even the supreme sacrifice is worthless.

2. Love is opposed to all the childish rivalries at Corinth (13:4-7); it would seem that the life and example of Jesus Christ have inspired the positive features listed. When all is put in terms of him, then it is indeed true that love is patient and kind, rejoices in the right, bears all things, believes all things, hopes all things, endures all things. In Jesus the love of God has revealed itself in human form. *Agapé* is not possessive love and is much more than affection: it finds expression in action; it is a love that is all-embracing and never exclusive. The negative features reflect the behaviour of the Corinthian community. Love has no place for jealousy or boasting, arrogance or rudeness. Love does not insist on having its own way, is not irritable or resentful, it does not rejoice at wrong. Christians have been called, through love, to be servants of one another (Gal 5:13).

3. A series of declarations stresses the transience of charisms (13:8-13): prophecy and tongues will cease and knowledge will pass away. Inevitably so, because prophecy and knowledge are imperfect. They are realities of this present age; they will have no place in the age to come. Here we see things in the blur of a mirror (the cloudy ancient mirror); charismatic knowledge as such is enigmatic, imperfect. Of all the gifts of God the three that abide are faith, and hope, and love; but the greatest of them is love.

This chapter 13 is no digression. Paul has made his point. He has, right in the middle of his treatment of the charisms, raised prominently the standard of love. This is the yardstick against which all the charisms must be measured. More accurately, it is the supreme gift that is the measure of all the others. By his chapter 13 Paul has paved the way for an answer to the question of the Corinthians: which spiritual gift should one prefer? And his answer is, firmly, that gift which contributes to what is fruitful and what contributes to the life of the community.

Gospel
Lk 4:21-30

A continuation of the previous Sunday's reading, this passage gives the reaction to Jesus' homily. The audience reaction is wonder and puzzlement: they think well of Jesus whom they know, they are lost in admiration at his gracious words – but can he, the humble son of the humble Joseph, really apply to himself the words of Isaiah and put himself forward as such an extraordinary personage? Most probably the reply of Jesus (vv. 23-24) answers an objection raised by the people of Nazareth on a later visit – hence the reference to miracles at Capernaum which does not, obviously, fit in the context of an inaugural appearance (as this purports to be).

In its present situation v. 23 refers to a demand that Jesus should back his claim by miracles and v. 24 explains why he cannot do this: he shares the fate of every prophet – rejection by his own people. The passage vv. 25-30, with its description of a violent reaction of the people, really belongs to the close of the Galilean ministry (this passage is composite). Not accepted by his own people, Jesus, like his great prophetic predecessors, will turn to the Gentiles who, by implication, will receive him. The people rise in fury (vv. 28-30) when they understand him to mean that the benefits they have rejected will be offered to the Gentiles (see Acts 13:46, 50). The ultimate fate of Jesus at the hands of his own people is foreshadowed, but his hour is not yet come (see 9:51; Jn 7:30, 45; 8:59).

According to Deut 13:1-5, a false prophet was to be put to death. The citizens of Nazareth thought they had their man and were ready to carry out a threat once made against Jeremiah (Jer 11:12). But the Father has arranged the schedule for Jesus, and the time will come when there will be no escape (see Luke 20:15; 23:33); for Jesus committed the ultimate political gaffe of finding fault with his own people. (Danker, p. 110)

FIFTH SUNDAY OF THE YEAR

First Reading
Is 6:1-8

Last Sunday it was the call of Jeremiah; today the call of Isaiah. He seems to have been an aristocrat and, apparently, a native of Jerusalem. 'The vision of Isaiah the son of Amoz which he saw concerning Judah and Jerusalem in the days of Uzziah, Jotham, Ahaz and Hezekiah, kings of Judah' (Is 1:1) – that title tells us nearly all we know of Isaiah. We can date his mission, in terms of the first and last kings listed, to between 783 and 687 B.C. Isaiah, not surprisingly, was rooted in the traditions of Jerusalem and David, and firmly believed in the promise made to David. For, in Judah, the promise to David, the Davidic covenant (2 Sam 7), had replaced that of Sinai, and Zion with its temple was the new holy mountain. Hope for the future rested in the Davidic line: 'your house and your kingdom shall be made sure for ever before me; your throne shall be established for ever' (2 Sam 7:16). The king of Judah was 'son of God' (7:14).

The covenant with David was understood as a promissory covenant after the pattern of that with Abraham. No condition attached to the promise; though individual kings might fail, the dynasty would be eternal. The existing order of the nation was willed by God and was founded by God. Yahweh would dwell forever among his people, would reign on Mount Zion. He would be their shield against their foes; no enemy would destroy the holy city and the blessed dynasty. This conviction was the theological basis of Isaiah's hope in the face of seemingly inevitable disaster. Because of it his message was, first and last, trust in Yahweh.

In 740 B.C., the year of the death of King Uzziah, Isaiah had his inaugural vision in the temple. Yahweh appeared to him as an oriental monarch, surrounded by a corps of seraphim who proclaimed the holiness of God. The divine presence was veiled by smoke – equivalent to the cloud that shields human eyes from his awesome glory. God revealed himself to Isaiah as the all-holy One. Holiness, in the Bible, means separation, being removed from sin and things of this world. The prophet's first reaction was fear and trembling (v. 5); but then, cleansed of his sins, he responded without hesitation to the divine call (v. 8). His mission was to be difficult, for the people would refuse to listen to his preaching (vv. 9-10). These verses are applied to rejection of the teaching of Jesus (Mk 4:10-12, parr), to his signs (Jn 12:37-40), and to rejection of Paul's preaching (Acts 28:25-28). In Isaiah, however, was a ray of hope: a 'remnant' will remain faithful (v. 13).

Isaiah insists on faith – the practical conviction that Yahweh alone matters; one must lean on God alone (8:13;28:16;30:15). He vainly sought, in Ahaz, the faith which would turn the king from trust in his political shrewdness and enable him to stand, unperturbed, in the face of threats and even in the face of hostile armies. Bluntly, he warned him: 'If you do not stand firm in faith, you shall not stand at all' (7:9). Later, when Hezekiah, counting on Egyptian help, toyed with the notion of revolt, Isaiah opposed him too, and for the same reason: Yahweh, and he alone, will save the nation. The God of Isaiah is the

'Holy One.' This holiness, thrice proclaimed by the seraphim, expresses his majesty and his transcendence. Furthermore, for Isaiah, Yahweh is the 'Holy One of Israel': this transcendent God is a God who acts in history on behalf of his own people. The title expresses the mystery of an all-holy God who yet stoops down to frail and sinful humankind.

Second Reading

1 Cor 15:1-11

In 1 Corinthians 15 Paul energetically defends the reality of resurrection from the dead. He starts by appealing to the resurrection of Jesus and quotes an early creed: 'I handed on to you as of first importance what I in turn had received: that Christ died for our sins in accordance with the scriptures, and that he was buried, and that he was raised on the third day in accordance with the scriptures, and that he appeared to Cephas, then to the Twelve' (vv. 3-5). The statement 'he was buried' underlines the reality of Jesus' death. The statement 'he appeared to' expresses the conviction of the first Christians that Christ had returned to the stage of history. Paul (vv. 6-7) adds a series of witnesses not mentioned in the gospels and ends (v. 8) with his own experience on the road to Damascus. Significantly, he makes no distinction between the appearance to himself and the appearances to the other witnesses. It is all the more noteworthy, then, that in none of the three accounts, in Acts, of the Damascus-road episode (9:1-19; 22:5-16;26:10-18) is it stated that Paul actually *saw* the Lord. A great light ('brighter than the sun') shone round him and a voice spoke to him. Yet, he is absolutely convinced that it was indeed the Lord.

Paul uses the word *óphthé* to state that Christ appeared to Cephas, to the other witnesses listed, and to Paul himself. The word can be rendered 'he showed himself.' It means that the risen Jesus manifested himself as present in some fashion so that Paul, and the others, can say, 'I have seen the Lord.' What is involved is a divine initiative leading to a real experience of the presence of the Lord and a firm conviction of the reality of his presence.

But how can one talk about resurrection from the dead? Never is there any attempt to describe the resurrection of Jesus because it was realized that it was a happening beyond our experience. Only symbol and imagery, not literal prose, could tell *this* story. Something had happened to these men and women which they could only describe by saying that they had 'seen the Lord' – that the Lord had 'shown himself' to them. The phrase did not refer to some general Christian experience but rather to a particular series of occurrences confined to a limited period. Such occurrences, on the threshold of ordinary human experience, just would not submit to precision of detail. 'The original witnesses were *dead sure* that they had met with Jesus, and there was no more to be said about it' (C.H. Dodd).

Gospel   Lk 5:1-11

Luke has left until now the call of the first disciples which Mark has at the very beginning of the ministry (Mk 1:16-20); their immediate response, prepared by the rumour of his ministry (Lk 4:14, 37), is more understandable.

The passage is composite and we may distinguish three elements: a detailed setting of a discourse of Jesus (vv. 1-3); a miraculous catch of fish (vv. 4-10a); the call of Simon (vv. 10b-11).

The miracle story is another version of that related in John 21:1-11 – which suggests that it originally stems from a post-resurrection setting. 'Lake of Gennesareth' (v. 1) is Luke's more precise designation of the popularly named 'Sea of Galilee'. Throughout Luke the 'lake' is more a theological than a geographical factor: it is the place of manifestations which demonstrate the power of Jesus (see 8:22-25). Simon's words (v. 5) underline the miraculous nature of the subsequent catch: since the night, the proper time for fishing, has yielded nothing, this daytime attempt is, humanly speaking, doomed to failure. The name 'Simon Peter', here only in Luke, is found in John 21.

Peter, profoundly moved by the miracle, sank on his knees and spontaneously declared his unworthiness. He addresses Jesus as 'Lord' (in place of 'Master', v. 5). The title 'Lord' and Peter's description of himself as 'a sinful man,' perhaps referring to his denial, would point to an original post-resurrection setting. James and John too are overcome by religious awe and Jesus speaks the reassuring words: 'Do not be afraid' (see 1:13, 30; 2:10). The symbolism of the miraculous catch is now made clear: henceforth Peter will be a fisher of people; already he stands forth as the leader. The implied call is, however, not addressed to him alone; others too follow Jesus (v. 11). Luke, typically, specifies that they left 'all' (see 5:28; 11:41; etc.).

SIXTH SUNDAY OF THE YEAR

First Reading   Jer 17:5-8

Here we have a snatch of wisdom poetry contrasting the wicked (those who trust in humans) and the righteous (those who trust in God). A barren desert shrub is contrasted with a fruitful tree beside a flowing river. To rely on weak human nature, on the flesh and the things of the flesh as the Bible puts it, can only mean spiritual death. To trust in God means to rely on God, to turn to him as to the one source of life. Psalm 1 (read as responsorial psalm) conveys the same message in the same imagery. Those who trust in God are the *anawim*, the poor, whom Jesus, in today's gospel reading, declares blessed. This is an application to the individual of the prophets' message that when the people abandoned the Lord and put their trust in armies and alliances their cause was lost. It was generally the experience of Israel's history that the more kings and people turned to human means, the less they did in fact experience their need of God.

Second Reading
1 Cor 15:12.16-20

In 1 Corinthians 15:1-11 Paul had insisted on the reality of the bodily resurrection of Jesus. In today's passage he brings out the meaning of it for Christians.

The Corinthians, in view of their sharp distinction between soul and body and their acknowledgment of the immortality of the soul, with parallel depreciation of the body, denied that there was any resurrection from the dead; (at least some of them did). Paul's argument is that if there is no resurrection from the dead (v. 12) it follows that Christ has not been raised (vv. 13, 16); Paul's preaching is in vain (v. 14) and he has been misrepresenting God (v. 15); the faith of the Corinthians is meaningless (vv. 14, 17) and they are still in their sins (v. 17); those who died in hope of resurrection have perished without hope (v. 18). He had already demonstrated (vv. 1-11) that the first conclusion (Christ has not been raised) is false – and so the whole Corinthian thesis collapses. Indeed, Christ has not only risen – he is 'the first fruits of those who have died' (v. 20). In other words, the resurrection of Jesus is not something that happened only to him; it reaches to us. And not only as it concerns our future resurrection. Already, as risen Lord, Jesus himself is present to us and with us in our striving to give substance to the kingdom. He is Emmanuel – God-with-us. We must not overlook however, the special importance of 1 Corinthians 15.

The real point at issue here is the importance of the body, and Paul gives it so much space because he felt he had to convince the Corinthians that motives and commitments became real only when embodied in a pattern of behaviour modelled on that of Christ. He is fighting for an understanding of the human person as a psycho-somatic unity. (Murphy-O'Connor, p. 137)

Gospel

Lk 6:17.20-26

Our gospels have two, notably different, versions of the beatitudes: Matthew 5:3-12 and Luke 6:20-23. Matthew has nine beatitudes. Luke has only four – but with four corresponding 'woes' (6:24-26). Both versions have grown from an original core going back to Jesus, the additions and adaptations being due to the evangelists. We can, without much trouble, discern a form of the beatitudes which would stand as a common basis for the developments of the evangelists and which may reasonably be regarded as representing the beatitudes of Jesus. These are three:

> Blessed are the poor, for the kingdom of heaven is theirs.
> Blessed are those who hunger, for they will be filled.
> Blessed are the afflicted, for they will be comforted.

Luke and Matthew have in common the three beatitudes of Jesus. They have also in common a fourth: the blessedness of those who suffer persecution for the sake of Christ. This was likely added in the tradition but, for practical purposes, we may regard it as a beatitude of Luke (Lk 6:22-23). In Luke's version of the beatitudes this standpoint of the beatitude of the persecuted because of Christ is extended to the previous beatitudes (vv. 20-21) which now also directly call to Christian readers. Jesus has spoken to the poor as such, the afflicted and the hungry; their very distress was enough to make them privileged before God. Luke has applied these promises to his readers with the manifest desire of encouraging them in their own painful situation. The beatitudes are now addressed to poor Christians. The promised blessedness will wonderfully compensate them for their present privations. But they ultimately owe their blessedness to their status as disciples of Christ.

In Luke's vocabulary the 'poor' are the indigent, people who lack the necessities of life. The 'hungry' are the poor considered in the concrete circumstances of their lives; they have not the wherewithal to obtain food. In contrast, the 'rich' are those whose possessions insulate them from need; they are sheltered from hunger, the lot of the poor. The 'full' are people who are fully satisfied. These terms illustrate the realism of Luke's assessment of the respective situations of rich and poor. Deprived of material goods, and by themselves unable to obtain these goods, the poor are faced with lack of food – while the rich enjoy a prosperity that enables them to gratify their desires.

The 'laughter' of the third woe expresses the satisfied wellbeing of the fortunate ones of the world; the 'tears' of the third beatitude express the distress of those who know in their world only privation and suffering. The beatitude is addressed to unhappy people, crushed by their circumstances. Again, in the fourth woe the 'flattered' are the fortunate ones while the 'reviled' are suffering and persecuted Christians. Luke fixed his intention on the implication of the beatitudes: they clarify the mission of Jesus, the role of Saviour which he is called upon to exercise in favour of those who believe in him, especially in favour of those who suffer for their faith in him. These beatitudes now apply to Christians in the painful conditions which persecution brings. This narrowing is a practical pastoral manner of coping with a crisis-situation. In Luke's catechesis the beatitudes become a means of encouraging believers in the midst of the difficulties in which they are caught. In their distress the victims of persecution assuredly have the right to apply to themselves the consoling promises of the beatitudes.

Luke is the evangelist of the rich and the respected. That is to say, he wants to motivate them towards a conversion in keeping with the social message of Jesus. If he is 'evangelist of the rich', his message is challenge – not at all palatable to the wealthy. He is an exceptionally keen critic of the rich. But he does envisage their conversion which, as he sees it, is possible only by way of radical renunciation – renunciation of half of their possessions, and by painful specific conduct – risky loans, cancellation of debts (see 10:8-9; 6:30).

SEVENTH SUNDAY OF THE YEAR

First Reading
1 Sam 26:2.7-9.12-13.22-23

Saul, who had welcomed the talented David into his service, soon became jealous of David's success and popularity. He had become convinced that David was a dangerous rival; he determined to get rid of him and pursued him with paranoid resolve. David was hounded through the wilderness of Judah until, in desperation, he put himself beyond Saul's clutches by becoming a vassal of a Philistine prince, Akish of Gath (1 Sam 27:1-7). Chapter 26 tells of an occasion when the pursuing Saul was at the mercy of his quarry – only to have his life spared (see 1 Sam 24). David had come upon Saul and his men by night and, with his comrade Abishai, was able to make his way to the side of the sleeping king. Abishai would have pinned Saul to the ground with the king's own spear, but David would have none of it. In his eyes, Saul, as king of Israel, was a sacred person, an anointed one whom the Lord had chosen. He spared his enemy and carried off Saul's spear as proof that he bore him no ill-will. This passage is chosen for today's reading in view of Jesus' injunction to love of enemies (Gospel reading).

Second Reading   1 Cor 15:45-49

The link between Christ's resurrection and the resurrection of the dead is worked out in 1 Corinthians 15 in terms of the parallel between Adam and Christ. The parallel rests on the idea of the Spirit as a power of the risen Christ; otherwise the corporate personality of Christ could not be invoked. Paul, of course, firmly asserts the reality of the resurrection and passes quickly to the manner of the resurrection and the nature of the risen body (vv. 35-38). On the analogy of the seed that springs to new life, the resurrection will bring about a profound transformation of the body (vv. 35-44). What is sown a physical body, sharing the natural and corruptible principle of life, like that of the first Adam, common to all creatures, will be raised a spiritual body, like that of the last Adam (Christ), freed from the laws of earthly matter, incorruptible, immortal (vv. 45-49). The raising of the body is the achievement of the Father who restores it through the power of the Spirit (Rom 8:11). Resurrection means that the earthly body will be raised into a spiritual body, wholly permeated with and domiciled by the life-force of the divine Spirit (1 Cor 15:44).

It is clear that Paul, by insisting on the resurrection of the *body*, is stressing the reality of a true and integrated human life beyond death – it is no partial existence. Of this he is convinced. But he is coping with a reality wholly beyond his experience. Wisely, he does not really attempt to describe the nature of the risen state; he is content to insist that the resurrection-body is very different from the human body that we know; it belongs to a new order (vv. 35-41). In this life, the body is physical, the instrument of the *psyché*, the principal of mortal existence. The risen body will be spiritual, the perfect instrument of a human's *pneuma*, which, in the new life, will be completely possessed by the Spirit.

When he further declares that 'it is not the spiritual that is first but the physical' (v. 46), Paul appears to have in mind a Hellenistic-Jewish view which saw in Genesis 1:27 the creation of the 'ideal human' and in 2:7 the creation of the earthly human, Adam. He insists that the opposite is the truth. Though the Apostle does not say so, explicitly, it can hardly be doubted that his Christian awareness of life in the Spirit here and now, and the baptismal transformation of the Christian, guided his treatment of the resurrection. The Christian, already filled with the Spirit and living by the 'law of the Spirit', already feeding on the 'spiritual food and drink' (1 Cor 10:4) is surely being prepared to be a 'spiritual body' in the resurrection life.

Gospel
Lk 6:27-38

Matthew's Sermon on the Mount (Mt 5-7) defined Christianity in terms of perfect righteousness and in terms of a religion that is more interior and demanding than that of official Judaism. Luke (6:20-49) is concerned rather with emphasizing the essential trait of that message – charity. It is around this theme of charity that the elements of the central section of Luke's discourse are grouped: the duty of loving one's enemies (vv. 27-36), the obligations of fraternal charity (37-42). It seems that Luke is far less interested in defining the spirit of Christianity than in pointing out the conduct which can give concrete expression to that spirit.

The inspiration behind Luke 6:27-36 is clear from the admonition 'Love your enemies' (v. 27a) – repeated in the conclusion (v. 35a). It is an instruction on the love of enemies, finely rounded off by v. 36. The enemies are those who injure by thought (hate), word (curse), or deed (abuse); the Christian reaction is *agapé*, a love that manifests itself in action, as the context shows. The striking on the cheek is a calculated insult; Jesus is referring to insults suffered by his disciples *precisely as disciples*. As Luke understands this saying, its message, couched in typical hyperbolic Semitic terms (v. 29), is that the most precious and most indispensable earthly things, such as honour and clothing, are nothing when balanced against the claims of *agapé*. Characteristically (v. 30), Luke adds 'everyone', and his reference to the 'taking away' and 'not asking back' stresses the generosity of love. The 'golden rule' (v. 31) is neither as original nor as profound as commonly imagined. The ultimate motivation is God's merciful love (v. 36). In vv. 32-33, in place of the 'tax collectors' and 'Gentiles' of Matthew 5:46-47, Luke, more delicately, has 'sinners'; v. 34 is a third example added by Luke. Love must be universal and disinterested. In Matthew 5:48 the perfection of the heavenly Father is somewhat intimidating; characteristically, Luke (v. 36) stresses the mercy of that Father. And he adds (v. 37) that we ought not to pass judgment on the motives or actions of others; and when we are injured by others, we ought to maintain a spirit of forgiveness.

After the Beatitudes and woes demarcate those to whom the kingdom pertains, the following exhortations are directed to those who have heeded the voice of the prophet and 'repented.' With the transition sentence in 6:27, 'I declare to you who are listening', Luke shows Jesus as the teacher of morality for the restored people of God. From verses 27-35, Jesus develops the proper understanding of the law of love by which this community lives. The ethical standards set by these commands is remarkably high, and they take on added significance by following so closely the final blessing and woe. The command to love enemies, do good to those who hate, bless those who curse and pray for those who scorn is not, we are to understand, hypothetical, but is to be taken as the norm for those who are in fact hated, scorned, set aside, reviled and cursed. (Johnson, p. 111f)

EIGHTH SUNDAY OF THE YEAR

First Reading   Sir 27:4-7

Jesus ben Sirach has the modest aim of teaching piety and morality; his book abounds in practical religious counsels. Here, in four sentences, three with picturesque comparisons, he makes one point: that a person's talk shows what one is. The passage illustrates Jesus' words read in today's gospel: 'Each tree is known by its own fruit ... for it is out of the abundance of the heart that the mouth speaks' (Lk 6:44-45).

Second Reading   1 Cor 15:54-58

Throughout chapter 15 Paul has been speaking of the resurrection of Christ and the resurrection of believers which results from it. The final resurrection will be the completion of Christ's victory over sin and death. Contemplating this, Paul cannot help seeing in the resurrection the fulfilment of Old Testament prophecy: 'Death shall be no more' (Is 25:8; see Rev 21:4), or, as Paul read it in his Greek Bible: 'Death has been swallowed up in victory'. Death, which once was a tyrant, has in the words of the prophet Hosea (13:14), lost its sting. The parousia will be the great moment when Death is finally and definitively vanquished. Paul is accustomed to link Death, Sin and Law (three tyrannical powers) and he does so here (v. 56). Sin leads to the false mode of being that stands in opposition to the way of God; it is the way of 'death'.

What does Paul mean by his assertion that 'the power of sin is the law'? His view is that Sin exercised its power by forcing men and women to give blind obedience to the Law, thereby stripping them of the freedom to make personal decisions – which responsible freedom is the only way of authentic being. In Christ believers have already been freed from Sin and Law (Rom 6:17-18; 7:7); at the parousia they will be freed from Death. At the prospect, Paul breaks into thanksgiving (v. 57). In conclusion he assures his Christians that they have access to such encouragement and grace through Jesus and his Spirit who is at work in us, that all the labour can be endured. The work we achieve is the work of the Lord within us, who is able to make all difficulties bearable.

Gospel
Lk 6:39-45

In 6:37-42 it is no longer a question of love of enemies (6:27-36) but of love of the brothers and sisters; the passage brings out the concern of each for the welfare of all – a Christian has concern for one's brother/sister. In Matthew the warning not to judge others (7:1-2) is followed, logically, by the parable of the Mote and the Beam (7:3-5); Luke has found two sayings inserted between them and, consequently, these sayings are somewhat out of place (Lk 6:39-40). Matthew 15:14 gives the proper context of Luke 6:39 (it refers to the Pharisees); it has been added in Luke's source through a rather vague association of ideas: blindness = mote or beam in the eye. The saying in v. 40 was inserted because of the vague link with v. 39: a teacher is one who leads the blind. Luke, seemingly, understands it to mean that one cannot undertake to guide others until one has a good grasp of the Christian way of life. To avoid being a blind guide one must exercise self-criticism (41:42). The following passage shows that the true Christian teacher must be a genuinely good person. The saying about the two trees (vv. 43-44), instead of illustrating a warning against false prophets as in Matthew (7:15), has become a recommendation addressed to the disciples: a person is known by the fruit one bears.

With the preceding message in mind this may mean that only a good disciple can win good converts. In v. 45 we have two sayings which are found, in inverse order but in a similar context, in Matthew 2:34-35. While the fruits of Luke 6:43-44 are 'good works', those of v. 45 are 'words'; the addition was made on the grounds of the recurrence of 'good' and 'evil.' Luke draws attention to good works (authentic and sound teaching) as to a special type of 'good fruit.'

It has been suggested that Jesus showed himself loveless by engaging in what appears to be abrasive critique of lovelessness. But it must be remembered that he did not discourage correction of others in the community. Rather, he attacked the spirit of isolationism that subverts, in the name of religion, the outreaching love of

God. Also, it may seem odd that Luke, who desired to bring together diverse parties in the Church, should repeat such abrasive sentences. But forthrightness is no crime. To conceal one's own potential for evil is. Besides, no surgeon ever healed without a cut. But shun that one who enjoys the cutting more than the healing. (Danker, p. 155)

NINTH SUNDAY OF THE YEAR

First Reading   1 Kgs 8:41-43

Solomon is the king-priest who officiated at the dedication of the temple he had built (1 Kgs 8). Naturally, such a liturgical occasion called for a suitably elaborate prayer. And Solomon rose to the occasion. In authentically high-priestly fashion (the high priest, on the Day of Expiation, first sacrificed for himself, Lev 16:6), Solomon first prays for himself (vv. 23-26). Then he prays for his people, that the temple may be their place of efficacious supplication: if a person sins against one's neighbour; if the people suffer defeat; if there is a disastrous drought; if there be famine: in all cases suppliants will find a ready hearing (vv. 27-30). Even the foreign sojourner will be received (vv. 41-43). These verses reflect the situation after the Babylonian exile, at a time when Israel was becoming more conscious that its religious heritage and its messianic destiny were intended not for itself alone but for all nations. Israel was brought to a realization that it had a mission, namely, to bring salvation also to other nations. The remarkable protection of Israel throughout its history would persuade humankind that Yahweh was the true God.

Second Reading   Gal 1:1-2, 6-10

Readings from Galatians will continue to the fourteenth Sunday inclusive. A brief introduction to the letter is in order.

Galatia had been evangelized by Paul early in his second missionary journey (50-52 A.D.) and *Galatians* was most likely written during the apostle's stay at Ephesus (54-57). The purpose of the letter is clearly defined: to refute the errors of the agitators who had come to disturb the faith of the Galatians by teaching the necessity of observance of the Mosaic law; and, positively, to vindicate Paul's 'gospel': justification (salvation) through faith in Christ, and not through observance of works of the Law. There is general consensus that the agitators were Jewish Christians from Judea who advocated circumcision and Torah (Law) observance. There are five texts in which Paul directly refers to the agitators: 1:7; 3:1; 4:17; 5:7-12; 6:12-13. Paul is intent on establishing the divine origin of his Torah-free gospel: 'Paul an apostle – sent neither by human commission nor from human authorities, but through Jesus Christ and God the Father ... ' (1:1). He respected the Jerusalem Church of Peter and James, but he was certain of his own independence.

In reading Galatians we must remind ourselves that Paul is not engaged in polemic against Judaism. Indeed, he himself was a Jewish Christian and his quarrel was with fellow Jewish Christians. He had no problem with traditional Jewish religious customs; his point was that such observances should not be imposed on Gentile Christians. For Paul, his letter was, first and foremost, a defence of the right of Gentiles to enter the Church on the basis of their faith in Jesus Christ without adopting the cultural practices of Jewish Christians. Paul was clear that what God had done in Christ is all that is needed for salvation. In relation to our contemporary situation we accept that faith in Christ is essential for full membership in the Church, while cultural and national differences are a matter of little importance.

There is no doubt that when he wrote Galatians Paul was an angry man. That fact is clear from the very style of the letter. He departs from his otherwise invariable custom of a 'thanksgiving' after the initial address and, instead, breaks into a pained: 'I am astonished ... ' (Gal 1:6). The agitators who are, successfully it appears, persuading the Galatians to take on observance of the Mosaic Law, evoke memories, that still rankle, of former opponents of his in Antioch – those 'false believers secretly brought in, who slipped in to spy on the freedom we have in Christ Jesus, so that they might enslave us' (2:4). Luke, I believe, has provided the key to Paul's impassioned reaction. In Luke's account of the Antioch situation (Acts 15:1-21), the Pauline opponents, described as 'some believers who belonged to the sect of the Pharisees' (15:5), and were natives of Judea, had gone to Antioch to confront Gentile Christians: 'Unless you are circumcised according to the custom of Moses, you cannot be saved' (15:1). Both Acts 15 and Galatians 2 agreed that Paul's view won the day: one could be Christian without becoming a Jew. The 'Pharisee sect' had suffered a resounding defeat. But this upset did not signal the end of them. Paul had to sustain their assaults throughout his ministry.

In Galatians 2:15-21 Paul gives us a resume of his gospel; much of the doctrine of Galatians is compressed into these few verses. The Jerusalem leaders Paul names (Peter, James, John) were able to accept his stance because they, too, believed that salvation was through Christ alone,. Nor did Paul object to the fact that the Judeo-Christians of Palestine remained faithful to Mosaic observances. Yet, he saw the inherent danger and realized that the true Christian doctrine involved freedom from legalism in theory and in fact. We cannot win salvation by observance; we must accept it as a free gift from Christ. The same basic teaching, in different terms – redemption by the death and resurrection of Christ – runs through the letter.

Although Paul's primary concern was to defend the rights of Gentiles, his doctrine of justification has important ramifications for the life of the individual believer. Paul proclaimed that he had been crucified with Christ and that he now lived by faith in the Son of God 'who loves me and handed himself over for *me*' (2:19-20). Because Christ 'gave himself for our sins' (1:4) all are equal before God. In Galatians 3:23-29 Paul takes a firm antinomian stand. He characterizes the Law as a *paidagogos*, 'disciplinarian'. The 'pedagogue', in Graeco-Roman society, was a slave who looked after the education of his master's son. While his writ ran he had considerable authority. But once his ward reached majority, that was the end of the pedagogue's role. Paul, writing for himself and his fellow Jewish Christians, argued that, in their regard, the Law had long served its purpose. He and they had come of age and were mature children of God. They had been baptized into union with Christ and, by that rite, had publicly proclaimed their union with him.

In 3:26-29 Paul quotes and adapts a baptismal declaration. The introduction reads: 'For in Christ Jesus you are all children of God through faith. As many of you who were baptized into Christ have clothed yourselves with Christ' (3:26-27). This is the setting of the remarkable pronouncement: 'There is no longer Jew or Greek, there is no longer slave or free, there is no longer male and female; for all of you are one in Christ Jesus' (3:28). Paul was almost obsessed so concerned was he to abolish the religious distinction between Jew and Gentile. In contrast to the specifically Jewish rite of circumcision, he saw baptism as a rite which bonded people from all different national and social backgrounds. He saw too that, through baptism, women might become fully members of the people of God – a status that could not be theirs in a religious system marked by male circumcision.

Paul's attitude to slavery was less clear (see 1 Cor 7:17-24). A factor here is the economic importance of slavery in the Roman Empire – a system which Paul could not realistically challenge. There is, though, the implication of his letter to Philemon: in sending back to his master a runaway slave, now become a Christian, he invites that master to welcome Onesimus as a 'brother' (Philemon 15-17).

'There is no longer male and female' – this statement is crucial. Paul has in mind Genesis 1:27 – 'male and female he created them.' In Jewish tradition this was primarily understood in terms of marriage and family. But Paul is asserting that patriarchal marriage is not what constitutes the new community in Christ. Again, this is a repudiation of inequality.

> Distinctions of race, class, and sex have been dissolved by the new creation that has occurred in Christ ... In this world, racial, social and sexual differences painfully separate people from each other, but for those who form the new eschatological person they cannot deny one full access to God's people, for God is impartial. (Matera, p. 146f)

The issue of Jew and Gentile was soon a non-issue – simply because the Christian movement had become wholly Gentile. It was not Paul but later Christians who brought about the overthrow of slavery. The equality of women and men in the Christian community has not yet become a Christian reality. The signs are that our generation is witnessing a surge which, one hopes, will issue in that desired result.

'For freedom Christ has set us free' (5:1). The tautology is firmly deliberate. Paul really believed in freedom, believed in it as an essential value of genuinely Christian life. He was aware of two enemies of freedom: exaggeration, as at Corinth – 'all things are lawful for me' (a Corinthian slogan, 1 Cor 6:12; 10:23) – and a yearning for security, as in Galatia. Paul's concern with the Galatians was that they were welcoming the agitators who offered them the security that came from clinging to Torah (Law), thus relieving them of responsibility for personal decision. Henceforth their life would be mapped out for them: they had only to do or to avoid as the Law prescribed. They were ready to shrug off responsibility and let an external moral directive carry the burden of decision. That is why he cried, in exasperation: 'You foolish Galatians!' (33:1). Paul wanted Christians to accept responsibility for their decisions. One cannot abdicate responsibility to the surrogate 'conscience' of law. 'For freedom Christ has set us free. Stand firm, therefore, and do not submit again to a yoke of slavery'.

Commentary on Galatians 1:1-2.6-10

In v. 1 Paul points to the moment of his conversion as giving him the right to call himself an apostle. Evidently, his apostleship was being challenged on the ground that he had not been commissioned by Jesus as the Twelve had been. He insists that his commission did indeed come from the risen Lord. His apostolate was as authentic as theirs.

The indignation of Paul at the situation in Galatia accounts for the fact that this is the only one of his letters which does not contain an initial thanksgiving; instead (vv. 6-10) he starts off abruptly with an expression of pained surprise at the fickleness of the Galatians, and with a sharp reproof. In Paul's view the fundamental truth about Christianity is that it is a religion of grace and not of merit ('another gospel'). Troublemakers were insisting that the way of standing right with God was by the observance of rules. Paul saw this striving for merit as a distortion of the Good News. And there is no other version of the Good News apart from the gospel he had proclaimed. His adversaries had, seemingly, accused him of being a time-server. The tone of this letter is certainly not that struck by one who is trying to win favour (v. 10).

Gospel   Lk 7:1-10

The Sermon (6:17-49) had been spoken in the hearing of Israel ('the people', v. 1); it may be that in turning directly to the episode of the centurion Luke wishes to foreshadow the Gentile mission. This may explain why (unlike Matthew) Jesus does not meet the centurion: according to the plan of Luke in Acts the Gentile mission is to follow the Ascension. The story, indeed, may anticipate Acts 10:35 – 'in every nation anyone who fears him and does what is right is acceptable to him.' The centurion (certainly a Gentile, v. 5) may be an officer of Herod Antipas; he could also have been a Roman centurion in charge of a small post at Capernaum.

The centurion sent 'elders', distinguished members of the Jewish community of Capernaum, to Jesus; it was a service he could have made bold to ask and which they would have been glad to perform because of what he had done for them. He is obviously, like Cornelius (Acts 10:1-2), a 'God-fearer', one of the numerous class of Gentiles attracted to Judaism, but distinct from proselytes who took on full Jewish observance. These 'God-fearers' were freely admitted to the synagogue worship; they came to know and appreciate the main tenets of the religion and to observe certain Jewish practices. The man is aware that Jesus, as a Jew, might be loath to incur the ritual defilement involved in entering a Gentile house (vv. 6-7; see Acts 10:28; 11:4); but his words, together with his action in sending an embassy rather than directly approaching Jesus, serve to emphasize the man's humility – a theme dear to Luke. The centurion (v. 8) is confident that Jesus can heal by a word: as a soldier, and subject to authority himself, he knew how a word of command could bring results.

Jesus's declaration (vv. 9-10) that the faith of this Gentile is greater than Israel's prepares the reader for the later acceptance of the gospel by the Gentiles (see Acts 28:28).

TENTH SUNDAY OF THE YEAR

First Reading   1 Kgs 17:17-24

The widow of Zarephath had been approached by Elijah during a famine in Israel and had given him a meal in spite of the scarcity of food. She was rewarded with the promise that her scanty supply of meal and oil would not run out while the famine lasted (17:8-16). But now (vv. 17-24) she has been grievously afflicted, by the loss of her son. Elijah restores him to life.

The parallel with the raising of the young man of Nain (gospel reading) is unmistakable. In both cases it is the hand of God which is discerned in the activity of his servant: Elijah is recognized as a 'man of God'; in Jesus, it is clear that 'God has looked favourably on his people.'

Second Reading   Gal 1:11-18

Paul is still (see 1:6-10) vindicating his gospel. When he asserts (vv. 11-12) that his 'gospel' has come to him by direct revelation, he has in mind not all his understanding of the faith but the particular doctrine of justification without the works of the law – a gospel that is truly open to all. This was something he could not have thought up for himself: it went clean against his Jewish upbringing and his bitter reaction to the Christian movement; he was quite clear that Christianity and Judaism would not mix (v. 14). No one other than the risen Lord himself could have led him to his daring vision; the Lord had won him for himself on the Damascus road (vv. 15-16; see Phil 3:12).

The experience was so powerful that he made no attempt to contact the leaders of the community but went off to work out for himself its awesome implications (v. 17). Indeed, his first visit to Jerusalem was not until three years after his conversion and it was then a private visit (v. 18). He did not need confirmation nor approbation. At the same time, he was well received by Peter and James.

Paul is making the point that they had no problem with his 'gospel'.

His Galatian adversaries were wrong-headed.

Gospel   Lk 7:11-17

This is a passage peculiar to Luke who has inserted the miracle at this point in his gospel as a preparation for the reply to the Baptist ('the dead are raised', v. 22). Nain lies about 8 miles southeast of Nazareth. The added poignancy of the death of a widow's *only* son moves Jesus to compassion. Here only is this sentiment explicitly attributed to him by Luke; but, indeed, the compassion of the Son of God is a major *theme* of the gospel. 'The Lord' (v. 13) henceforth, in Luke, appears regularly as a title of Jesus. It is a Christian title (see Rom 10:9; Phil 2:11), implying divinity, and Jesus was not addressed as 'Lord', in this full sense, during his ministry. The body of the young man, wrapped in a shroud, lay on a stretcher (not in a coffin); life was restored by the mere word of Jesus (vv. 14-15; see 1 Kgs 17:23). 'Fear' (v. 16) is the normal reaction to a manifestation of divine power, quickly followed by praise of God. The people see in Jesus a great prophet, like Elijah or Elisha, who also raised people from the dead (1 Kgs 17:17-24; 2 Kgs 4:18-37). His deed is a merciful intervention of God in favour of his people. In Jesus, God has indeed visited his people.

ELEVENTH SUNDAY OF THE YEAR

First Reading   2 Sam 12:7-10.13

Chapter 7 of 2 Samuel tells of Yahweh's promise to David: 'Your house and your kingdom shall be made sure for ever before me; your throne shall be established forever' (7:16). In a prayer (7:18-29) David thanks the Lord. Before long we are sharply reminded of the sheer humanness of the king. He, too, can compound a crime by an attempt at cover-up. It is clear that his adultery with Bathsheba was an open secret; her husband Uriah was quite aware that he had been cuckolded (11-1-13). David's next move is wholly unworthy of one who, before, and again, displays greatness – he engineered the death of Uriah (11:14-25). It is cold-blooded murder.

The only redeeming feature is that, when challenged by a prophet, David acknowledges his double sin (12:1-15). (It is deplorable that the lectionary omits Nathan's clever parable [vv. 2-6]; it *should* be read). We may not fully appreciate the remarkable significance of the episode. After all, David was undisputed master: King of Judah and

Israel and a petty emperor to boot. In any other society of the time he might have had any woman of his desire for the taking. But, in the setting of Yahwism, the king too was subject to the law of his God. David had to resort to murder if he would have the wife of another (his subject). In a different setting a prophet would not have so brazenly challenged his king, as Nathan did, and kept his head.

More surprisingly, the prophet obviously expected the confession and repentance of his king. Truly, Yahweh is not as other gods. Not even the king may flout his law. And it is to David's credit that he sees it so. His prompt and direct response (v. 13) shows something of the quality approved by Jesus in the gospel reading.

Second Reading
Gal 2:16.19-21

In Galatians 2:15-21 Paul gives a resumé of his gospel; much of the doctrine of Galatians and Romans is compressed into these few verses. We have noted that the specific purpose of Galatians is to defend the doctrine of justification by faith in Christ without the works of the Law. The Jerusalem leaders were able to accept his stand because they too believed that salvation was from Christ alone. Nor did Paul object to the fact that the Judaeo-Christians of Palestine remained faithful to the Mosaic observances. Yet he saw the inherent danger and realized that the full Christian doctrine involved freedom from the Law in theory and in fact. We cannot win salvation by our own observances; we must accept it as free gift from Christ.

The same basic teaching, in different terms – redemption by the death and resurrection of Christ – runs through the letter. Crucified with Christ, the Christian is dead to the Law in order to share in the life of the risen Christ (v. 19); even while still in the flesh one is animated by the life of Christ and spiritualised through the faith (vv. 20-21). 'I have been crucified with Christ' (v. 19), Paul can declare because, through faith and baptism (Rom 6:3-11) the Christian has been identified with the phases of Jesus' passion, death and resurrection; one can therefore 'live to God.' One can declare: 'Christ lives in me' because one experiences a union with Christ, the glorified Lord, who has become at the resurrection 'a life-giving Spirit' (1 Cor 15:45). This Christ is the vital principle of Christian activity. Paul can declare: 'I live by faith in the Son of God' because he realises in faith that his real life comes from his surrender to the power of the Son of God within him. He is in love with that Son of God him who loves him and died for him. He will not now insult that love by spurning the gracious gift of God and vainly strive to earn justification (v. 21)

Gospel   Lk 7:36-8:3

Nowhere more clearly than in this passage (7:36-50), the story of the
'woman in the city who was a sinner', do we see Jesus as Luke saw him.
The context, too, is admirable: here, indeed, is the 'friend of sinners'
(v. 34). The story has links with the other anointing stories: Mk 14:3-
9; Jn 12:1 – the story had assumed various forms in the stage of oral
tradition. Here the Pharisee (Simon, v. 40), though he had invited Jesus
to dine with him, had been coldly formal in the reception of his guest
(vv. 44-46).

Though 'sinner' is of wider connotation, the impression is that this
woman was a prostitute and was well known as such (v 30). Luke has
courteously refrained from naming her and she must remain anonymous. There are no grounds for identifying her with Mary Magdalene
(8:2). She was a woman who had previously encountered Jesus and
had received his forgiveness. She made brave and extravagant gestures: she kissed and anointed the feet of a reclining Jesus, to the
evident scandal of his Pharisee host. Jesus, on the other hand, accepted
her presence and ministering with gentle courtesy. And his verdict was
clear and to the point: 'Her great love proves that her sins have been
forgiven' (v. 47). Simon's reasoning was (v. 39): if Jesus was so
unaware of the character of the woman that he had now incurred the
ritual uncleanness of contact with a sinner, then he could not be the
prophet whom many believed him to be.

The moneylender of the parable (vv. 41-43), who remits the debt
simply because his debtors were unable to pay, is hardly typical of his
calling. It is manifest that close behind him stands a God who is ready
to forgive any debts; such is God, Jesus says, so infinitely good and
merciful. In the parable, and throughout the narrative, 'love' means
'thankful love', 'gratitude'; so the question of Jesus would run:
'Which of them would be the more grateful?' While Simon had
omitted those gestures of esteem and affection with which an hon-
oured guest was received, the woman has so prodigally supplied them
(vv. 44-47). What Simon is being told is the application of the parable:
This woman, despite her sinful past, is nearer to God than you, for she
has, what you lack, gratitude.

It is typical of Luke that he took care to introduce these women
disciples of Jesus (8:1-3). Faithful to the end, they were present at the
foot of the cross (23:49) and at the burial (23:55-56), and became
witnesses of the resurrection (24:1-11). One of these women was Mary
Magdalene. Because of the, wholly unjustified, traditional identification of Mary Magdalene with the anonymous woman of Luke 7:36-50,

it is a matter of simple justice to rehabilitate Mary.

Mary Magdalene Tradition has been cruel to Mary Magdalene. Indeed, she could well qualify as the most sinned against victim of sexist prejudice. Her characterization as a reformed prostitute has gone almost unchallenged. The fact is: there is not a single shred of evidence to sustain that portrait of her. She has had the ill fortune to emerge for the first time in Luke's gospel immediately after his story of 'the sinner' (7:36-50). Whether or not that 'sinner' was a prostitute (not at all clear) has nothing to do with the subsequent reference to 'Mary, called Magdalene, from whom seven demons had gone out' (8:2). Traditionally, the 'seven demons' have been interpreted as demons of sexual immorality and Mary has been identified with the anonymous woman of chapter 7 (who was taken to be a prostitute). The only logic here is the sick logic of misogyny. From parallel texts it is clear that possession by 'seven demons' means that Mary was a mentally ill woman, healed by Jesus. To class her as a 'sinner' is calumny.

One is not suggesting that a one-time sinner might not become a follower of Jesus and a saint. But there is no justification for classifying Mary Magdalene as a reformed prostitute. Perhaps the whole of feminist unhappiness with the Church is just there. The thoroughly positive presentation of Mary Magdalene in the Synoptic – and more so in the Johannine – traditions has been adroitly manipulated. The threatening Mary has been cut down to size: she is the proverbial prostitute with the heart of gold.

TWELFTH SUNDAY OF THE YEAR

First Reading   Zech 12:10-11

The second part of the book of Zechariah (chapters 9-14), much later than chapters 1-8, dates from the fourth century B.C. The passage 12:1-13:6 is an oracle on the deliverance and purification of Jerusalem. It is not at all easy to determine the meaning of our short reading (vv. 10-11). For our purpose it is best to look to the sense given them in the New Testament. The 'spirit of compassion and supplication' is that Spirit poured out on the disciples at Pentecost. This new spirit, promised for the last times, was a central element in the prophecies (e.g. Ezek 37:1-14; Joel 13:1). The one 'whom they have pierced' is seen by John (19:37) as Jesus, in his role as suffering servant of the Lord (Is 52:13-53:12), the sinless one whose sufferings atone for the sins of others and whose way to vindication is through pain and humiliation. The text of Revelation 1:7 ('Look! He is coming with the clouds, every eye will see him, even those who pierced him') is based on a combination of Daniel 7:13 and Zechariah 12:10, a combination which occurs also in Matthew 24:30. John looks to the coming of Christ as judge at the end of time.

Second Reading   Gal 3:26-29

In Galatians 3:23-29, Paul takes a firm antinomian stance. He characterises the Law as a *paidagógos*, 'custodian'. The 'pedagogue,' in Greco-Roman society was a slave who looked after the education of his master's son. While his writ ran he had considerable authority. But once his ward reached majority, that was the end of the pedagogue's role.

Paul, writing for himself and his fellow Judaeo-Christians, argues that, in their regard, the Law had long served its purpose. He and they have come of age and are full-blooded children of God. They have been baptized into union with Christ and, by the rite, have publicly proclaimed their union with him. They have 'clothed themselves' with Christ as a garment – an Old Testament expression for the adoption of someone's moral dispositions and outlook (Job 29:14). They have become heirs of the promises made to Abraham, but not through observance of the law: it is faith in Christ which makes one a true child of Abraham and heir of the promise made to the patriarch (v. 29). Of the three contrasts set out in v. 28, the Jew-Greek and slave-free forms are no longer vital issues but the third, 'no male and female' is very much with us.

> If the exclamation 'no male and female' as part of the early Christian baptismal formula is meant to refer to the original and essential human unity envisaged in Gen 1:27, then it is of the three pairs the most profound, the one whose consequences drive most deeply into the heart of what it is to live in Christ. Paul's message with all three is that there is equal access to salvation, to the grace of Christ, and that there is no advantage or disadvantage to belonging to either side. It is a proclamation that the differences and destructive tensions that are felt can be overcome, primarily and ultimately in the final coming of Christ, but also *now*. (Osiek, pp. 42-43)

Gospel
Lk 9:18-24

Luke gives no indication of the setting of Peter's confession. He has deliberately avoided mentioning Caesarea Philippi (Mk 8:27) lest it distract from the central place of Jerusalem in his gospel and also because Galilee is the scene of the first part of Jesus' mission. The sequence – multiplication of loaves, Peter's confession (9:10-20) – is found also in John 6:1-69. Typically (vv. 18-19), Luke refers to the prayer of Jesus (see 3:21; 5:16; 6:12). Even after the multiplication of loaves the people still think of Jesus in the same terms as before (v. 19) – see the rumours which Herod Antipas had heard (9:7-8). Luke here provides the true answer. Peter's phrase, 'the Messiah of God' (v. 20) – in place of Mark's 'the Messiah' – is an Old Testament expression: the one whom God has anointed, his Messiah. Luke (v. 22) has omitted the intervention of Peter and the rebuke of Jesus (Mk 8:32-33) – he has spared the apostle. In Mark's gospel, Peter's profession of faith, followed by the prediction of the passion, marks a turning point: the public ministry is over, Jesus goes to his death; in Luke's plan the ministry goes on.

More important is the assertion that Jesus' messiahship involves suffering, repudiation and death. A word to the disciples opens out into an invitation to all (v. 23). Three conditions are listed: denying oneself, that is to say, not to be preoccupied with oneself and one's personal interests, but to have in mind only him whose disciple one would be; taking up one's cross by patiently bearing trials and so dying to the world (see 1 Cor 15:31) – the 'daily' taking up of the cross indicates a spiritual interpretation of a saying of Jesus which originally pointed to martyrdom (see Mk 8:34); these conditions prepare the way for the third – the following of Jesus by the acceptance of his way of life. To 'save one's person' (v. 24) is the opposite of 'denying oneself' while 'losing one's person' means just that; Luke has explained what the renunciation demanded of a disciple of Jesus entails. The obstacle to self-denial (a necessary condition for following Jesus) is the attraction of the world. In other words, one must choose between Jesus and the world.

THIRTEENTH SUNDAY OF THE YEAR

First Reading
1 Kgs 19:16.19:21

The call of Elisha is the origin of the familiar expression that the mantle of so-and-so falls on another. When Elijah cast his cloak over Elisha, he was claiming him as his own – he also endowed him with his own power and personality. Elisha's response is total for, in slaughtering the oxen and burning the plough, he is precluding a return to his old way of life. Luke, in particular, will draw on the stories about Elisha in his teaching on the nature of Christian discipleship. Jesus's call to discipleship will have more urgency than that of Elijah and he expects a more prompt answer than that of Elisha.

Second Reading   Gal 5:1.13-18

'For freedom Christ has set us free' (v. 1). Paul, the former Pharisee, believed passionately in *freedom*. He had known, too long, the slavery of a rigid religious system, the bondage of a religion of law and precept. Christ had set him free from all that and he gloried in his freedom. He ached for his disciples to value the freedom that was theirs; he was sad, and angry, when freedom that was theirs was not truly appreciated: 'stand firm, therefore, and do not submit again to a yoke of slavery' (v. 1). He understood very well the awesome responsibility of freedom and scrupulously respected the conscience of his disciples: he would not compel them – they must make their personal decisions. But Christian freedom is never licence to do as one pleases; it is always motivated – and constrained – by love. 'For though I am free with respect to all, I have made myself a slave to all' (1 Cor 9:19).

In John, the contrast 'flesh' and 'spirit' means the merely human and the realm of the divine. In Paul's 'flesh' (v. 13), however, we find a firm overtone of sin – it is self-indulgence. The ultimate sin is the false assumption that one lives from one's own self rather than from God.

In vv. 16-18 Paul establishes the major contrast of this unit (5:16-26): the Spirit and the flesh. This contrast, however, is not to be understood in terms of body and soul. The Spirit (*pneuma*) is the Spirit of God while the flesh (*sarx*) refers to unredeemed humanity: humanity turned in and upon itself. Those who have been incorporated into Christ have received the Spirit. Conversely, those who have not been incorporated into Christ have not received the Spirit; they are carnal (*sarkinoi*) because they dwell in the realm of the flesh, i.e. unredeemed humanity. Consequently, the whole person (body and soul) is either spiritual or carnal depending upon the realm in which he or she dwells. Thoughts as well as actions can be carnal if they do not proceed from the Spirit. Conversely, the most material activity can be spiritual if it proceeds from the Spirit ...

In Paul's theology Spirit and flesh are two realms which stand in total and utter opposition to each other. Whereas the flesh seeks to please itself, the Spirit seeks to please God. These two realms cannot peacefully coexist, nor can there be any compromise between them. They are opposed to each other so that the Galatians cannot do whatever they want. (Matera, p. 206)

To live by (lit. 'walk by') the Spirit (v. 16) is to live one's life according to the standards of the Spirit. It is only logical that the Spirit which is the principle of Christian sonship should be the principle of Christian living. Paul warns that even Christians, despite their union with Christ and their endowment with the Spirit, still must struggle with the 'flesh' which could prevent them from doing what, as Christians, they ought to do. The Christian choice is clear because 'to set the mind on the flesh is death, but to set the mind on the Spirit is life and peace' (Rom 8:6). If they submit themselves to the Spirit who dwells within them, they will break free, not only of the 'flesh' but of the extrinsic and limiting norm of the Law. In Paul's view the Law – for 'law' read 'legalism' – has no place in the life of a Christian. It belongs to a past (3:23-26); it is an instrument of 'flesh'.

Gospel
Lk 9:51-62

A new section of Luke's gospel begins at 9:51 – the so-called travel account (9:51-18:14). The sayings and narratives of this section are fitted into the framework of a journey to Jerusalem. V. 51 is the title of the travel account. The 'taking up' of Jesus comprises his death, resurrection and ascension as one event in the same way as do the Johannine terms 'glorification' and 'elevation': he returns to his Father. The Samaritans, always hostile to Jews (Jn 4:9), absolutely refuse to receive one who is apparently going on pilgrimage to Jerusalem. James and John, living up to their reputation as 'sons of thunder' (Mk 3:17), expect Jesus to act like Elijah (2 Kgs 1:10-12). Jesus rebukes them (v. 55): his way is one of mercy, not destruction.

The next passage (vv. 57-62) introduces three would-be followers of Jesus. In v. 57 the point is made that the disciple of Jesus must be, like him, a homeless wanderer. In vv. 59-60 it is not implied, of course, that the father has just died: the man's excuse is that he must wait until his father is dead before he can become a disciple – he appeals to the demands of the fourth commandment. Others who are 'dead', insensitive to the call of Jesus, will take care of the man's obligation to his father. Luke adds the commission to proclaim the kingdom of God: discipleship implies missionary activity. Like Elisha (1 Kgs 19:19-21) the third man (vv. 61-62) wants to return to take leave of his people: Jesus is more demanding than Elijah. His reply is in proverbial form: the man who is suitable for the proclaiming of the kingdom is one who gives himself to it without reserve like the ploughman who must give his whole attention to ploughing a straight furrow.

The sayings teach, in forthright language, that sacrifice and total self-commitment are demanded of a disciple of Jesus. They suggest, too, that life's most painful choices are not between good and evil but between the good and the best. Taken together, the two scenes of the reading (vv. 51-55, 57-62)

> serve to correct wrong ideas of what it means to follow Jesus. Discipleship does not consist in zealous punishment of those who reject Jesus and his mission; nor does it consist in qualified following. All of this comes from the teacher who walks resolutely toward the goal. (Fitzmyer, p. 827)

FOURTEENTH SUNDAY OF THE YEAR

First Reading   Is 66:10-14
The reading is a stanza of a poem (66:1-16) written after the return from Babylonian exile. The poet is convinced that deliverance from that trial must herald the last age; he sings of the New Jerusalem. It is summons to all who love her to rejoice over the glory that will be hers. The city is addressed as a mother who nurses her children at her breast – a moving image of peace, contentment and love. Like the other hymns on Jerusalem in this later part of Isaiah, this one too prepares for the image of the heavenly Jerusalem in the New Testament (e.*g.*, Gal 4:26; Rev 3:12; 21:2-4). But there is more to it. In v. 13 the image changes as God takes on the mother-role: 'As a mother comforts her child, so I will comfort you'. We can rightly speak of the mother-love of God. See Isaiah 49:14-15.

Second Reading   Gal 6:14-18
It was Paul's practice to dictate his letters. He had, however, written in his own hand the conclusion of Galatians (6:11-18) – that by way of his signature. In vv. 12-13 he has his final fling at the Judaizers who would impose circumcision and the observance of the Mosaic law on the Galatian Christians. For his part, he will have none of their self-reliance. He will lean on the grace and favour of God manifest in 'the cross of our Lord Jesus Christ,' that is to say, in the whole Christ-event.

He takes 'world' in much the same sense as 'flesh' – all that stands at enmity with God. Paul has died to this 'world' (2:19; 5:24). Through the power of Christ the Christian becomes 'a new creation.' Incorporation into Christ is incorporation into a new creation where there is neither Jew nor Greek, slave nor free, no male and female (3:28).

> For Paul, this new creation is a rule (*kanón*) of conduct by which the Galatians must lead their lives: they must live in Christ as a new creation ... Consequently 'the Israel of God' (v. 15) refers to those Gentiles and Jewish believers who walk according to the new creation established by God's act in Christ. In this verse, then, 'the Israel of God' includes the Galatians, yet goes beyond them. Paul extends a greeting of peace and mercy to the Galatians, and then to all of those who, like them, conduct themselves according to the rule of the new creation. (Matera, p. 232)

The 'new creation' is reminiscent of John and his 'rebirth' (Jn 3:3-8). Both Paul and John speak with great realism. They insist that Christian life is a new existence; it is a new shaping of one's life by the life-giving principle that is the Spirit of Christ. Paul's glorying in the cross is not empty rhetoric; he bears the scars of his way of discipleship (v. 17). The marks (literally, 'stigmata') are not metaphorical but very real, wrought by illness (4:13), flogging (Acts 16:22), stoning (Acts 14:19) – all for the sake of Christ. See 2 Cor 11:23-29.

Gospel
Lk 10:1-12.17-20

The passage 10:1-16 is parallel to 9:1-6 (the mission of the Twelve). It does not seem that this sending of the seventy foreshadows the universal mission of Jesus' disciples (as has been suggested); in 24:47 the Gentile mission is entrusted to the Twelve. The office of the seventy (v. 1) is not that of the messengers of 9:52, a material one, but a mission of preaching. Two, obviously distinct, sayings follow (vv. 2-3); taken together they reflect the experience of the first missionaries: their own zeal and the opposition they encountered. The warning (v. 4) not to waste time on civilities (elaborate, in the oriental manner) underlines the urgency of the mission. 'Peace' (*shalom*) is the Jewish greeting. One who 'shares in peace' (v. 6) is, literally, 'son of peace'. 'Son of peace', a Hebraism, means one worthy of peace. Clearly, the greeting is meaningful, a blessing. Food and shelter (v. 7) are not alms but wages (see 1 Cor 9:14).

The mission is not a private sally but a public proclamation of the kingdom. The kingdom is near, so they are not to waste time on those who will not receive them; the message must be brought to others (vv. 10-11). The unreceptive town (v. 12) will not go unpunished; 'on that day' means on the day of judgment. Jesus, sent by the Father, has sent the disciples; rejection of them is rejection of God (v. 16).

The ability to cast out demons had, understandably, made a deep impression on the disciples (v. 17). The power had come to them from Jesus (v. 19) and it is by their faith in him that they have been successful. The real cause for rejoicing is that the kingdom has come; for Satan it is the beginning of the end – his fall will be lightning fast (see Jn 12:31). The disciples have received power over the enemy of humankind in all fields (v. 19); serpents and scorpions (though these may have a metaphorical sense, see Ps 91:13) exemplify evils in nature, the work of Satan (see Acts 28:3-6). The assurance of being numbered among the elect is the ultimate reason for rejoicing (v. 20). The image of the 'book of life' is a common Old Testament one (see also Rev 3:5; 13:8; 17:8; 20:12, 15).

FIFTEENTH SUNDAY OF THE YEAR

First Reading   Deut 30:10-14

In the third discourse of Deuteronomy (chapters 29-30) Moses is depicted as exhorting the people to commit themselves to the Lord by observing his covenant. First, he reminds them of the Lord's beneficence towards Israel (29:1-15). Next, he warns against infidelity to the Lord (29:16-21) and interprets the Babylonian exile as the Lord's punishment of Israel's infidelity (29:22-29). He then proceeds to promise Israel's return from exile (30:1-10). As in Jeremiah (31:31-34) and Ezekiel (36:22-32), this return is accompanied by an interior renewal on the people's part, involving the 'circumcision of the heart' (30:6). The basic structure of the covenant remains: Israel's life and prosperity depend upon the observance of the Lord's 'commandments and statutes' (30:10). But whereas, previously, these commandments and statutes were considered as external to humankind, now they are presented as being within, as flowing from within (30:11-14). The principle of human moral behaviour and service of the Lord is to be seen as emanating from existence as true human beings.

Second Reading   Col 1:15-20

Today and the following three Sundays, second readings are from Colossians. Pseudonymity (the attribution of a writing, by the author, to another than oneself) was a well-known and accepted literary convention in New Testament times – in both Hellenistic and Jewish circles. More and more it is being accepted that Colossians is pseudonymous. This means that a disciple of Paul, one who revered the great apostle, faced up to the problems and difficulties of his later age in the manner he believed Paul would have done in his own day. Colossae, a hundred miles east of Ephesus, seems never to have been visited by Paul. The approximate date of the letter is 60 A.D.

The author wrote this letter because of a dangerous error which threatened to disrupt the Colossian community. What the disturbers propose to the Colossians, in the first place, are observances touching the calendar (2:16b), dietary laws (2:16a, 21-23) and circumcision (2:11-13); the Jewish character of these observances is manifest. Besides, behind it all stands the Jewish law (2:14) with its obsolete air of being a 'shadow of things to come' (2:17). Then, too, the 'cult of angels' (2:18) refers to ideas about celestial or cosmic powers common among Jewish groups such as the Essenes. In contrast, the author's one concern is to maintain the absolute supremacy of Christ; his interest in the 'powers' is secondary.

In 1:15-20, 'Paul' sets forth his understanding of Christ's role in relation to the world and to the Church. The use of three prepositions ('in', 'through', 'for') establishes his relation to the world. All the laws which govern the creation and government of the world reside in him. He is the centre or reservoir of all creative force – all things were made *through* him. He is the principle of coherence for every creature (all things were created *for* him) – and 'in him all things hold together'. Christ, God's wisdom incarnate (Wis 7:26) is 'the image of the invisible God' (v. 15). As such, he reveals God to humankind.

If we wish to know what the Christian God looks like we have only to regard the man Jesus of Nazareth, 'for in him all the fullness of God was pleased to dwell' (v. 19). On the other hand, because he is 'the first-born of all creation', Christ is the revelation of humankind. For, if the 'fullness' of God dwells in Christ so does the 'fullness' of humanity. Jesus is not partly human and partly divine: he is *wholly* both. He is the image of God because he is the perfect human being (Gen 1:26). He is the perfect human because his life is an expression of the reality of God.

In relation to the Church he holds absolute supremacy – he is its head, its ruler, the source of its vitality (v. 18). And, as 'the first-born from the dead' he is source of the new life of the new family of God.

Gospel   Lk 10:25-37

The introduction (vv. 25-29) is essential for an understanding of The Good Samaritan. The lawyer's question was meant to embarrass Jesus; he, adroitly, put the onus on his questioner, who found his reply (from Deuteronomy 6:5 and Leviticus 19:18) winning the approval of Jesus. So the lawyer tried again and asked for a definition of 'neighbour.' This time he must have felt that the 'Master' would have been hard put to reply for he had raised what was, in fact, a much-discussed problem. The Pharisees would have excluded all non-Pharisees, while the Essenes of Qumran would go even further and declare that all the 'sons of darkness,' that is, all who did not belong to the sect, should be hated. All would agree that, even in the broadest interpretation, the terms should be limited to Jews and proselytes. It is expected that Jesus, too, will respect the broad limits; it remains to be seen whether he will narrow them appreciably.

Though it is not explicitly stated it is certainly implied that the man waylaid on the road to Jericho was a Jew (v. 30). His nationality is not expressly mentioned because the very point of the parable is that the lawyer's problem is not going to be solved in terms of nationality or race. Priest and Levite refused to become involved in what, one way or another, was sure to be a messy business (vv. 31-32). Jesus does not accuse them of callousness, he does not pass judgment on their conduct. They are men who lack the courage to love; dare we say that they represent the common man? After priest and Levite it might have been expected that the third traveller – a series of three is typical of the popular story – would turn out to be a Jewish layman; the bias would be anticlerical. The drama is that the third man, and hero of the story, is one of the despised Samaritans. He has been designedly chosen to bring out the unselfishness of love. The man applied first-aid to the wounded traveller and carried him to an inn; and he did not consider that his obligations had thereby ended. Whatever a cynic might have thought of his conduct so far, the man turns out to be very much the realist. He did not naively presume on the charity of the innkeeper but paid him, in advance, to look after the victim.

At the end, Jesus got the lawyer to answer his own question. Yet, did he really answer the original question? In v. 29 he asked: 'Who is my neighbour?' while the question that Jesus puts in v. 36 is rather: 'To whom am I neighbour?' The lawyer was concerned with the object of love and his question implied a limitation: my neighbour is one who belongs to such and such a group. Jesus looked to the subject of love: which of the three had acted as neighbour? The lawyer's question was not answered because it was a mistaken question. One cannot determine theoretically who one's neighbour is because love is not theory but practice. One's neighbour is any person who needs one's help, says the parable; the wounded man was neighbour to the priest and Levite just as much as he was to the Samaritan, but while they would have theorized in the manner of the lawyer, he acted. The traveller was neighbour to all three; the Samaritan alone was neighbour in return. The lawyer had learned his lesson and answered correctly (v. 37).

Though the final recommendation of Jesus was addressed to the lawyer it holds a message and a warning for all Christians. We must not pause to ask ourselves: 'Is this person really my neighbour?' Such a question has no place in Christian life. Christian charity knows no bounds and oversteps all man-made limits. The pity is that there are so few 'Samaritans' among us.

Stunning is the use to which Jesus turns the parable. The point, we learn, is not who deserves to be cared for, but rather the demand to become a person who treats everyone encountered – however frightening, alien, naked or defenceless – with compassion: 'you go and do the same'. Jesus does not clarify a point of law, but transmutes law to gospel. One must take the same risks with one's life and possessions that the Samaritan did! (Johnson, p. 175)

SIXTEENTH SUNDAY OF THE YEAR

First Reading   Gen 18:1-10

The story teaches that God can 'appear' to his servants in the circumstances of daily life. Abraham, sitting contentedly in the shade of his tent during the heat of the day, was startled by the sudden appearance of three strangers. It will emerge that they are Yahweh and two heavenly companions. But Abraham reacts with instinctive hospitality. With delightful oriental understatement the 'morsel of bread' (v. 5) turns into a lavish feast (vv. 6-8). Yet, the setting remains familiar and relaxed. And it is the setting of the solemn promise of a son to Abraham (v. 10). Sarah's eavesdropping and her scepticism (v. 12) contribute to the light-heartedness of the scene. The transcendent God deals familiarly with his friend and watches over the details of his life. Such intimacy between God and humankind foreshadows the extreme condescension of God who became man among humankind.

Second Reading   Col 1:24-28

'Paul' the prisoner suffers for his converts: he has his share in the
reconciling work of Christ. He is minister of that 'mystery hidden for
ages': the calling of the Gentiles to salvation and to heavenly glory
through union with Christ. The centre of this mystery is the person of
Christ who brings salvation to *all* through their incorporation in his
Body. The letter preaches to the pagans that Christ is working in their
midst preparing them for a glorious destiny. 'Paul,' for his part, does
not merely bear suffering patiently; he rejoices in it because he sees it
as the completion of Christ's suffering for the Church (v. 24).

At first sight, this would imply that Christ's suffering is in some
way deficient – which can hardly be the intent of the writer. It seems
that we should consider the sufferings of Christ under two distinct
aspects. As an expiatory sacrifice the passion of Jesus was all-
sufficient – he was 'offered once to bear the sins of many [i.e., all]'
(Heb 9:28). But the Son of man who came to serve suffered also in and
through the exercise of his ministry. Such 'ministerial' afflictions will
be – must be – shared by his ministers and agents through the life of
the Church. And, because the Church is his Body, then Christ himself,
in his servants, will suffer to the end of time. Recall the word to Saul:
'I am Jesus, whom you are persecuting' (Acts 9:5).

Gospel   Lk 10:38-42

From John 11:1 we know that the 'village' (v. 38) was Bethany, on the
eastern slope of the Mount of Olives. In John 11:1-44 the sisters have
the same contrasting temperaments. The familiar relationship between Jesus and the family of Bethany, explicitly remarked in John
11:5, is here strikingly exemplified: the exasperated Martha does not
hesitate to point out that it is partly Jesus' fault that she is left on her
own to make all the preparations (v. 40). He gently chides her for her
agitation (v. 41). There is textual confusion with regard to v. 42a. The
longer reading, impressively attested ('few things are needful, or only
one'), refers to the needless preparation of Martha – one dish will
suffice. The shorter reading ('one thing is needful'), however, may
well be authentic: Martha is told that the one thing necessary is the
person of Jesus, the Lord, and the word which he imparts. Mary,
drinking in the words of Jesus (v. 39), has chosen the good portion
('undivided devotion to the Lord,' 1 Cor 7:35).

Obviously, Mary is here presented as the ideal disciple who sits at
the Lord's feet; it would be wrong to read into the story a contrast
between 'contemplative' and 'active' life – with a consequent depre-

ciation of the latter. The immediately preceding parable of The Good Samaritan underlines the essential place of loving service, of action. Martha's fault is not that she is busy but that she was 'distracted' – 'anxious', 'troubled' – she had made herself too busy. Surely the lesson is that Christian service is the fruit of contemplation.

> Of extraordinary significance ... is the recognition – in contrast to later rabbinic and ecclesiastical attitudes – that a woman is as much entitled as a man to receive instruction from an eminent teacher of divinity [see 10:39]. Martha, in turn, is offered liberation from dependency on household routines as a prime instrument for evaluating female identity. (Danker, p. 225)

SEVENTEENTH SUNDAY OF THE YEAR

First Reading   Gen 18:20-32

In our passage Abraham emerges as an intercessor pleading for Sodom. This intercessory role highlights an important aspect of biblical prayer. It was taken for granted that God had endowed some of his servants with a special grace of efficacious intercession. This is a gift which may cost its possessor dear – as one may see in the case of Moses (Ex 32:30-32; Deut 9:18-19). Abraham, in prayer, displays a refreshing outspokenness. Look at his plea, here, for the people of Sodom. We catch the flavour of a bargaining bout in an oriental bazaar with prices being ruthlessly slashed. Abraham's clever opening gambit is designed to put Yahweh on the defensive. There is a smack of blackmail: Yahweh is surely not going to wipe out the righteous! 'Far be it from you to do such a thing, to slay the righteous with the wicked ... Shall not the Judge of all the earth do what is right?' (vv. 24-25). This is putting it up to God and no mistake. And, having made his point, Abraham is prepared to lower his price: forty-five, forty, thirty, twenty, ten. He realizes that lower than ten he cannot go and so the matter rests. But he had made a valiant try (vv. 22-23).

This is story. That the author could, in such an uninhibited manner, present such a lively dialogue between a human and God, reveals a profound understanding of God. He is a transcendent God, but he is not a remote God, and surely not a fearsome God.

Second Reading   Col 2:12-14

Because Christ is *in* his body the Church (see Col 1:27), it follows that Christ's life, death and resurrection are continuing, abiding realities within the Church. Thus, because Christ, the 'head,' has died to the 'flesh' with all its demands, the Christian should no longer submit oneself to human traditions. Baptism is the Christian's integration into Christ's death and resurrection; one dies and rises spiritually. Those who had been dead because they were sinners 'die' to their sins because they go through the experience of dying with Christ. They renounce sin and càn have nothing more to do with it (see Rom 6:2). Baptism identifies the baptized with Christ's resurrection so that one begins to live a new life. But we must guard against a mechanical understanding of baptism which gives the idea that reception of the sacrament assures one of salvation. The new life received at Christian initiation must be developed through a life-long struggle against all that threatens it.

Gospel   Lk 11:1-13

Luke has provided a wholly credible setting for the Lord's Prayer (v. 1). It is not only that the disciples were, understandably, taken by the mien of Jesus in prayer to the Father. They had come to see themselves as a group apart, a group, in their own eyes, as distinctive as that of the followers of the Baptist. It was time for them to have their very own prayer. And that prayer will remain, for all time, the characteristic prayer of the disciples of Jesus. Matthew (6:9-13) and Luke have given two versions of the prayer. The first, obvious, difference is that Matthew's form is longer. More importantly, Matthew has preserved the original, strongly eschatological, flavour of it, while Luke has adapted it to the modest pattern of day-by-day Christian living.

Luke's simpler 'Father' (in place of the solemn 'Our Father in heaven' of Matthew) represents the intimate *Abba* of Jesus' own address to the Father. He calls on his disciples to come to the Father in the same uninhibited manner. 'Give us each day our daily bread' is a childlike request for the ordinary needs of life. Christians, even as they do look to a goal beyond earthly confines, must yet steadfastly live out their lives in the only world they know. They have need of the concern of One who will care for them. The Father who arrays the lilies of the field and feeds the birds will not neglect his children (Mt 6:25-33; 12:22-31). The disturbing truth is that daily bread is not for all and that little ones do go in need. But this is because we have not taken the whole message to heart: 'But strive first for the kingdom of God and his righteousness, and all things will be given to you as well' (Mt 6:33)? Chesterton may have had the right of it when he remarked that Christianity had not failed because it had not been tried.

Luke has softened the Semitic starkness of the call to forgiveness (see Mt 6:12). It remains, for him, an inescapable obligation: 'forgive ... for we ourselves forgive.' Do we – can we – sincerely pray this prayer? An honest answer will tell us something of the quality of our Christianity. A sage comment:

> The Lord's Prayer was not meant to be a rigid formulation for the petitioner. The church today is also at liberty to modify, revise, and restate the Lord's Prayer ... Yet liturgical commissions know how strongly people can feel and react to any tampering with time-hallowed phrases. (Danker, p. 228)

EIGHTEENTH SUNDAY OF THE YEAR

First Reading
Ecclesiastes 1:2, 2:21-23

The book of Qoheleth (Ecclesiastes) comes after the book of Job (it was written, likely, in the third century B.C.) and marks a further development in biblical thought. Here, as in Job, the problem of personal retribution is taken up, and once again the traditional doctrine is found wanting. The accepted doctrine of retribution, in its simplest form, is that the good are rewarded and the wicked punished in this life. Furthermore, it maintained a necessary link between suffering and sin; if a person suffers it is because one is a sinner. Job was able to show that suffering does not presuppose sin in the sufferer and can be quite independent of guilt. But what about the reward of the virtuous person?

It is precisely this other side of the picture, the view that the just person must be happy, that Qoheleth questions. He observes that when a person, even a righteous person, has all one wants, one is not content. Qoheleth refuses to take a mechanical view of Providence. For him God is no accountant keeping a rigid balance sheet and doling out life and death, happiness and misery, in strict proportion to a person's virtue or guilt. God is in no way answerable to humankind.

'Vanity of vanities' is the keynote. What seems to be cynicism is honest realism. Qoheleth casts a cold eye on human life, and he does not flinch from what he sees there. He has the courage to admit that the things which are supposed to satisfy one do not satisfy. He tests our customary values and finds them wanting: he offers a test of pleasure (2:1-11); a test of wisdom (2:12-17); a test of work (2:18-23). One example of 'vanity' is all the toil and affliction which a person can put into acquiring wealth, for the benefit of an heir, and whether the heir will turn out to be a wise person or a fool, one cannot really know. Qoheleth has had the courage of question and to challenge because his vantage point is one of faith. He questions not because he doubts but because faith is a way through darkness: humans cannot know the work of God. And, at the end of all, he is content to acknowledge that, because God is in his heaven, all is well with the world (3:11-14; 5:2; 8:12; 9:7).

Second Reading   Col 3:1-5, 9-11

Today's reading sums up some of the conclusions that follow from the fact that the Christian through baptism shares in the life of Christ. One consequence of the Christian's spiritual death and resurrection with Christ (2:12-13) is that one's true 'home' is now 'above' (3:1). The spatial imagery is meant to bring out the quality of the new life; 'seeking the things that are above' means leading a good life in this world. 'Earthly' existence means a life of immorality (v. 5). 'Paul' is not preaching indifference to the world and its needs. What he wishes to get across is that the believer cannot model oneself on the behaviour of the world (see Rom 12:2) but on the behaviour of Christ whose life one shares. It is by living the new moral life that the Christian divests oneself of one's old nature and 'puts on' Christ, *the* image of God (1:15), thus becoming, like Christ, the image of the Maker (3:9-10). In the last analysis, the image of God is the Church, that is, the community of all those who allow their lives to be changed by the example of Christ.

Gospel   Lk 12:13-21

The request by 'one in the crowd' for a ruling in a matter of inheritance (v. 13) becomes an occasion of a warning against 'greed' or cupidity (v. 15) and the setting of the parable of The Rich Fool. The parable illustrates the peril to which 'greed' exposes one. In v. 21, the conclusion of the parable, Luke expresses his basic verdict: 'So it is with those who store up treasures for themselves, but are not rich toward God'. Instead of laying up treasure on earth, to be enjoyed in this life, the rich man should have remembered to 'be rich toward God', he should have been laying up 'an unfailing treasure in heaven' (v. 33).

In Luke's eyes the error of the rich man consists positively in having thought only of his 'soul' – in the biblical meaning of the seat of desire and satisfaction, the principle of life (v. 19). He stored up his harvest in view of enjoyment here and now. His conduct reflects the sentiment of the discontented heir (v. 13); it corresponds to the outlook of people who are concerned about what they eat and drink and put on (v. 22). It is the conduct of pagans (v. 30).

> The word 'soul' (*psyché*, v. 19) in the story of the wealthy farmer requires special attention. In 12:19-20 it specifies human beings in their totality, possessing life as that which animates them and having a personal identity that transcends and outlasts mere bodily existence. This farmer made the mistake of confusing his real self with his body. He is like a certain man who trained for the dental profession and at age thirty looked forward to retirement at age forty so that he might enjoy his country estate, ignoring the fact that his trained talents were needed by people. (Danker, p. 248)

The fortune of the rich fool is not presented as having been dishonestly acquired; his plans are not immoral. His fatal error is to have thought only of this life. His neglect of the afterlife has not allowed him to take account of the manner in which he ought to have used his wealth for the benefit of the poor. It is on this score that Luke has regarded him as blameworthy. His fault comprises three inseparable factors: forgetfulness of God; forgetfulness of eternal life; forgetfulness of his obligations to the poor. He is truly a 'fool,' because he has not known how to use wisely the wealth which he has.

NINETEENTH SUNDAY OF THE YEAR

First Reading   Wis 18:6-9

In the most important centre of the Diaspora (the numerous Jewish communities 'dispersed' throughout the world of the time), Alexandria, the latest Old Testament writing, the Book of Wisdom, appeared about the middle of the first century B.C. The second part of the book (chapters. 11-19) is a midrash in homily form. The work takes its point of departure from a short summary of the biblical narrative of Israel's desert wanderings (11:2-4). In v. 5 the author states a pattern which he discerns in the Exodus events: the Israelites were benefited by the very things that punished the Egyptians. He illustrates this observation in five antithetical diptychs. Our reading is the beginning of the fifth diptych (18:5 19:22) where, in terms of the tenth plague and the exodus, he shows how the Egyptians were punished and Israel glorified.

A feature of the technique is the handling of the biblical story with great freedom. Here, in vv. 5-19, the point is made that in return for their determination to slay Israel's male infants, the Egyptians were punished through loss of their first-born sons. Note the repetition of the basic theme in v. 8. The homily recalls for the Alexandrian Jews that once before the Jews had suffered in Egypt and the Lord had come to their rescue. It sets forth an historical basis for trust in God.

Second Reading   Heb 11:1-2.8-19

Today and the next three Sundays, second readings are from the Letter to the Hebrews. This magnificent epistle was written by an unknown, immensely gifted, Hellenistic Christian to encourage Jewish Christians who, in face of difficulties and persecution were tempted to drift from Christianity. The author exhorts them to cling to the Word of God as unveiled in Christ and to persevere in faith. The force of the argument rests altogether on the person and work of Jesus: Son of God, eternal high priest, offering a perfect sacrifice. It is most likely a document of the second Christian generation and may be reasonably dated in the 80s.

The central theme of Hebrews, the priesthood of Christ, is formulated by reference to Jewish theological categories: Christ is superior to angels, to Moses, to the levitical priesthood; and Christ's sacrifice is superior even to the high-priestly liturgy of the Day of Atonement. Such Old Testament concepts were well appreciated by first-century Jewish converts though not, even then, by all; inevitably, they lose something of their relevance after twenty centuries. Despite this, we meet throughout the letter religious truths of perennial validity. The author intended his treatise to be a 'word of exhortation' (13:22). The whole is a splendid statement of the saving work of Christ and constitutes for us today a moving word of exhortation when we may be tempted to 'fall away from the living God' (3:12).

A special worth of Hebrews is its contribution to Christology. For the author Jesus is Son of God; but he is the Son who 'had to become like his brothers and sisters in every respect' (2:17), a Son who 'in every respect has been tested as we are, yet without sin' (4:15). He is the human being who stands in a relationship of obedient faithfulness towards God (3:16) and who stands in solidarity with human suffering. Thereby he is a mediator: a true priest who can bring humankind to God. If he bears 'the exact imprint of God's very being' (1:3) it is because we see in him what makes God God; he shows us that God is God of humankind.

The consistently negative evaluation of the whole levitical system might suggest that, for the author of Hebrews, the Old Testament holds nothing of value for Christians. Not so: there is, among other things, the inspiring example of faith of the great men and women of Israel, with the reminder that faith is necessary for those who would move onward to draw close to God. Faith is the assurance of the fulfilment of our hope. For faith is oriented to the future and reaches out to the invisible. Grounded on the word of God, it is a guarantee of heavenly blessedness; it persuades us of the reality of what is not seen as yet and enables us to act upon it. This is brought out most clearly in chapter 11.

The realization that the saints of the Old Testament, their noble ancestors in the faith, are witnesses of the great race which Christians must run, will give them heart and encourage them to persevere. Nor are these merely interested onlookers. As in a relay race, the first runner have passed on the baton of faith – they are deeply involved in the outcome of this race run by Christians. But the example that is best calculated to sustain the patience and courage of Christians is that of their Lord who was humiliated and crucified only to rise again and enter into his glory. Jesus is the 'pioneer' – that is, chief and leader – offering the example of faith strong enough to enable us to endure the sufferings of a whole life (12:1-11).

Commentary on Heb 11:1-2.8-19

In 11:40 the author deals with the faith of the Old Testament patriarchs, with the reminder that faith is necessary for those who move onward to draw near to God (v. 6). Examples of enduring faith are marshalled from the traditions of the patriarchs; the exegesis is midrashic in tone. V. 1 offers a descriptive, 'existential,' definition of faith: concerned with the assurance which suffering, persecuted Christians have that faith is a guarantee of the unseen realities in which they hope, of the heavenly homeland which they approach (vv. 6,14). Faith and hope blend – yet faith stands out as the basis of hope.

The 'assurance of things hoped for': for Hebrew's readers faith would be that by which they already had a title of possession to the things they hoped for, so that if they kept their faith they would have an unshakable assurance, based on God's own promise (10:36; 6:17-20) of those things.

'The conviction of things not seen': faith anchors us firmly in the things to which we have a title in the heavenly world (6:18-20) and gives us a firm conviction of that world's reality, proved despite its invisibility. The faith of Abraham and Sarah is instanced in vv. 8-12.

'And he set out, not knowing where he was going' – a splendid comment on Genesis 12:1. Abraham is a type of our pilgrimage toward heaven.

Vv. 13-16 are an interlude in which the author makes some general observations on the examples he has proposed. The faith of Abraham emerges again in vv. 17-19 – grim testing of his faith in readiness to sacrifice his only son (Gen 22:1-4).

Gospel   Lk 12:32-48

A 'little flock' in a hostile world, the disciples must not be discouraged but must look with confidence to a Father who has chosen them for his kingdom (v. 32). In v. 33 Luke has rewritten a saying that may have originally been close to Matthew's version (Mt 6:20-21); the danger of riches and the value of almsgiving are favourite themes of Luke. The following passage, 12:35-48 – on watchfulness and faithfulness – is a compilation of parables and sayings on the common theme of *The Waiting Servants* (vv. 35-38). The short v. 35 ('Be dressed for action and have your lamps lit') is Luke's introduction to the series of parables (vv. 36-48) on watchfulness and faithfulness with an exhortation to constant vigilance. The skirts of the long outer garment were tucked into the belt for freedom of movement; the lamp must be ready and lit – the ancient oil lamp cannot be lighted by pressing a switch! The servants are expected to sit up for their master who is returning from a wedding. This last detail has all the signs of allegorical development – a reference to the messianic banquet – once the parable had been referred to the parousia.

At any rate, in v. 37b, Luke has an addition which points to the identity of the master because, unlike any earthly master (see 17:7-10), he himself will serve the faithful servants. Two texts spring to mind: 'I am among you as one who serves' (22:27) and 'I, your Lord and Teacher, have washed your feet' (Jn 13:14). This 'Teacher' is manifestly the Lord who, at his coming, welcomes his faithful servants to the Messianic Feast. And now, the 'Blessed' of Luke 12:37-38 takes on the sound of eschatological judgment. One might add that the knocking and the opening of v. 36 evokes Revelation 3:20 – 'Listen! I am standing at the door, knocking; if you hear my voice and open the door, I will come in to you and eat with you, and you with me.' The true disciple will hear the voice of the Teacher who is friend.

The Thief at Night (vv. 39-40). This little parable points to the uncertainty of the hour at which the Lord will return – he will come 'like a thief in the night' (1 Thess 5:2; Lk 17:24; 21:34-35). The householder is not in the same situation as the servants of the previous parable. They knew the night of their master's return – though not the precise hour – and so they could keep watch; but the householder has no idea when his house is going to be burgled. Therefore the moral, expressed in v. 40, is not so much vigilance, as before, but preparedness: the Son of man will appear as judge at an unexpected moment.

The Servant: Faithful or Unfaithful (vv. 41-48). The question of v. 41 refers to the preceding parable of the Waiting Servants. The parable proper (vv. 42-46) deals with the alternative conduct of a servant whom his master would place in charge of his affairs while he himself was absent on a long journey. Especially significant, in v. 42, is the change of 'servant' (*doulos*) to 'manager' (*oikonomos*) (see Mt 24:25). When Luke wrote, Hellenistic Christians saw their leaders as God's managers. They are God's deputies, acting not in their own name but in his. Hence, they are not masters of the community but men dedicated to its service. As stewards, God's stewards, they are more than ever *servants*. In Acts 20:17-35 Paul movingly outlines, in personal terms, the quality of community service. For Luke, service is the essence of office in the Church.

Vv. 47-48 introduce the fresh idea that the punishment of disobedience will be in proportion to knowledge of the Master's will. They are likely not from Jesus but constitute a community saying: their caustic tone is foreign to him. Whatever the provenance and the original meaning of the verses, there is no doubt of their meaning in the Lucan context. The office holders (the 'managers') are those who know the will of their Lord and have the duty to make it known. If they do not live according to this knowledge they deserve a greater punishment than others. The purpose of these words is to summon those who hold office in the community to faithful and selfless service of their Lord and of the Christians in their care.

TWENTIETH SUNDAY OF THE YEAR

First Reading
Jer 38:4-6.8-10

Throughout his book, the sufferings of Jeremiah are described with a grim realism that recalls the description of the Passion of Jesus. There are no miracles here, no legion of angels: Jeremiah is abandoned to his enemies and is powerless. And he makes no impression on them. It is not surprising that Christians have seen him as a type of Christ. In chapter 38 we read that Jeremiah was brought before the princes and charged with treason. This was during the Babylonian siege of Jerusalem – the year of the fall of the city in 587 B.C. Feelings ran high. The princes demanded the prophet's execution. Since King Zedekiah lacked the courage to withstand them, Jeremiah was thrown into a cistern and left to die. He was rescued through the good offices of one Ebed-melek. Zedekiah sent for him and interviewed him secretly (vv. 14-23). Jeremiah, having warned the king that his cause was hopeless, requested – and got – more lenient treatment, being kept in the court of the guard until the city fell (v. 28).

Second Reading   Heb 12:1-4

After his survey of Old Testament figures of persevering faith (chapter 11) the author of Hebrews returns to the present and exhorts his readers to persevere in their own faith, regardless of cost. Christian existence in this world is likened to a school of endurance and a toughening through hardship in which the training and formation are divine. The 'cloud of witnesses' refers to the saints of the Old Testament presented as spectators in a stadium. They have run their race. They are keen and involved fans of this race of Christians, willing them to persevere. Of course, the great race has already been won: Jesus is the winner. But, like our popular city marathons, what matters is to participate and to finish the course.

Jesus is 'the pioneer and perfecter of our faith' (v. 2). 'Pioneer' here means chief or leader, offering an example of his whole life, sufferings brought to a climax on the cross, knowing that the reward of divine exaltation awaited him afterward in heaven. As such he is an example (greater than the entire 'cloud' of Old Testament examples) for Christians who suffer in this world but are assured in faith of the promised reward awaiting them in heaven (11:1, 13-16). If Christ endured so much at the hands of his sinful adversaries, we ought to take heart from his example and remain firm in the face of our adversaries (v. 3). In v. 4 'sin' is especially, but not exclusively, the sin of apostasy.

The statement, 'you have not yet resisted to the point of shedding your blood,' is perhaps still athletic terminology: you have not yet given of your utmost. But the message is clear: the Christian, too, like his Master, must be ready to struggle – perhaps even unto death – against all obstacles on the road to God.

Gospel   Lk 12:49-53

The coming of Jesus marks a time of decision, a crisis in which no one can be neutral. Proper to Luke (vv. 49-50), these verses may first be considered independently of their context. The fire which Jesus wishes to see kindled is that which purifies, a fire lighted on the Cross (see Jn 12:32). The 'baptism' is the Passion which will 'plunge' Jesus into a sea of suffering. Jesus is the bringer of salvation to humankind but he is aware that the way to salvation is through suffering – through fire and water (see 24:41-44). But Luke has understood the saying in relation to vv. 51-53: Jesus is the 'sign of contradiction' (2:34-35). Jesus is 'set for the fall and rising of many in Israel' (2:34): people will be for or against him (vv. 51-53). The description of family dissension (a dramatic presentation of the division he brings) is based on Micah 7:6. In this passage of Luke we discern another Johannine contact because it is a feature of the fourth gospel, to be met with again and again, that Christ, by his very presence, causes division: people must be for or against the light (see Jn 8:12; chapter 9).

Jesus had to be 'baptized,' to be submerged in opposition, hatred, pain and even death in order to fulfil the will of his Father and save sinners. His followers would be called on to share in some degree in their Lord's lot. Their loyalty to him would be costly. They would have to learn from his example to endure the shame and the pain that their following of him might entail.

> Jesus' opponents were of the opinion that the best way to permanence for an institution was to proceed in an orderly and systematic way. Observance of time-honoured rules and regulations effected such a process. But Jesus was unconventional and no team-player. In the judgment of some of Jerusalem's hierarchy, his words and actions only helped to create chaotic conditions. In sum, he was not too helpful in maintaining either respect for ancestral traditions or stable relationships with the Roman imperial establishment. (Danker, p. 257)

TWENTY-FIRST SUNDAY OF THE YEAR

First Reading   Is 66:18-21

This passage shows, clearly, the influence of Ezekiel (3:23; 11:22-23; 43:1-9): the glory of the Lord will be manifest to all nations. As a result, the pagans will be converted and receive a share in Israel's blessings. The author describes, in panoramic vision, Jews making their way back from the ends of the earth to worship in the restored city of Jerusalem. They bring with them people from the non-Jewish world to do homage to the one God. The author's hope that the Gentiles would be saved was to be fulfilled when the humble man from Galilee of the Gentiles (see Mt 4:15) invited all peoples to his heavenly banquet (see Lk 13:22-30).

Second Reading   Heb 12:5-7.11-13

This passage is a continuation of last Sunday's reading. It is useful to compare Proverbs 3:11-12. 'Discipline' is the whole process of education and training by which young people are helped to shape themselves in those qualities of mind and body which characterize the real adult – strong, sober and able to cope with the problems that life will bring one's way. A true father sees to it that his son receives *paideia* ('discipline,' 'training') – vv. 7-8. The hardships the readers are experiencing are a sign that they enjoy God's fatherly concern.

V. 9 offers an argument *a fortiori*. If we respect our earthly father, how much more should we respect our heavenly Father. God trains his children for their ultimate goal (vv. 10-11). His *paideia* leads to the 'peaceful fruit of righteousness,' the heavenly tranquillity and security of the person who is disciplined.

The overall message for the Christian is that suffering is a necessary ingredient in the building up of a mature Christian person. Suffering may exasperate but it is part of the human condition and it has constructive as well as a destructive dimension.

Gospel   Lk 13:22-30

In this passage various sayings of Jesus which are found isolated in Matthew have been built into a parable. The question of v. 23 – 'Lord, will only a few be saved?' – was a current one and the regular answer was that all Israel would have a place in the future kingdom; even the ordinary people, though 'ignorant of the law' (Jn 7:49), would not be excluded – only tax-collectors and suchlike, 'sinners,' would be debarred. (One must firmly keep in mind, that, despite all early – and later – Christian scruples, Jesus was and is 'friend of sinners'). Though the question is concerned solely with the salvation of Israel it is still one that Jesus refused to answer directly. Instead, he warned his questioners that an effort is demanded of them: it is no easy matter to lay hold on eternal life (see Mt 7:13).

The second part of v. 24 – 'for many, I tell you, will try to enter and will not be able' – is explained by the following verses. In v. 25 we are dealing no longer with a narrow door but with a closed door, and the image is now that of the messianic banquet. A comparison with Matthew 25:10-11 indicates that the master here is Jesus himself. The Jews had not accepted him, they had not entered into the kingdom while they had the chance; now it is too late, the door is firmly closed. This explains, too, why those of v. 24 are unable to enter. While in Matthew 7:22-23, the rejected ones are unworthy Christians, here (vv.

26-27) they are still the Jews. It is not enough for them to have eaten with him; they had not accepted him and now they are cast off. Their chagrin will be all the greater when they see not only their own ancestors but the Gentiles, too, present at the banquet (vv. 28-29). V. 30 is a familiar secondary conclusion added here in view of the contrast between Gentiles and Jews (vv. 28-29).

Today's reading strikes a universalist note that is typical of Luke. Men and women from the four corners of the world will share in the messianic kingdom (v. 29) and the Jews will have no advantage over the Gentiles (v. 30). Yet Jesus does not offer salvation at a bargain price. Only those who follow the path pointed out by Jesus, only those who enter the narrow gate, will gain access to the Kingdom.

TWENTY-SECOND SUNDAY OF THE YEAR

First Reading   Sir 3:17-20.28-29

In praise of one who is meek, gentle, kindly, affable, humble. Meekness involves a consciousness of one's own weakness (even when one holds authority). Ben Sirach treasured the Jewish wisdom which was based on the Law and he believed that the 'fear of the Lord' – commitment to God – was the beginning of true wisdom (1:14). A humble person is open to the Lord and never rejects wisdom, no matter where it comes from. Ben Sirach declares God's love for the person who approaches him with gentleness and an open heart. Not only does God appreciate the underlying strength of meekness, but friends welcome the modest person and neighbours appreciate one's willingness to learn. Pride and self-glorification raise a barrier to God's graciousness and to communion with our fellows.

Second Reading   Heb 12:18-19.22-24

The passage 12:14-29 of Hebrews is an eschatological warning. It opens with the admonition (vv. 14-15) that Christian life consists in striving for peace with our fellow men and women on earth and for a share in God's own holiness (12:10). The Christian must not dally with distractions and diversions along the way.

Then, in vv. 18-24, Sinai and Zion are contrasted. The heavenly city, goal of the Christian's pilgrimage (13:14), at last appears in detail. At the same time the contrast of the two covenants, two orders of salvation, is made with the symbolism of two mountains – Sinai, the mountain where the old covenant was made, and Zion, the mountain of the heavenly Jerusalem. Midrashic embellishment emphasizes the element of dread in the relations between God and humankind under the old covenant (vv. 18-21). The 'heavenly Jerusalem' (v. 22) belongs to the heavenly world of valid spiritual realities and of humankind's meeting with God (Rev 3:12; 21:2, 10; Gal 4:26); it belongs to the messianic age ushered in by Christ.

The 'now' and the 'not yet' of Christian existence in this world is shown; the author speaks of those who are still on their journey to heaven; and yet, because they already possess in an anticipatory way the good things to come, he can speak of them as having already arrived. 'The assembly of the first-born who are enrolled in heaven' (v. 23) are the elect the elect of the Old Testament and the first generation of Christians. Christ (see vv. 18-21) is the mediator of the final covenant (v. 24). The 'sprinkled blood' recalls the ritual of the Day of Atonement (9:1-10). Where the blood of Abel had cried out to God for vengeance (Gen 4:10) the blood of Jesus achieves reconciliation. This reconciliation and union through the blood of Christ is the consummation of that 'peace' and 'holiness' which Christians strive after as their goal (Heb 12:14).

Gospel   Lk 14:1.7-14

In 14:1-24 four episodes are set in the context of a meal to which Jesus had been invited; our reading has two of them. Jesus receives, and accepts, an invitation from a Pharisee (see 7:36; 11:37); his adversaries hope that they may discover grounds for further accusations against him. At first sight, vv. 7-11 seem to offer a lesson in etiquette. Luke, however, calls the passage a 'parable.' Later on, the scribes are characterized as those who love 'the places of honour at banquets' (20:46); in our text, such conduct, presented in parabolic guise, is censured and made the object of a warning. One who has seated himself 'in a place of honour' must yield place to the eminent guest for whom that place had been reserved and, since the intermediary places will have been filled, must take the lowest place (vv. 7-9). For v. 10 compare Proverbs 25:7 – 'It is better to be told "come up here" than to be put lower in the presence of a noble.' The key to the passage is v. 11, a saying which occurs, too, in 18:14 as a generalizing conclusion to *The Pharisee and the Publican*. Here, however, is its proper place. The passive stands for the action of God ('For all who exalt themselves will God humble, and those who humble themselves will God exalt'), and the future tense refers to the judgment (see 14:14).

We are taken beyond the perspective of human relations and

assured that God is no respecter of persons. Now the drift of the parable is clear. If the scribes and pharisees arrogated to themselves privileges and demanded preferential treatment, they did so on the grounds of their observance of the Law, on their standing as religious men. They took for granted that God would see things in this way too and render them like preferential treatment, the first places in the kingdom; here they are quietly warned that they may be fortunate to get the lowest places. It is not difficult to see that the warning could with reason, if not always with profit, have sounded down the centuries, and could continue to ring in the ears of the professional religious men of the Christian Church.

No more than the preceding parable is the passage on the choice of guests (vv. 12-14) meant as practical advice. Rather, Jesus teaches that a limited and interested love is worthless in the sight of God (see 6:32-34). The passage is a commentary on 6:35 – 'But love your enemies, do good, and lend, expecting nothing in return. Your reward will be great, and you will be children of the Most High; for he is kind to the ungrateful and the wicked.' Those who act from motives of disinterested charity will receive their reward at the resurrection – they will take their place at the messianic feast (v. 14). Here Luke's concern for the poor and afflicted is manifest. He sees the following parable of *The Great Feast* (vv. 15-24) as an illustration of vv. 12-14.

TWENTY-THIRD SUNDAY OF THE YEAR

First Reading   Wis 9:13-18

The Book of Wisdom, though written, in Greek, about 50 B.C. is, by its author, attributed to Solomon. Wisdom 9:1-18 is 'Solomon's' prayer for wisdom. Our passage, the conclusion of the prayer (vv. 13-18), insists that no one can arrive at God's counsels without wisdom. God is all-wise (v. 13). In contrast, faced with the mysteries of the universe, the meaning of history, and the mind of the Creator, people are ignorant (vv. 16-17). God does not leave humankind in its ignorance and uncertainty but bestows the gift of knowledge. The answer to life's problems is in the hand of God; he is generous with his gift of wisdom to all who humbly ask for it (v. 18). The 'holy Spirit' of v. 17 is Wisdom personified. But Paul can call on the association of 'spirit' with 'wisdom' here to teach that the Spirit communicates a wisdom that is not of this world and that enables those who accept it to understand and appreciate the divine plan (1 Cor 2:6-16).

Second Reading   Philemon 9-10.12-17

The shortest of Paul's writings, little more than a postcard of some 25 verses, the letter to Philemon is vintage Paul. Properly understood, it has proportionately as much to say as some of the longer Pauline letters. Often enough one can effectively express in few words what can get lost in verbiage.

A first observation is that the letter is addressed to 'Philemon our dear friend and co-worker, to Apphia our sister, to Archippus our fellow soldier, and to the Church in your house.' We are talking of a ministerial team: Philemon, Apphia, Archippus – with the woman Apphia being obviously an equal member. When one compares Romans 16, which lists several women actively engaged in the apostolate, as well as Philippians 4:2-3, one realises that, in the Pauline understanding of Church, women stood shoulder to shoulder with their brothers.

Philemon, it appears, was a native of Colossae in Asia Minor, and had been converted by Paul himself (v. 19). His slave Onesimus had run away and had somehow reached Paul in prison (v. 10); he, also, became a Christian and was active, with Paul, in the ministry. He was still a runaway slave, and Paul felt obliged to send him back to his master. He took care to provide a covering letter. With notable delicacy (though he does not refrain from making some telling points) he urged Philemon to welcome back as brother his erring slave who was now, too, a Christian. In v. 11 there is a play on the slave's name: 'Formerly he was useless to you, but now he is indeed *useful* both to you and to me' – the Greek *Onesimos* means 'Useful One.'

The onus, however, is firmly on Philemon. A truly Christian response must be free, not a matter of duress. Paul tells Philemon, bluntly enough, what he *ought* to do, but he refuses to order him. 'Though I am bold enough in Christ to command you to do your duty, yet I would rather appeal to you on the basis of love' (vv. 8-9). His real concern is expressed a few lines later: 'I preferred to do nothing without your consent in order that your good deed might *be voluntary and not something forced*' (v. 14). Paul was in no doubt about his own authority, and could command if he had wanted to. But he regarded a command that *must* be obeyed as a form of compulsion, a limiting of the *free decision* that is essential for authentic growth; and he will not issue a binding directive in the area of moral decision. (In practical matters he had no hesitation in issuing directives). And there is, perhaps, after all a sting in the tail: 'One thing more – prepare a guest room for me' (v. 22). Paul hoped to be released from prison and planned to visit Philemon – an embarrassing visit if Philemon had not done what Paul had requested!

This little letter – because it is Pauline – makes another significant contribution: it puts before us the fundamental attitude of the early Church to slavery. In the social pattern of the age the abolition of slavery was impossible. A Christian slave, however, should be regarded and treated as a brother and not as a chattel. For that matter, in v. 21, 'knowing that you will do even more than I ask', Paul seems to be asking Philemon to emancipate Onesimus. He hints that Philemon should allow Onesimus to return to work with him. In time, the leaven of the gospel would create such relations between master and slave that the system of slavery would become obsolete. And when it was revived by 'Christians' (African slaves in the New World), it came again to be recognized as blatantly un-Christian.

Gospel

Lk 14:25-33

Luke has set the two parables (vv. 28-30; 31-32) in the context of self-renunciation (v. 33); he underlines the cost of discipleship. The exhortation (vv. 26-27) is couched in its strongest terms ('hate' here means detachment), and the situation envisaged in the (relatively) rare one in which a person is called upon to choose between the following of Christ and one's own relatives. In v. 27 'to carry the cross' means to be prepared to face death. The disciple of Jesus should be prepared to lay down life; he or she is like one condemned to death, carrying the instrument of execution (see Jn 19:17).

The twin parables (vv. 28-32) drive home the lesson that discipleship does involve commitment; it cannot be undertaken thoughtlessly. Though the parables appear to repeat each other they are, in fact, complementary. In the first, the builder is free to undertake his construction or not; he is considering the matter in the abstract. The king, on the other hand, is already up against it: his country has been invaded (the other king is 'advancing against him'); therefore he must act. For, indeed, these are the two factors in the call to follow Christ: we have to count the cost both of accepting that invitation and of rejecting it. One who comes to Christ must come with one's eyes wide open.

The parables may seem discouraging but they are to be understood in much the same way as the saying of v. 26. The following of Christ is at all times a serious business and, in certain circumstances, it can be a very serious business indeed. This is true, for instance, in time of persecution. It is scarcely less true in the modern world where the

Christian is called upon to renounce so much that is taken for granted by others. If one does come after the Master one must be prepared to take up one's cross and carry it (v. 27), while at the same time one cannot, without sin, fail to live up to one's obligations as a Christian. The encouraging thing is that Christ who calls, knows the cost involved and knows, too, human frailty, and will lavish his grace on one who really strives to answer his call. V. 33 is a practical consequence of the parables rather than their moral.

> Following Jesus is no invitation to trivial adventure. A Church that encourages its followers to play it safe and to conform with the substandard practices of surrounding society not only invites disaster but loses all claim to association with the revolutionary cause of the Kingdom. The invitation to commitment expressed in v. 33 echoes 6:46-49 and is as total as any dictator could wish. Everything depends on the decision. A Church that does not spell this out clearly to prospective members or to its constituency proves false to the good news. Indeed, failure to do so has led the institutionalized Church to pussyfoot on a variety of issues. (Danker, p. 273)

TWENTY-FOURTH SUNDAY OF THE YEAR

First Reading   Ex 32:7-11.13-14

Exodus 32 is the episode of the 'golden calf': while Moses is conversing with Yahweh on the mountain, the people conspire with Aaron to make gods for themselves. In vv. 7-10 God informs Moses of what the people have done. 'Your' people he calls them as if they no longer belonged to him, and in v. 10 there is a hint that he can make himself another people. Then Moses turns to God and *intercedes* for the people (vv. 11-13). Moses was an intercessor (see Ex 15:25; 17:11-16). But he is, too, a supreme example of the truth that God's gift of efficacious intercession is one which may cost its possessor dear. Later in the chapter we discover an instance of the heroic generosity of Moses the intercessor (vv. 30-32): 'But now, if you will only forgive their sin – but if not blot me out of the book that you have written.' Moses, conscious of his responsibility, is prepared to put his neck on the block. It is highly reminiscent of Paul who, many centuries later, in his turn still prays for the 'hard-necked' people: 'For I could wish that I myself were accursed and cut off from Christ for the sake of my own people, my kindred according to the flesh' (Rom 9:3). No trace here of 'I'll keep you in my prayers'! The intercessor enters into the anguish of the situation and lays himself open to God.

A feature of Old Testament prayer is forthrightness – a remarkable outspokenness in addressing God. Here (v. 11) Moses questions the wisdom of God in turning against his people. He reminds God, firmly, of his promise to the patriarchs (v. 13). Surely God is not going to welsh on his promise! In v. 12 there is a touch of blackmail: 'Why should the Egyptians say ... ' God will make himself a laughing-stock if he permits his people to perish. Not much of a god he is, the nations will say, if he is unable to protect his own. Therefore, 'turn from your fierce wrath; change your mind and do not bring disaster on your people' (v. 12). 'And the Lord changed his mind about the disaster that he planned to bring on his people' (v. 14). Did he have any choice?

Second Reading   1 Tim 1:12-17

The two letters to Timothy and the letter to Titus have, since the eighteenth century, been known as the Pastoral Epistles. 1 Timothy and Titus are of essentially similar literary character; 2 Timothy has a more personal tone than the others. All three have been written by the same author, a man of the third Christian generation, who wrote *ca* 110 A.D. (It may be that 2 Timothy was indeed written by Paul.) He had invoked the names of the well-known disciples to deal with the problems of the community, or communities, of his concern. Paul is, for him, the ideal apostle. And the pastoral directives, needful for his situation, found greater weight when they were presented as issuing from Paul.

The Pastorals differ from the Pauline letters not only on the ground of different authorship but more fundamentally because they reflect a greatly changed Church. A feature of Paul's outlook is his eschatological expectation; he can contemplate the parousia of the Lord happening in his own lifetime. In Pastorals the view clearly is that the Church must make adjustments for a prolonged stay in the world. This involves a preoccupation with institution and with orthodoxy. Natural enough, too, is a concern with 'good citizenship'. Christians are expected to be model exponents of the moral and social virtues. In this way it was hoped that they would win respect and acceptance among their contemporaries in the Roman world (contrast Revelation).

Despite the emphasis on structure no clear structural pattern emerges – certainly no obvious hierarchical institution. Indeed, one man stands out: Paul – he is the real figure of authority. As for doctrine, a clear tendency runs through: traditional teaching is not interpreted but is firmly inculcated as an existing and permanent norm.

The Pastorals present a Church coming to terms with life: an eminently sensible Church concentrating on structure, orthodoxy and respectability. It is a sort of Church with which we are familiar because, historically, the Christian Church has followed the Pastoral model. Not an exciting Church.

Commentary on 1 Tim 1:12-17

Our reading gives (in autobiographical guise) on account of the conversion of Paul. He had experienced the mercy of God and had received the call to God's service even though he had opposed and injured the infant Church. That fact served to highlight the quality of God's generosity and underlies our duty to thank and honour him. The formula 'the saying is sure' occurs five times in the Pastorals (1 Tim 1:15; 3:1;4:9; 2 Tim 2:11; Titus 3:8); it introduces a formal statement about Christ as saviour. All the 'sure sayings' are sayings which offer reliable directives for faith and life and help the communities to answer important and new questions. V. 15, the 'sure saying' of our passage, may be paraphrased: 'Christ Jesus did not come into the world to make us sinners.' His mercy and patience transform sinners into 'just' people (v. 9).

Gospel   Lk 15:1-32

See the Fourth Sunday of Lent (pp. 59-60, *supra*) for a commentary on the introduction to this passage (vv. 1-3) and on the parable of The Prodigal Son (vv. 11-32). Here we shall look at the two parables of vv. 4-10.

The Lost Sheep (vv. 4-7). Jesus tells of the shepherd who went in search of the sheep that was lost and of his joy when he had found the stray. The solicitude of the man is such that he leaves the ninety-nine in the desert, that is, in the scanty pasture of the Judean hill-country, while he searches for the other. And his joy at finding the lost sheep is so great that he must tell his neighbours of it. The moral of the story is stated in emphatic terms: God will rejoice ('joy in heaven' is a circumlocution) that, together with the just, he can also welcome home the repentant sinner. Or we might render the verse: 'Thus God, at the Last Judgment, will rejoice more over one sinner who has repented, than over ninety-nine respectable persons, who have not committed any gross sin.' That is why Jesus seeks out sinners while the scribes and Pharisees, by caviling at his conduct, are criticizing the divine goodness.

The Lost Coin (vv. 8-10). Peculiar to Luke, this parable is parallel to the other; it is typical of the evangelist that he has brought a woman into the picture. The 'silver coins' (or 'drachmas') represent a modest sum but the loss of even one coin is of great concern to a woman in humble circumstances. She had to light a lamp because the small windowless house – the only opening being a low door – was in near darkness. The phrase 'before the angels of God' (v. 10) is a periphrastic rendering of the divine name: 'God will rejoice' (see v. 7; 12:8-9).

The two parables consider the conversion of a sinner from God's point of view: he rejoices that the lost should return home, because they are his; he rejoices because he can forgive. God has sent his Son 'to seek out and to save the lost' (19:10), and Jesus' actual concern for sinners is a concrete proof that God does more than desire that sinners should repent.

TWENTY-FIFTH SUNDAY OF THE YEAR

First Reading   Amos 8:4-7

Amos is the earliest of the Old Testament prophets whose words have been preserved for us in book form. The heading of the book (Amos 1:1) tells us that Amos was a peasant of Tekoa (about six miles south of Bethlehem) and that he was active during the reign of the contemporary kings, Uzziah of Judah and Jeroboam II of Israel. Since his ministry was clearly set in the height of Israel's prosperity, it must have been well into the reign of Jeroboam II (783-743) – a reign which marked the apogee of Israel – in other words, around the year 750 B.C.

'Peasant' he may have been, but his poetic genius is as evident as that of the Irish 'peasant' poet Patrick Kavanagh.

The passage Amos 7:10-15 gives a more detailed picture of Amos' background. He spent part of his time as a shepherd and part as a 'dresser of sycamore trees' – this expression refers to a method of helping the fruit to ripen. The mission in Israel of a prophet from Judah is a striking indication that a common religious tradition spanned the divided kingdoms. When Amaziah, priest of Bethel, warned Amos that he should earn his living in Judah – by accepting fees like the professional prophets (see 1 Sam 9-8; 1 Kgs 14:3; 2 Kgs 8;8), Amos replied that he was not a *nabi* (prophet) of that sort, nor was he one of the 'sons of the prophets': ninth-century prophetic groups. Amos had received a personal call.

Amos was the great champion of justice who vindicated the moral order established by God and enshrined in the covenant. He castigated the disorders that prevailed in an era of hectic prosperity. To his eyes, the symptoms of social decay were glaring. Wealth, concentrated in the hands of a few, and these the leaders of the people, had corrupted its possessors; oppression of the poor was rife; the richly-endowed national religion, with its elaborate ritual, provided a comfortable, self-righteous atmosphere. It was this dangerous complacency that the prophet set out to shatter. Amos did not speak in riddles; his message was uncompromising and unmistakable. He savagely assailed the oppression of the poor and the cheating of the poor, as well as the corrupt judicial system which denied them any hope of obtaining justice (2:6-8; 3:9-11; 5:7, 10-12, etc.).

Our short reading is an eloquent example. With biting sarcasm he depicts the 'religious' employers waiting impatiently for the end of holy days so that they can engage in lucrative business. Those sabbaths and holy days – what a shameful waste of valuable time! Though law forbade Israelite merchants to make use of a dishonest measure (Lev 19:36; Deut 25:14-15) they are here represented as tampering with the *ephah* (dry measure) and *shekel* (unit of weight) – and selling 'the refuse of the wheat.' By such sharp practice it is the vulnerable poor and needy who are being bought and sold. Someone has, rather neatly, called Amos the Oscar Romero of the eighth century B.C.

Second Reading   1 Tim 2:1-8

The passage is about the prayer of intercession and, because the setting is community prayer, it is about the Prayer of the Faithful. The Christian community is summoned to pray for its civil rulers, at that time its pagan rulers, and to pray, not as one might expect, that they themselves might be left in peace but that their rulers should share in the salvation God wills for all peoples. The Old Testament is very sure that God is a saving God. If his saving grace reaches first to Israel there is not lacking an appreciation that it will spread out to all humankind.

Most firm of all is the declaration in v. 4 here: 'God our Saviour, who desires everyone to be saved and to come to the knowledge of the truth.' That this should be is logical. It is the inevitable expression of God's loving concern for humankind. Salvation is offered to *all* and is offered to all as *gift*. Whether some, ultimately, are not saved we do not know. What we should be clear about is that there is one way, and one way only, in which anyone can be 'lost.' It is the way of rejection of God's loving gift. God is love and his purpose is love. Can any child of his, finally and definitively, turn his or her back on infinite love?

God alone knows. Let us take comfort in the assurance: God wills the salvation of *all*, for there is only one God, and one mediator, Jesus Christ who gave himself as a ransom *for all*.

Gospel
Lk 16:1-13

The parable of The Astute Manager (16:1-8) was one which Jesus' readers would have readily understood. They would have appreciated the humour of his bold characterization: his putting forward of a disreputable man as a spur to resolute decision and action. The manager (steward) was accused of embezzlement. Until he produced his books he had a breathing space. He rewrote contracts – in favour of his master's creditors and in view of a kickback! It was a neat scam. The master (who had to honour the contracts duly made in his name) grudgingly applauded the resourceful conduct of his unscrupulous manager. Jesus would wish that his disciples show as much resourcefulness in God's business as men of the world do in their own affairs. Outside of Palestine the parable quickly raised the problem of how this unscrupulous man could be, in any sense, an example.

Vv. 10-13 are meant to answer the difficulty raised by the steward's conduct. He is no longer an example but a warning. It is noteworthy that these additions leave the substance of the parable unchanged, but they do bear witness to the interpretation of a parable which is now applied by the early Church to the community. It is, however, an application that is very much in the line of the parable as Jesus spoke it. The resolute action which he recommends does embrace the generosity of v. 9, the faithfulness of vv. 10-11 and the rejection of mammon in v. 13. The early Christians did not miss the point of the parable; but, applying it to themselves, they necessarily caused a shift of emphasis. They were able to bring its teaching to bear on their daily lives because they lived in the atmosphere of the decision it urgently enjoined: they had accepted the Kingdom.

Luke is more precise. In vv. 1-9 the crafty manager, a dishonest man (v. 8), is brought forward to teach Christians the wise use of money: to make friends with it so that at death, when money fails, their friends can welcome them (their benefactors) into eternal dwellings. To use money wisely is to give it to the poor and so ensure one's eternal lot. The woe of the rich is linked to the horizon on which their eyes are fixed: 'where your treasure is, there will your heart be also' (12:34). And even if the rich hear the word, 'they are choked by the cares and riches and pleasures of life, and their fruit does not mature' (8:14). Their 'hearts are weighed down with dissipation and drunkenness, and the worries of this life ' (21:34). They become incapable of looking beyond this present life. Such is the conviction of Luke. He, obviously, has to do with a Christian community wherein many were prosperous.

The parable of The Astute Manager says in positive terms what the parable of The Rich Fool (12:13-21) says negatively. The steward is, at least, prudent: his example teaches people to use their earthly goods for the sake of a heavenly future. Just as the 'Woes' (6:24-26) are addressed to the rich, the episode of 'the rich ruler' illustrates the extreme difficulty a rich person faces in finding salvation (18:18-27).

The case of Zacchaeus shows that an exception is always possible. Jesus declares of him in effect: 'Today salvation has come to this house' (19:9). But in Luke's narrative this verdict is strictly linked to the declaration of the rich tax-collector: 'Look, half of my possessions, Lord, I will give to the poor; and if I have defrauded anyone of anything, I will pay back four times as much' (v. 8). Zacchaeus is saved but his fortune is gone back to the poor and to those who have been the victims of his exactions. Inexorably, Luke maintains his position that the proper use of wealth is to distribute it to the poor.

Even though the sayings of 16:9-13 are complementary to the parable of The Astute Manager, it is not unfair to say that the ultimate message of the parable, as Luke understands it, is given in v. 13 – 'No slave can serve two masters; for a slave will either hate the one and love the other, or be devoted to the one and despise the other. You cannot serve God and wealth (Mammon).' It is not simply a question of two ways of using money but of the impossibility of any compromise between the service of God and the service of wealth – for Mammon takes on the character of an idol.

Yet, it is not really a struggle between God and Mammon. The conflict is situated in the human heart, in the psychological inability of giving oneself wholly to two masters, neither of whom can be served by half-measures. The service of the one or of the other must be exclusive. One has to make a choice. The situation of the wealthy man is tragic: his wealth ties him to Mammon. How difficult it is to free himself and put himself wholly at the service of God. And thus Luke's closing recommendation remains: 'And I tell you, make friends for yourselves by means of dishonest wealth (mammon) ... '

TWENTY-SIXTH SUNDAY OF THE YEAR

First Reading
Amos 6:1.4-7

Amos saw that nothing short of a radical change of life-style could save Israel (5:4-6, 14-15) and he feared that it would not happen. He warned those who looked to the 'Day of the Lord' as the time of triumph of God's people over all its enemies, that the Day would be darkness and not light (5:18). Amos speaks to the wealthy of both Judah and Israel: those who are at ease in Zion, those who feel secure in Samaria. His description of the wealthy, lying in their ivory beds, eating lamb and stall-fed veal, playing music, drinking wine, anointing and garlanding themselves, speaks for itself. Their crime is that they could not have cared less for the plight of the poor (the very sin of Dives in the gospel parable). Nor were they aware that their conduct was a formula for disaster, undermining the fabric of the nation. For them Amos has a chilling warning: they will head the band of those whom the enemy will lead off to exile. Within a generation the kingdom of Israel was overrun.

Second Reading
1 Tim 6:11-16

In this passage of his letter, the author, building on a baptismal tradition, spells out what he means by 'life.' The gift of eternal life offered and received in baptism comes from a God who is God of life (v. 13) At baptism the Christian makes 'the good confession' (v. 12), makes one's profession of faith, in imitation of Christ Jesus who, before Pilate, made 'the good confession' (v. 13). That example underlines the seriousness of Christian commitment.

There are several lessons. As Jesus was faithful to his call in face of a hostility that led to his death, Christians facing persecution should be faithful to God's call. Jesus' suffering emphasized the reality of his humanness; Christians should make their profession as full human persons. As Christ Jesus made the good confession in accord with a true understanding of who God is, Christians must make their confession in accordance with 'the sound words of our Lord Jesus Christ' (v. 3). Christians who live in hope of 'the appearing of our Lord Jesus Christ' are urged 'to keep the commandment' (v. 14). By 'the commandment' the author means the pursuit of 'godliness,' affirmation of the word, adherence to sound teaching, and faithfulness to the Saviour Christ Jesus during persecution.

Gospel   Lk 16:19-31

In Luke's mind the two parables of his chapter 16 (The Astute Manager and Dives and Lazarus) have the same theme: the use of money. The Astute Manager (vv. 1-8: see previous Sunday) is to teach the disciples (v. 1) the proper use of money; Dives and Lazarus (vv. 19-31) is to point out to the Pharisees the danger in which they stand by selfishly hoarding their wealth (v. 14). Dives was a worldling who did not look beyond the good things of this life (v. 19). In sharp contrast is the crippled ('who lay') beggar Lazarus – the name means 'God helps.' The dogs, wild scavengers, add to his misery since he is unable to keep them at bay. He would have been glad to have – if they had been offered to him – the pieces of bread with which the guests wiped their fingers and which they then dropped on the floor (vv. 20-21).

The rich man might (according to Luke's understanding of v. 9) have made of Lazarus a friend to welcome him into the eternal habitations. It is important to observe that nowhere is it suggested that Dives' wealth is ill-gotten nor that Lazarus is a victim of his oppression. The sin of Dives is that, cushioned by his lavish life-style, he is simply oblivious to the presence of a beggar at his gate. The contrast between the two in the next life is more pronounced – but they have exchanged roles (v. 22). Death was currently described as 'going to be with Abraham' or 'being gathered to Abraham,' that is, to join the patriarchs. Lazarus is given the place of honour at the right of the patriarch. The phrase 'to Abraham's bosom' is explained by John 13:23 – 'one of his disciples, whom Jesus loved, was reclining next to him (literally, upon the bosom of Jesus),' that is, at his right side and leaning backward toward him. The rich man's burial, in keeping with his wealth, merely emphasised the futility of his life, for he went to the place of torment.

Jesus' story reflects the current Jewish notion of Sheol as it had been adapted in the wake of belief in resurrection and retribution after death. It was imagined to have two compartments: in one the just quietly awaited the resurrection while in the other the wicked were already being punished (vv. 23-24). Abraham does not disown Dives: as a Jew he is, according to the flesh, his son, but this is not enough to save him (vv. 25-26). The rich man realized that his present state was a punishment, not a change of fortune only, and that Lazarus was being rewarded not for his poverty but because God is vindicator of the poor. The abyss not only divides the two compartments of Sheol but marks a definitive separation between the two classes of dead. In all this Jewish imagery we are not given anything resembling a 'topography of hell.' Besides, it is a description of the intermediate stage, before the Last Judgment.

This is one of the double-edged parables and, true to form, the greater emphasis is on the second point (vv. 27-31). But, just as in the first part, we are given no real description of hell, so here we can learn nothing of the psychology of the damned. The reaction of Dives is described from an ordinary point of view: his present sorry state has at last opened his eyes and he is understandably desirous that his brothers should escape his fate (vv. 27-28). Abraham answers that the five, who evidently led much the same sort of life as their unhappy brother, have 'Moses and the prophets,' that is, the Old Testament. A text of Isaiah meets exactly the situation of Lazarus: what God asks of his people is 'to share your bread with the hungry, and bring the homeless poor into your house; when you see the naked to cover him' (58:7). The man makes one more bid (v. 30). Surely, if Lazarus were to come back from the dead his brothers would at last be moved and repent. The reply is that a miracle will not help those who have made no use of the means God has put at their disposal.

We must look to the broader context of Luke's attitude towards wealth. Why is it 'easier for a camel to go through the eye of a needle than for someone who is rich to enter the kingdom of God' (18:25)? The first 'woe' replies: because the rich 'have received their consolation' (6:24). The declaration of Abraham is more explicit: 'Child, remember that during your lifetime you received your good things, and Lazarus in like manner evil things; but now he is comforted here, and you are in agony' (16:25).

There is no doubt that Luke regarded the rich as unhappy and he invites us to pity them. The broad way along which they walk is not the path which leads to the Kingdom.

TWENTY-SEVENTH SUNDAY OF THE YEAR

First Reading   Hab 1:2-3; 2:2-4

We know nothing whatever of the person of Habakkuk; he seems to have been a contemporary of Jeremiah. The book opens with a dialogue between God and the prophet: a first complaint (1:2-4) regards the prevalence of injustice in Judah and a first divine response (1:5-11) foretells the coming of the Babylonians as agents of divine justice. The complaint of vv. 2-3 is something that we might have thought to be a characteristic of Jeremiah. This text assures us that

Jeremiah was not just being temperamental. Other prophets, too, could feel the burden of their office and be as candid in their complaining.

A second complaint (1:12-17) concerns the tyranny of the Babylonians, now masters of Judah, and the divine response (2:1-4) promises that God's intervention will not fail to save those who trust in him. Habakkuk faces up to the scandal of God's action in history and of his treatment of Israel. How can he, who hates sin, use the ruthless Babylonians, 'who transgress and become guilty, whose own might is their god' (1:11), to chastise his own people who, though far from guiltless, are at least 'more righteous' than their oppressors (1:13)?

The problem of evil on an international scale – the problem considered by Habakkuk – is also the preoccupation of many in our day. To him and to them the same divine answer is given: by strange and paradoxical means the all-powerful God prepares the way for the final victory of right and 'the righteous shall live by their faith' (2:4).

Second Reading   2 Tim 1:6-8.13-14

Timothy is called upon to rekindle the gift of God within, the grace of consecration which he received when he was officially invested as an apostle, a grace of courage and of power. He is urged to accept his share of suffering for the Gospel and to bear these sufferings cheerfully as 'Paul' did (1:6-8). For, God has called us not because of our deeds but freely, in virtue of his grace, now manifested through the appearance of our Saviour Jesus Christ who has destroyed death and brought life and immortality to light (1:9-10).

'Paul' suffers for the Gospel but he is not ashamed of his sufferings (so neither should Timothy). He had been appointed preacher and apostle and teacher and he is confident that he will stand firm in his charge to the end; Timothy, too, with the help of the Holy Spirit, will faithful to the Gospel (vv. 10-14). The reminder of the power of 'the Holy Spirit living in us' from baptism that enables us to bear witness to our faith in and our love of Jesus Christ is relevant for Christians in every age.

Gospel   Lk 17:5-10

The passage Luke 17:1-10, instruction of the disciples, is a mosaic of sayings. The primary meaning of *skandalon* (vv. 1-3a) is not 'stumbling-block' but 'bait,' 'snare' a snare or a lure by which one is liable to be led into sin. In practice it is inevitable that there should be scandal, but the one who deliberately leads astray the 'little ones' (humble believers) will be severely punished.

In vv. 3b-4 Luke's emphasis on repentance is typical as is also his 'seven times *a day*' – a spirit of forgiveness must be an unfailing attribute of a Christian.

The request of v. 5 is an editorial introduction to the following saying: the disciples ask for a greater confidence in God. It is the nature of faith that matters: a grain of authentic faith – perfect confidence in God – can achieve great things. In Matthew and Mark reference is to the removal of 'this mountain'; Luke's version reflects the Greek idea that nature cannot change: trees do no grow in the sea.

The parable of The Unprofitable Servant (vv. 7-10) is one which would have shocked Jesus' hearers not because of the use of the term *doulos* ('slave') but because of the manner in which this servanthood is to be lived before God. The picture he has painted is starkly clear. A slave has no claim on his master – neither wages nor thanks – quite independently of how much he may have done for his master. His service is utterly taken for granted. The application of the parable : 'So you also, when you have done all that you were ordered to do, say, "We are worthless slaves; we have done only what we ought to have done!"' (v. 10) strikes at the roots of an ethical attitude of some at least in contemporary Judaism. In their religious consciousness, God 'owed' humans salvation in view of the just person's fidelity to the Law. But Jesus sets a person in *direct* relationship to God, that is, without the Law intervening. He establishes a person as a *doulos* over against God, standing in obedience to the personal and acknowledged sovereignty of God. There is no doubt that the parable belongs to Jesus' criticism of the theology of his contemporaries: he pronounces a radically negative verdict on the idea of reward. What he does acknowledge is something quite different: the reality of divine recompense, of God's sheer goodness.

Luke begins chapter 17 with the phrase, 'He said to his disciples'; but then, in v. 5, the *apostles* (the inner group) ask for an increase in faith, and the parable would seem to be addressed to them. It would appear, then, that Luke has especially in mind the missioners or itinerant preachers of the Gospel. They are reminded of the attitude they ought to have: the consciousness of being slaves who serve their Lord without any claim on a reward. This attitude must inevitably, too, colour their relationship with those whom they serve in the Lord's service. But the lesson remains a general one. All disciples, God's slaves, have no *claim* to reward for doing what God expects of them; they must humbly acknowledge that they are only poor servants.

A call to commitment is not an invitation to omnicompetence.

Many so-called lay people have gifts for ministry that their officials do not possess. Redistribution of tasks and revision of traditional views of ordination may be necessary to carry out more effectively God's programme (see Acts 1:7-8). The Church, its officials, its ministers, and all Christians who are engaged in special services are slaves of Jesus Christ, not of tradition. (Danker, p. 289)

TWENTY-EIGHTH SUNDAY OF THE YEAR

First Reading   2 Kgs 5:14-17

The healing of Naaman the leper by Elisha the prophet (2 Kgs 5:1-18) is a close parallel to the gospel story. A cure of leprosy is wrought on both occasions and an impressive example given of unreserved gratitude. It is a pity that the lectionary reading is a mere snippet because the Naaman story is delightfully told. Naaman hears of 'the prophet who is in Samaria' from an Israelite slave-girl carried off in a raid (5:1-5). There is the consternation of the King of Israel who receives a letter from the Syrian king: 'I have sent to you my servant Naaman that you may cure him of his leprosy.' 'Am I God?' he exclaims, and fears a trap; the Syrians, he thinks, are trying to pick a quarrel (vv. 6-7). Naaman, bidden by a messenger from the prophet to bathe seven times in the Jordan, is highly indignant – he had expected to be honourably received. He was induced by his retinue to do as the prophet had asked (vv. 9-14). And then came the cure which leads Naaman to acknowledge Yahweh as the supreme and only God. He had encountered Yahweh in Yahweh's own land; he takes the precaution of carrying two mule-loads of Israel's soil with him so that, in Damascus, he may worship Yahweh standing on his Israel island.

Second Reading   2 Tim 2:8-13

'Paul' reminds Timothy that the work of proclaiming the gospel will not be easy; it will result in hardship, even in opposition and persecution. 'Paul' himself is in bonds, like a common criminal, for the sake of the gospel. However, he takes comfort from the fact that, though he may be bound, the word of God which he proclaims is not bound and accomplishes its effects in the hearts of the elect.

The passage closes with a quotation (vv. 11-13) from a baptismal hymn: at baptism the Christian dies and rises with Christ, but the sacrament imposes the obligation of endurance and fidelity. There is more involved here than the spiritual death and resurrection of the

Christian. Involved too are the problems, difficulties, hardships, and opposition inherent in living the Christian message from day to day in a hostile world.

Gospel
Lk 17:11-19

In v. 11 Luke again (see 9:51; 13:22) reminds us that Jesus is journeying to Jerusalem; the indications of this verse (still at the starting-point) prove that the journey is a literary construction. The lepers remain at a distance as the Law demanded (vv. 12-14; see Lev 13:45). Leprosy (a term which in the Bible covers a variety of diseases, Lev 13) is the ultimate uncleanness which cuts the afflicted one off from the community as being a source of ritual defilement to others. The Law was helpless in regard to leprosy; it could only defend the community against the leper. Jesus' command (v. 14) implied the granting of their request – the priests would verify the cure and authorize them to return to normal life (Lev 14:1-32) – but also tested their faith.

All had shown faith in the word of Jesus but one only, a Samaritan, returned to thank him (vv. 15-16). By implication the others were Jews; mutual hatred (see 9:53) was forgotten in their common misery. The nine, sons of Abraham, had apparently accepted the miracle as a matter of course; but Jesus praises the gratitude of the 'foreigner' (one of the mixed Samaritan race). Again (see 7:9; 10:30-37) a 'stranger' puts Jews to shame and already the contrasting attitude of Jew and Gentile to Jesus and his gospel is foreshadowed.

TWENTY-NINTH SUNDAY OF THE YEAR

First Reading
Ex 17:8-13

The narrative relates the first battle of Israel after their deliverance from Egypt. Their victory, however, is based not on their might or prowess but on the power of God mediated through the intercessory power of Moses. The text does not clearly say that Moses prayed. No words are recorded and the battle seems to be decided by the raising and lowering of his hands. Moses' hands are presented as mediating power which is in turn regarded as a sign of the direct intervention of God himself.

The incident is symbolic of the spiritual struggles with which people of all ages have to reckon including our own battles against selfishness and sin.

Second Reading   2 Tim 3:14-4:2

'Paul' instructs Timothy to abide in the sound doctrine which he has
been taught since his childhood because, in the first place, he knows
that it is based on reliable foundations – he had been trained by people
of sincere faith, his grandmother Lois and his mother Eunice (1:5).
There is great emphasis in the Pastorals on the personal relations
through which the Christian tradition is passed on. Secondly, he has
long been familiar with sacred scripture (the Old Testament). The
authority of these writings is rooted in God who is their author.
Timothy's education is not over; it is an ongoing process that will last
as long as life itself. Scripture is the indispensable equipment ('for
every good work') of the apostle. 'Paul,' then, encourages Timothy to
be zealous in preaching the message of Jesus, availing of every
opportunity to do so 'whether the time is favourable or unfavourable'
– traditionally, 'in season and out of season.'

Gospel   Lk 18:1-8

Luke makes clear his understanding of this parable of The Unjust
Judge: the disciples should pray at all times and persevere in it (see 1
Thess 5:17). Yet he still has in mind the coming of the kingdom: it will
come in response to the prayer of God's elect for vindication. In reality,
like The Friend at Midnight (11:5-8), the parable originally had a
different emphasis. The judge, described as unjust in v. 6, is of a type
that was all too common in Israel, and the Old Testament also refers
very often to the helpless widow. It is implied that the widow has right
on her side, but the judge is not interested in the rights of a penniless
plaintiff; if he is to give a decision in favour of anybody it has to be
made worth his while to do so.

   Jesus would have asked his hearers to contemplate, if they would,
a God cast in the image of the unjust judge. Could they really imagine
that he was remotely like that? It is the widow who holds *Luke's*
attention – with the bonus that he had now balanced his male-role
parable (11:5-8) with this female-role parable. The widow, aware that
she cannot pay the bribe expected by this venal judge, has no recourse
but to pester. If she makes enough of a nuisance of herself he will grant
her request merely for the sake of peace and quiet. What a bold picture
of prayer to God this is!

   The parable is rounded off by an *a fortiori* argument. If this cynical
judge will, in the end, yield to the importunity of the persistent widow,
surely it is to be expected that God who is not a judge at all but a loving
Father will yield to the importunity of his children! No, he will not

delay. As always, the problem is not with the constant God; it is with his inconstant creature. Is there the faith that will support this confident and persevering prayer (v. 8)? Each Christian must answer for herself or himself.

THIRTIETH SUNDAY OF THE YEAR

First Reading   Sir 35:12-14.16-19

In the section immediately prior to this, Ben Sirach discusses human generosity; this leads him to treat of the generosity of God to human-kind. In a corrupt society where money brings power, and where injustice can be smoothed over by bribery, the poor man's situation is pretty hopeless. If we add a prejudiced inequality of the sexes, the poor woman is in even worse straits. Without financial backing and social influence the poor cannot get legal redress when they are wronged and so are often forced to accept unfair treatment from the better-off. But God is a just judge: he shows no partiality for the rich or the powerful or for those in high places.

The 'poor of Yahweh,' the *anawim* (the term includes a broad spectrum of suppressed persons: widows, orphans, captives, the destitute, the sick), is a familiar theme in the prophets. Towards these God assumes the role of protector, defender, their guarantee of justice. Ben Sirach continues in this prophetic line of thought when he says: 'He will not ignore the supplication of the orphan, or the widow when she pours out her complaint' (35:17).

Second Reading   2 Tim 4:6-8.16-18

'Paul' realizes that this, his second Roman captivity, will end with his execution; hence, he can speak of his blood about to be poured out as a libation to God (see Phil 2:17). Although his death is in sight his confidence is unshaken: The Lord will reward his efforts with a 'crown of righteousness.' Demas – a companion of the first captivity (see Col 4:14; Philemon 24) – has now deserted 'Paul,' while Crescens, Titus and Tychicus are absent on missionary work. Only Luke is with the Apostle and now he dearly wishes to have Timothy and Mark come to him – these three are like that inner circle of Jesus' disciples, Peter and James and John. He wants Timothy to bring a cloak, books and parchment left at Troas, and the disciple is warned against a certain Alexander. The life-like touches of v. 13 show the skill of the author; he has got really into his role of Paul. He has 'Paul' protest that during his time of trial, deserted by his friends, his sole support was faith and prayer. Now, with new strength, he can predict that 'the Lord will rescue me from every evil attack and save me for his heavenly kingdom' (v. 18).

Gospel   Lk 18:9-14

The parable of The Pharisee and the Tax-collector (18:9-14) does fit neatly into the ministry of Jesus. Both characters are drawn from life: the righteous one and the outcast. And the parable is spoken as a warning to the righteous (v. 9).

So often the Pharisee of this parable has been called a hypocrite. It is an error which clouds the pathos of the parable and blunts its impact. The sad fact is that the man is sincere and his claims are true. He is scrupulously honest, a faithful family man, a meticulous observer of the Law (as the tax-collector by definition is not). The Law enjoined only one fast a year (on the Day of Atonement) but he, a pious Pharisee, fasts each Monday and Thursday. And, far beyond the demands of the Law, he gives tithes of all his possessions. He is sincerely convinced that he stands right with God. After all, he has done what he ought to do, and more. He can truly thank God that he is not like other men. The snag is that his 'prayer' is not prayer at all. That is why it is not heard.

It is this sort of person and this attitude Paul has in mind in Galatians and Romans. He had seen with clarity (for he, too, had been a convinced Pharisee) that one for whom the heart of religion is observance may feel that one can earn salvation. What one must avoid and must do are clear. If one is faithful, then a just God cannot but justify one. Such an attitude blunts the fact that salvation is gift. That is why the Pharisee could not recognise God's gracious gift in Jesus. And it is because the 'sinner' had no such illusion that he could instinctively see the gift for what it was. There is nothing mysterious in the fact that Jesus was a 'friend of tax-collectors and sinners' nor that this was scandal to the 'righteous'.

There is a wry point to the story about the good lady who, after a Sunday morning homily on our parable, was heard to remark: 'Thank God I am not like that Pharisee'! For 'pharisaism' is not only a late Jewish phenomenon. It is endemic in the Christian Church and has proved a hardy growth. The self-righteous Christian is not a rarity. Regular church-going and certain pious practices may seem to set one apart and guarantee salvation. Always, of course, it is a case of 'these you ought to have practised, without neglecting the others' – but the 'weightier matters' of justice, mercy and faith are what religion is all about (Mt 23:23-24).

The tax collector was a man bereft of hope, though not without faith. He had been robbed of hope by the righteous, so thoroughly branded an outcast that he had come to regard himself as such. If salvation depended on meticulous observance of the Law, as the Pharisees maintained, then he had no chance at all. But he cannot bring himself to believe that God is like that. Hoping against hope, he dared to come to the temple of God. And his prayer is the most moving of all prayers. It is a prayer that should sound an echo in our hearts, a prayer that should spring, unbidden, to our lips: 'God, be merciful to me, a sinner.' This is the prayer that God listens to and answers – 'this man went down to his home justified.' The second half of v. 14 ('for all who exalt themselves will be humbled, and all who humble themselves will be exalted') explicitly lifts this parable out of the ministry of Jesus, away from any narrow conflict of Pharisee and tax collector, and turns it into a lesson for Everyman.

> For Luke, prayer is faith in action. Prayer is not an optional exercise in piety, carried out to demonstrate one's relationship with God. It is that relationship with God. The way one prays therefore reveals that relationship. If the disciples do not 'cry out day and night' to the Lord, then they in fact do not have faith, for that is what faith does. Similarly, if prayer is self-assertion before God, then it *cannot* be answered by God's gift of righteousness; possession and gift cancel each other. (Johnson, p. 274)

THIRTY-FIRST SUNDAY OF THE YEAR

First Reading   Wis 11:22 -12:2

Wisdom 11:7-12:22 is a lengthy treatment of God's power and mercy. It stresses that God is omnipotent (11:17-22) and then argues that, precisely because he is all-powerful, he is merciful (11:23-12:22). Our reading makes the point that God spares humankind because he loves them. In short, God's relationship with everything that he has created can only be one of love and mercy. Only love can explain his having created anything in the first place and only love can explain his continued preservation of them in being. Because of his love, God does not desire the destruction or death of humankind. He is always ready to pardon their sin, desiring only that they repent and return to him. God is a patient lover. 'For you love all things that exist ... for you would not have made anything if you had hated it' (1:24) is an echo of

'And God saw everything that he had made, and behold, it was very good' (Gen 1:31). It is a firm biblical conviction that creation is *good*.

Second Reading   2 Thess 1:11-2:2

Paul visited Thessalonica for the first time probably in 50 A.D. His stay was short – a matter of a few months. Later, in Corinth, being assured by his emissary Timothy, that the young community was thriving, he gave expression to his relief in a letter to it. He seized the occasion to draw attention to certain shortcomings and to issue instructions. This first letter (1 Thessalonians) set the pattern for the subsequent Pauline letters.

A principal reason for a second letter (2 Thessalonians) was to set right erroneous views on the parousia. One practical issue was that some Thessalonians, expecting an imminent End, no longer saw any point in work. Because of the language of apocalyptic drama in 2:1-10 and because phrases have been copied from 1 Thessalonians, many scholars question Pauline authorship of 2 Thessalonians.

In the passage chosen for reading today, Paul tells the Thessalonians that the grace of God is necessary at every stage of their lives and not only at the start: the life of faith is a life-long journey. God's 'call,' a word Paul reserves for the saving activity of God, contains within it the power to enable one to respond and to continue responding in faith. Grace does not eliminate responsibility and co-operation; rather, it makes them possible. In 2:1-2 Paul assures his readers that the Day of the Lord has not happened (some of them seem to have thought that it had). Possibly, Paul's earlier teaching had led the Thessalonians to look for an imminent return of the Lord; there also seem to have been false rumours about (some purporting to come from Paul). In any event Paul (or somebody in his name) is concerned enough to write and set the matter straight. The parousia is not quite around the corner. There is a programme of eschatological events that must take place before that day can come.

Gospel   Lk 19:1-10

In this episode, Jesus shows himself a friend of 'tax collectors and sinners' and again his solicitude meets with criticism (see 15:1-2). Zacchaeus held a high position at an important customs post and had turned it to good account. Curious to see a man with such a reputation as Jesus had won, Zacchaeus forgot his dignity (vv. 3-4). It was Jesus who saw Zacchaeus: he 'must' come to the house of the tax collector, he who had come to seek out 'the lost' (v. 10). The joy of Zacchaeus is matched by the murmuring of those who did not understand the goodness of God (vv. 6-7; see 5:30; 15:2).

Touched by the gracious approach of Jesus (v. 8), the tax collector is a changed man – he is more generous than the ruler (18:23). The present tense describes not a present habit but a present resolve: henceforth he will give half of his goods in alms. Moreover, he will make fourfold amends (the requirement of Roman law in *furtum manifestum*) if he can ascertain that he has defrauded anybody. Luke's concern with the proper use of wealth (to give it away in alms!) is evident. Jesus declares to Zacchaeus in effect: 'Today salvation has come to this house' (v. 9). But in Luke's narrative this verdict is strictly linked to the declaration of the rich tax collector in v. 8. Zacchaeus is saved but his fortune is gone back to the poor. Inexorably, Luke maintains his position that the proper use of wealth is to distribute it to the poor.

Jesus turns to the murmurers (v. 9): Zacchaeus is a son of Abraham and has as much right to the mercy of God as any other Israelite (see 13:16): the visit of Jesus has brought salvation to the man and his family. V. 10 is very likely an independent saying which echoes the theme of the parables of chapter 15 and indeed of the whole gospel. The Zacchaeus episode is a striking illustration of it.

THIRTY-SECOND SUNDAY OF THE YEAR

First Reading
2 Macc 7:1-2.9-14

The second book of Maccabees, written in Greek, deals with the dramatic events of 176-160 B.C. An important feature of the book is its confident teaching on the after-life: the living can pray for the dead and make sin-offerings on their behalf (12:42-45), while the just who have passed beyond the grave intercede for those who still live on earth (11:11-16). The resurrection of the body is taken for granted (chapter 7; 14:46). These doctrines are facets of the sure faith and unswerving hope that pervades the book. And they highlight the loving mercy of God and his care for those who are faithful to him.

The book belongs to a literary form then popular in the Hellenistic world and known as 'pathetic history'; its characteristic was an appeal to the imagination and emotions of the reader. The rather lurid story of chapter 7 – the martyrdom of a mother and her seven sons – is typical of the genre. These martyrs were encouraged and consoled by their faith in the resurrection of the just. Important, too, is the clear statement on creation (v. 28).

The book makes a positive evaluation of the suffering and death of the just. Though the sufferings of the martyrs may be chastisement, their willing acceptance is an expiation which turns aside the anger of God. If Judas Maccabaeus wins victories it is because God has accepted the sacrifice (7:36; 8:5).

Second Reading   2 Thess 2:16-3:5

Paul himself (or, if the letter is pseudonymous, as is most likely the case, then the literary 'Paul'), while he was writing this letter, was suffering considerable opposition (3:2). He was writing to a people who had experienced hostility from the first preaching of the gospel (1 Thess 2:14-15; Acts 17:1-9). It is against this background of oppression and persecution that Paul writes his message of hope.

Today's passage consists of three prayers. The first (2:16-17) asks that the God of comfort and hope, and the Lord Jesus Christ, will continue to be with them encouraging them in goodness of work and word. Then Paul (3:1-2) asks that they pray for him in order that his preaching of the Gospel may triumph despite the hostility of faithless people. Conscious that God will be faithful to his promises towards them, he prays (3:5) that they may persevere in the love of God and steadfastness of Christ.

Gospel   Lk 20:27-38

Unlike the preceding questions in Luke (20:1-8; 20-26), the query of the Sadducees (vv. 27-28) is not concerned with the authority of Jesus or with his attitude to Rome; the issues it raises are religious and theological. At the same time, the motives of the questioners are no better. Sadducees, unlike the Pharisees, are 'those who say there is no resurrection': see Acts 23:8 – 'The Sadducees say that there is no resurrection, or angel, or spirit; but the Pharisees acknowledge all three.'

The question (v. 28) is based on the law of levirate marriage (a law which was no longer in force.) The provision of levirate (from the Latin *levir* = brother-in-law) was the following: if brothers dwelt together and one of them died childless, a surviving brother was expected to marry the widow and the first-born son of this union was legally regarded as the son and heir of the deceased (Deut 25:5-10). Doubtless this (vv. 29-33) was a stock question, designed to ridicule the idea of bodily resurrection from the dead.

Luke (vv. 34-36) sets up an emphatic contrast between 'those who belong to this age' (who take wives and marry) and 'those who are considered worthy of a place in that age and in the resurrection from the dead' (and who do not contract marriage). The reason for this is indicated in v. 36 – no marriage because no more death. Luke accentuates the connection of marriage with this present age and contrasts the world of the resurrection where no such link exists any more. The essential import of the saying is that it 'relativizes' marriage. Despite its human and religious importance, marriage pertains to the order of this world and will cease with the passing of this world.

In vv. 37-38 the argument is from Exodus 3:6; this text implies that the patriarchs are still alive because God could not be named after a dead thing – a rabbinical argument which impresses the hearers (v. 39). V. 38b ('for to him all of them are alive') means that all who await the resurrection have life from God, the source of life.

THIRTY-THIRD SUNDAY OF THE YEAR

First Reading
Mal 3:19-20a

The book of Malachi is really an anonymous writing. The name 'Malachi' comes from Malachi 3:1 where the word is a common noun, meaning 'my messenger.' The book (middle of the fifth century B.C.) is strongly influenced by Deuteronomy and is preoccupied with the cultic faults of priests (1:6-2:9) and people (3:6-12). The Day of the Lord is presented in a cultic setting and the world to come will see the perfect cult (3:4). God and sin are incompatible. Evil-doers will be punished on the Day of Visitation. The just will be the special possession of God – their names are already written in the 'book of remembrance' (v. 16). If the Day of the Lord will be, for sinners, as Amos put it: 'darkness and not light, and gloom with no brightness it' (Amos 5:20), for the just all will be brightness: 'For you who revere my name the sun of righteousness shall rise, with healing in its wings' (Mal 4:2). This is surely one of the loveliest verses in the Bible.

Second Reading
2 Thess 3:7-12

Paul had already exhorted the Thessalonian Christians to take pains to earn their living so that they would command the respect of outsiders and be dependent on nobody (1 Thess 4:11-12). The situation as reflected in the second letter shows no improvement. Paul is forced to state his message even more clearly: 'Anyone unwilling to work should not eat' (2 Thess 3:10). Evidently the Thessalonian situation was occasioned or aggravated by that community's attitude to the parousia: it was imminent (or had happened) so there was no further purpose in work. But the teaching makes sense apart from that context. Human work is a positive contribution to the creative work of God. God has made men and women (*ha-adam*) masters of his creation (Gen 1:26) that he might subdue it and bring it to the glorification of God (see Sir 17:3-10).

Gospel   Lk 21:5-19

In 17:22 Luke had treated of the parousia, the glorious return of Jesus. Here he takes up the subject again but this time, like Mark and Matthew, in close association with the question of the destruction of Jerusalem. Luke, writing in the decade 80-90, obviously knew of the fall of Jerusalem (70 A.D.); he is, too, conscious of the delay of the parousia. He handles two distinct themes. One is historical – the destruction of Jerusalem and the victory of the gospel. The other is eschatological – the end of this age and the parousia of the Son of man. Our reading is concerned with a prediction of the destruction of the temple and with the situation of Christians in a time of trial. V. 5 has 'some' in place of 'one of his disciples' (Mk 13:1); the discourse is no longer addressed only to the disciples.

Luke omits Mark's reference to the Mount of Olives (Mk 13:3); the setting is still the Temple. In Luke's scheme, during this last period in Jerusalem, Jesus is in the Temple by day and on the Mount of Olives by night. The phrase 'the days will come' (v. 6) introduces an oracle of woe: this splendid temple is doomed. The question of v. 7 concerns the destruction of the Temple; in his reply Jesus distinguishes this event from the end of the world: the fall of Jerusalem will not mark the End.

By his addition of the phrase 'the time is near' (v. 8) Luke strengthens the warning against false messiahs who preach that the end of the age is imminent. 'The end will not follow immediately' (v. 9) is a stronger expression than Mark's (13:7) and emphasizes the delay of the parousia: these events precede the fall of Jerusalem but they do not herald the End.

The editorial phrase, 'Then he said to them,' marks a transition from the warnings of vv. 8-9 to the prophetic passage which follows; Luke adds 'plagues,' 'portents and great signs from heaven,' and omits Mark's 'This is but the beginning of the birth pangs' (Mk 13:8) because he sees the beginning in the persecution of the disciples (vv. 12-19).

The language consciously echoes traditional Old Testament images of disaster and could well be applied to the destruction of Jerusalem, seen as a divine intervention and as a prefiguration of the end of the world. Of more immediate concern to the disciples is the persecution they must face. Luke omits Mark 13:10 ('and the good news must first be preached to all nations') because the gospel has been preached to 'the end of the earth,' that is, Rome (Acts 1:8; 28:30-31). Profession of faith in such circumstances will be the supreme testimony to the gospel (v. 13).

The wording of v. 15 recalls Acts 6:10 – the martyr Stephen. It is Christ himself (Mk 13:11 – the Holy Spirit) who will inspire the disciples – their victory will be really his. The world's hate, and martyrdom for some, will be their fate, yet they must remain confident (vv. 16-17).

Vv. 18-19 follow on vv. 14-15 (vv. 16-17 may be regarded as a parenthesis): steadfast, supported by Christ, the disciple will come through the persecution. In this context of persecution the optimistic atmosphere is that of Acts. But Luke intimates that Christians must anticipate a long period of tribulation. (See First Sunday of Advent, pp. 11-12.)

THIRTY-FOURTH SUNDAY OF THE YEAR SOLEMNITY OF CHRIST THE KING

First Reading 2 Sam 5:1-3

David had already been anointed king of Judah by his own people at Hebron (2:4). In today's reading we hear how the northern tribes ('all the tribes of Israel') acknowledged him as their king. David was now king of the united kingdom of Judah and Israel, God's anointed representative in ruling his chosen people. The term 'Anointed One' (Messiah) became in time a technical term for the future liberator of the people. The Israelites had expected from David and his successors a form of government that would be a reflection of the divine will. The historical kings did not meet their expectation. Hence the idea grew that a future liberator of the people, while being a human and Davidic figure, would be at the same time Son of God, 'coming on the clouds of heaven.' Jesus was the fulfilment of this expectation but not quite in the way Judaism had imagined. He was not the firebrand liberator of his people but the one who was anointed (made *Christos*) only after he had given himself up to death on a cross (Phil 2:5-11).

Second Reading   Col 1:11-20

It is widely accepted that Colossians 1:15-20 is basically a liturgical hymn taken over and adapted by the author of Colossians. In vv. 11-14, which may be regarded as an introduction to the hymn, 'Paul' gives thanks to God the Redeemer, who has 'delivered' and 'transferred', thus bringing out the theme of deliverance from captivity, evocative of the deliverance of Israel.

The 'kingdom of the beloved Son' is, most likely, the interim period between the resurrection and the definitive appearance of the Kingdom, that is, the time of the Church. In God's Church, entrusted to Christ, we find forgiveness of sins: the effect of baptism union with Christ (Acts 2:38; Mk 1:4).

First Stanza: Christ and Creation (vv. 15-17).

No clear distinction is made between the pre-existent and incarnate Christ.

'Image': in Wisdom 7:25-26 divine Wisdom is 'a pure emanation of the glory of the Almighty ... a reflection of eternal light, a spotless mirror of the working of God, and an image of his goodness'.

'First-born of all creation': in the light of Proverbs 8:22 this appears to mean that in Christ God has contemplated the plan of the universe.

'For in him all things were created' (v. 16) is an emphatic affirmation of the transcendence of Christ. The rest of the verse is an addition which makes clear that the angelic beings too were created in Christ and so they are subordinate to him.

Verse 17 is a summarizing conclusion to the first stanza.

Second stanza: Christ and the New Creation (vv. 18-20).

'He is the head of the body, the Church.'

The gradual development of the theme of the Church as the body of Christ which can be traced through Galatains 2:26-29; 1 Corinthians 6:13-17; 10:14-21; 12:12-27; Romans 12:5 here reaches its climax. 'The body' has become an accepted designation of the universal Church; by the introduction of the theme of 'head' the whole Christ is more adequately distinguished from the individual Christ. The second part of the verse corresponds structurally to v. 15 and so is part of the original hymn.

'That in everything he might be pre-eminent': it is a characteristic of Pauline theology (the letter is, on the whole, in line with Pauline theology) that the resurrection marked a new beginning not only for humanity (v. 20) but also for Christ. Through his resurrection he was 'constituted Son of God in power' (Rom 1:4), and 'become a life-giving Spirit' (1 Cor 15:45).

V. 19 – 'For in him all the fullness of God was pleased to dwell' –
is a difficult verse. Note that the Greek text has simply 'fullness'; the
addition 'of God' (NRSV) is gratuitous. The sense is that God willed
all fullness (*pleroma*) to dwell in Christ: it takes up and broadens the
thought of v. 16a – 'For in him all things were created' He is the head
of all creation. God reconciles a sin-divided cosmos to himself through
Christ (v. 20).

'The blood of his cross': 'Paul' associated reconciliation with the
cross, for in his theology the effects of redemption are attributed to the
blood of Christ (Rom 5:9) or to his death (1 Thess 5:10, 1 Cor 6:20,
etc.) The 'through him' is emphatic: reconciliation is exclusively
through Christ.

In Colossians the person and work of Christ are considered from a
point of view that is not only soteriological but cosmic as well. Now,
Christian salvation takes on the dimension of the universe. Christ is not
only head of the Church, whose members are his members and build
up his body; he is the head of all creation. To designate this situation
the author uses the term *pléróma* ('fullness'). And he finds the basis
of Christ's universal supremacy in his divine pre-existence as image
of the Father, and he sees him as the source and end of creation.

Gospel
Lk 23:35-43

Luke divides the spectators of the crucifixion into three categories: the
people looked on (see v. 27); the rulers mocked Jesus; the soldiers
joined in the raillery. In v. 35, Mark's title 'the King of Israel' is given
a turn more congenial to Luke's Greek readers ('The Christ of God, his
Chosen One') and points to the Servant of Yahweh (Is 42:1). The title
on the cross ('This is the King of the Jews') is the climax of the
mockery.

The 'good thief' episode is proper to Luke. While one of Jesus'
fellow-sufferers joined in the raillery, the other acknowledged the
innocence of Jesus, and provides an instance of healing forgiveness
during the passion. In rebuking his co-sufferer, 'the other' acknowledges that both of them had been condemned deservedly – 'but this
man has done nothing wrong' (23:41). The wrongdoer addresses
Jesus, 'Jesus, remember me when you come into your kingdom' (v.
42). The direct address, 'Jesus', without qualification, is unique in this
Gospel. The idea conveyed by 'into your kingdom' is that of Jesus
ascending into the kingdom from the cross. In dying, Jesus had passed
beyond time. The 'other' wrongdoer is asking to be remembered at the

moment of Jesus' vindication.

Typically, Jesus' response goes far beyond his expectation. 'Truly I tell you, today you will be with me in Paradise' (23:43). 'Today' means this very day; to be with Jesus in Paradise is to be with Christ in the full presence of God. 'Paradise' is a Persian loan-word, meaning park or garden; in the Septuagint it is used to render the 'garden of Eden' (Gen 28) and eventually came to mean the abode of the righteous. Here it is no more than an image. Instead of trying to situate 'Paradise,' it is more profitable to recall the words of Ambrose: *Vita est enim esse cum Christo; ideo ubi Christus, ibi vita, ibi regnum.* ('Life means being with Christ; where Christ is, there too is life and there is the Kingdom.') See Passion Sunday, pp. 75-76.

Holy Days

First Reading   Jer 1:4-9

Jeremiah, of all the prophets, is best known to us as an individual. His book contains many passages of personal confession and autobiography, as well as lengthy section of biography. He stands out as a lonely, tragic figure whose mission seemed to have failed. Yet, that 'failure' was his triumph as later ages were to acknowledge.

Jeremiah came from Anathoth, a village four miles north-east of Jerusalem. His father, Hilkiah, was a priest (Jer 1:1). His prophetic call came in 626 (1:2) while he was still quite a young man, and his mission reached from Josiah (640-609) to Zedekiah (697-587) and outlasted the reign of the latter. That is to say, he lived through the days, full of promise, of the young reformer king, Josiah, and through the aftermath, the tragic years that led to the destruction of the nation. It seems that Jeremiah was initially in sympathy with the aims of the reform but was disappointed at its eventual outcome. There is no doubt that he thought highly of the high-minded young king (22:15-156), but he quickly realised that 'you cannot make people good by act of parliament.'

Jeremiah has particular relevance for our day. His predecessors, as far as we know, accepted their prophetic mission with submissiveness – Isaiah indeed with eagerness (Is 6:9). But Jeremiah had to question; there is in him a trace of rebellion. He was not at all satisfied to accept, uncritically, traditional theological positions. He struggled, as the author of Job was to do centuries later, with the problem of retribution (112:1) and asserted the principle of individual (as against collective) responsibility (31:29-30).

But, mostly, it was his own prophetic office that was his burden, and it was indeed a burden far heavier and more painful than that of any other prophet. He needed, all the more, the support of his God. His obedience was so much the greater because of his questioning, because he felt its yoke, because it led to a feeling of being abandoned.

The call of Jeremiah is itself modelled on that of Moses (Ex 4:10-16) and has in turn influenced the account of later calls such as that of the Servant of the Lord (Is 49:1).

Patrick, like Jeremiah, was called from his earliest years, and never ceased to protest his unworthiness. Yet he was conscious that God had given him the Word to spread among the Irish people. It was this sense of vocation that was to keep him faithful to the end.

Second Reading   Acts 13:46-49

Chapter 13 of Acts begins (13:1-3) with the decision of the Christian community at Antioch (in Syria) to launch a mission to the Gentiles. This was a daring new departure because, up to then, the Christian movement was almost wholly Jewish. Barnabas and Saul (Paul), the designated missionaries, moved on to Cyprus and then on to Asia Minor (modern Turkey). At Antioch in Pisidia they preached, on the sabbath, in the synagogue – it was their policy to preach first to Jews. They had quite a favourable reception. A week later, however, the opposition had rallied. In reaction, Paul and Barnabas declared: 'We are now turning to the Gentiles.'

The conclusion of our short reading – 'When the Gentiles heard this they were glad ... Thus the word of the Lord spread throughout the region' – suits, admirably, the welcome of the Irish to the message of Patrick.

Gospel   Lk 10:1-12.17-20

The passage 10:1-16 is parallel to 9:1-6 (the mission of the Twelve) It does not seem that this sending of the seventy foreshadows the universal mission of Jesus' disciples (as has been suggested); in 24:47 the Gentile mission is entrusted to the Twelve. Two, obviously distinct, sayings (vv. 2-3) reflect the experience of the first missionaries: their own zeal and the opposition they encountered. The warning (v. 4) not to waste time on civilities (elaborate, in the oriental manner) underlines the urgency of the mission. 'Peace' (*shalom*) is the Jewish greeting. One who 'shares in peace' is, literally, a 'son of peace'. 'Son of peace', a Hebraism, means one worthy of peace. Clearly, the greeting is meaningful, a blessing. Food and shelter (v. 7) are not alms but wages (see 1 Cor 9:14).

The mission is not a private sally but a public proclamation of the kingdom. The kingdom is near, so they are not to waste time on those who will not receive them; the message must be brought to others (vv. 10-11). The unreceptive town (v. 12) will not go unpunished; 'on that day' means on the day of judgemnt. Jesus, sent by the Father, has sent the disciples; rejection of them is rejection of God (v. 16).

The ability to cast out demons had, understandably, made a deep impression on the disciples (v. 17). The power had come to them from Jesus (v. 19) and it is by their faith in him that they have been successful. The real cause for rejoicing is that the kingdom has come; for Satan it is the beginning of the end – his fall will be lightning fast (see Jn 12:31). The disciples have received power over the enemy of humankind in all fields (v 19); serpents and scorpions (though these may have a metaphorical sense, see Ps 91:13) exemplify evils in nature, the work of Satan (see Acts 28:3-6).

The assurance of being numbered among the elect is the ultimate reason for rejoicing (v 20). The image of the 'book of life' is a common Old Testament one; see also Rev 3:5; 13:8; 17:8; 20:12,15.

THE ASSUMPTION OF MARY
15 AUGUST

First Reading
Rev 11:19; 12:1-6.10

In a prophetic vision, John sees the holy of holies of the heavenly temple thrown open and the ark of the covenant visible to all (11:19). The fulfilment will come in the New Jerusalem when God will dwell with humankind (21:3). Here, as assurance to the faithful, the open temple finds a remarkably apposite parallel in Hebrews 10:19 – 'Therefore, brothers and sisters, we have confidence to enter the sanctuary by the blood of Jesus.' Christians have full confidence to 'draw near to the throne of grace' (Heb 4:16). That assurance in Hebrews, no less than in Revelation, is founded on 'the Lamb who was slain.'

Revelation 12 is based on two sources: a narrative describing the conflict between a pregnant woman and a dragon (vv. 1-6, 13-17) and a narrative depicting a battle in heaven (vv 7-12). This sandwich technique, reminiscent of Mark, indicates that the narratives must be understood in conjunction. The woman symbolizes the people of God bringing forth the Messiah; the dragon is the 'ancient serpent' of Genesis 3 – a later reinterpretation of the talking snake of the Genesis text.

By the 'birth' of the Messiah (12:5) John does not mean the nativity but the cross – the enthronement of Jesus. The woman's child was snatched from the destructive intent of the dragon to the throne of God: precisely by dying, Jesus defeated the dragon and was exalted to God's right hand. The expulsion of Satan from heaven in the result of the victory of Christ on earth; this is clearly brought out in the heavenly chorus of 12:10-11.

Second Reading   1 Cor 15:20-26

Some in the Corinthian community, in their Greek view that the human person was made up of two distinct and separable parts (soul and body) with the soul, in practice, being what mattered, despised the body. Logically, they denied resurrection from the dead (15:12). In 15:1-19 Paul not only unwaveringly affirms faith in the resurrection but vehemently defends an understanding of the human person as a psychosomatic unity. Moreover, by stressing the importance of the body, he vindicates the incarnational character of Christianity. His argument is in terms of the resurrection of Christ.

Then, in our passage (15:20-28) he describes the consequences of Christ's resurrection . In fact, not only has Christ risen – he is 'the first fruits of those who have died' (v. 20); his resurrection has implications for all. Paul illustrates the impact of Christ's resurrection on humankind with a contrast developed more fully in Rom 5:12-21: he sets Adam over against Christ. Adam brought death to humankind and this was a sign of deeper separation from God. Jesus Christ brought resurrection from the dead, and this is an efficacious sign of the saving nature of his death. The resurrection of Christ destroyed the definitive character of physical death; those who are in Christ will live forever (vv. 21-22).

Paul looks to the future, to the moment when all those in Christ will be raised, the moment of the Parousia, of the End (vv. 23-24). Why is there an interval between the resurrection of Christ and of those who belong to him through faith and baptism? It is because the mission of Christ was not complete at his death: 'He must reign until he has put all his enemies under his feet' (v. 25).

Having been exalted to the position of Lord through his resurrection (Rom 1:3-4; 14:9; 1 Cor 15:45), Christ still had to annihilate the hostile powers that yet held the great mass of humanity in subjection to a false value system. At his death the power of forces hostile to authentic human development had been broken, but they had not been definitively crushed. The evil influences operative in the 'world' act on those who are physically alive, and so these must be destroyed first (v. 24), but Death is the master of those who have died, and so its turn necessarily comes next (v. 26). When this definitive victory has been won, when the words of Ps 8:7 (referring to humankind before the fall) and Ps 110 (referring to the Messiah) have been fulfilled, then Christ will present his kingdom to God (v. 24), and he will remit into God's hands the authority given him for his mission (v. 38) The subordination of Christ, precisely as 'Son', to God could not be expressed with greater clarity, and is in total accord with the stress on his humanity in v. 21. (J. Murphy-O'Connor, *1 Corinthians*, p. 143).

Gospel

In the structure of the Lucan infancy narrative this passage, 'The Visitation', is a complementary episode, a pendant to the diptych of annunciations (1:1-38). Elizabeth is granted the perception not only that Mary is with child but that her child is the Messiah. Her canticle in praise of Mary (1:42-45) echoes Old Testament motifs and anticipates motifs that will be found in the gospel (11:27-28). This narrative serves as a hinge between the two birth stories, of John and of Jesus. And this meeting of women illustrates their respective situations. Elizabeth's pregnancy was not only a sign for Mary; it was also an invitation. The 'haste' of Mary was inspired by friendship and charity.

At Mary's greeting Elizabeth felt the infant stir within her – John, while still in the womb, is precursor (1:17) of the Lord. Enlightened by the prophetic Spirit she concluded that Mary is to be mother of 'the Lord.' That is why Mary is 'blessed among women' - the most blessed of women. Elizabeth went on to praise Mary's unhesitating acquiescence in God's plan for her – her great faith: 'And blessed is she who believed ... '

Mary's reply is her *Magnificat* (1:46-55). This hymn is the conclusion of, and the interpretation of, Luke's Visitation scene. In form a thanksgiving psalm, the Magnificat is a chain of Old Testament reminiscences and leans especially on the canticle of Hannah (1 Sam 2:1-10). There is no clear reference to the messianic birth – and this is surprising in view of the angel's message and the words of Elizabeth. Like the *Benedictus*, this psalm came to Luke from the circles of Jewish-Christian *anawim*. The hymn originally referred to a general salvation through Jesus Christ. It will readily be seen that, without v. 48, the *Magnificat* would fit smoothly into that Anawim setting. But we have the song in Luke's infancy gospel. There it stands between the Old Testament and the New and, like the rest of Luke's infancy narrative, captures the atmosphere of that unique moment. Luke presents the *Magnificat* as a canticle of Mary and we may, and should, read it as such.

Elizabeth had blessed Mary as mother of the Messiah; Mary gives the glory, in joyful thanksgiving, to the God who had blessed her, and through her, Israel: 'My soul magnifies the Lord.' The rest of the opening cry of joy (Lk 1:47) echoes the words of Habbakuk 'I will rejoice in the Lord, I will exult in the God of my salvation' (Hab 3:18). God had looked with favour upon his hand-maid, upon her who is the most perfect of the 'poor of Yahweh.' Here total acceptance of God's will has won for her, the Favoured One, everlasting glory. At once she turns the attention away from herself to the Almighty, the holy and merciful God, who has done great things for her. The Mighty One shows his power most of all in caring for the needy. In truth, the 'steadfast love of the Lord is from everlasting to everlasting on those who fear him' (Ps 103:17). All humankind will find hope in what God has achieved in Mary: loneliness turned into fruitfulness.

The interest then (vv 51-53) switches to Israel and to the manifestation of God's power, holiness and goodness in favour of his people. These verses are not concerned with the past, or not with the past only, but represent God's action at all times: what he has done in Mary and what he, through her as mother of the Messiah, has done for Israel, shows forth his manner of acting. He does mighty deeds with his arm, symbol of his power, when he reverses human situations – the proud, the mighty and the rich he has humbled and left empty, while he has lifted up and blessed with good things the poor of this world (the *anawim*).

This is nothing other than the message of the Beatitudes (Lk 6:20-21). For, if that message of Jesus were to bring about the desired change of heart, the poor, the marginalized, would come into their own. It is God's 'preferential option for the poor' – the option of a God who scrupulously respects human freedom. He awaits the response that will achieve the great transformation – but he looks for that response. The Magnificat anticipates Luke's concern throughout his gospel, for the poor. It is echoed in Jesus' programmatic statement: ' ... the poor have the good news preached to them' (4:18).

The closing verses (54-55) in the mouth of Mary, point to the final intervention of God. His sending of the Messiah is the decisive act of his gracious treatment of Israel, the people which, through his covenant with Abraham (Gen 17:7), had become his 'Servant' (Is 41:8-9). Mindful of his great mercy, he has fulfilled the promise made to the patriarchs: a promise made to a man is accomplished in a woman.

Elizabeth had singled out Mary's faith for special attention and she had done so rightly. Still, there remains the more mundane, but refreshingly human factor that Mary had travelled from Nazareth to Judea to share the joy of her aged cousin and to lend a helping hand. One may refer to the Cana episode (Jn 2:1-15). True, it a passage heavy with Johannine theology – and this is not the place to get involved in that aspect of the text. What matters here is that John has cast Mary as a charitable and practical woman who could be depended on to supervise, quietly but efficiently, a rural wedding. Each in his way, Luke and John have presented her as the woman for others. Not a surprise casting of her who is mother of 'the man for others.'

ALL SAINTS
1 NOVEMBER

First Reading   Rev 7:2-4, 9-14

The breaking of the seven scroll-seals by the Lamb (Rev 6:1-8:5) unleashed a series of plagues which follows the pattern of events in the Synoptic apocalypse (Mk 13; Mt 24: Lk 21). Before the breaking of the last seal the servants of God were sealed with the seal of the living God, 144,000 of them. The opening of the last seal will unleash the plagues of trumpets (8:6-11:19), which are modelled on the plagues of Egypt. The sealing of the elect recalls the immunity of the Israelites to the plagues that struck the Egyptians. John's unexpected twist is that his servants will be sealed for protection through the great tribulation. They achieve their victory, yes, but in the only Christian manner: 'for they did not cling to life even in the face of death' (12:11).

The 'great multitude' of 7:9-17 is not a group distinct from the 144,000 (itself a 'great multitude'): it is the same group now viewed beyond the great tribulation. In keeping with John's consistent outlook, these are presented as happy here and now; they stand before God and Lamb, celebrating a heavenly feast of Tabernacles (the most joyous of Jewish feasts). As martyrs – the ideal representatives of God's people – they have come triumphantly through the tribulation: the vision is prophetic, anticipatory. A 'great tribulation' was expected to precede the End; for John, the tribulation through which these martyrs come triumphantly is imminent persecution (see 3:10; 13:7-10). These are the victors of the prophetic messages of chapters 2 and 3. The striking paradox (made white in the *blood* of the Lamb) has a haunting beauty; and, as beauty, it speaks truth. It expresses God's and the Lamb's definition of victory: they have won by suffering death, not by inflicting hurt.

Second Reading   1 Jn 3:1-3

We can speak of a person being *named* to an office or a job. In a Semitic context, to be named ('called') is a more forceful expression. Our text says we are named God's children and, in case there should by any doubt, John adds: 'and that is what we are.' We know, that is, experience, our filial relationship to God. We have been born to a new life and share, mysteriously but really, in the life of God (1:29).

The fact of being a Christian, of being born of God, is permanent assurance that one is loved by the Father; each carries in his or her person the attestation of this love. (John will, of course, insist that the Christian live as child of God, 3:4-23). The unbelieving world is incapable of recognizing the true status of Christians because it has not come to know God. For John this means that it had failed to recognize Jesus. As for ourselves, we have to await the coming of the Lord, to see him 'as he is,' before we can arrive at full appreciation of our own Christian reality. Only then shall we see clearly that our future state will be like the glorified state of Jesus. But the process of becoming like Christ has already begun – a familiar stress in John.

Gospel   Mt 5:1-12

Our gospels have two, notably different, versions of the beatitudes: Mt 5:3-12 and Lk 6:20-23. Matthew has nine beatitudes. Luke has four only – but with four corresponding 'woes' (6:24-26). Both versions have grown from an original core going back to Jesus, the additions and adaptations being due to the evangelists. The beatitudes of Jesus are three:

> Blessed are the poor, for the Kingdom of heaven is theirs.
> Blessed are those who hunger, for they will be filled.
> Blessed are the afflicted, for they will be comforted.

These beatitudes do not refer to three separate categories but to three aspects of the same distressful situation. One may ask: what merit is there in being poor, hungry, afflicted? There is none. The 'blessedness' of the poor is in their very need, their distress. God is their champion – as he showed himself to be in Jesus.

Luke has these three beatitudes, plus a fourth: the blessedness of those who suffer persecution for the sake of Christ; and he, like Jesus, looks to the really poor and afflicted. Matthew's longer version contains only three quite new beatitudes: the merciful, the pure in heart, the peace-makers. We get a total of nine only because those of the poor/meek and last two (the persecuted) are duplicates. But there distinctive features in Matthew's beatitudes as a whole. The expression 'poor in spirit' points to a transformation of idea of 'the poor.' In current usage, the designation 'poor in spirit' applies to one who is detached from worldly goods, who is interiorly free in regard to money. In fact, it is frequently related to the possession of wealth: it is possible for an economically rich person to be 'poor in spirit.' That is because we take 'poor' in a specific sense, an economic sense, which may not be the biblical meaning. And that meaning, we now know from the Jewish texts of Qumran is 'humility'; the poor in the spirit are the humble. The parallel beatitude of 'the meek' confirms this meaning. These beatitudes, in Matthew, are no longer addressed to those who lack the necessities of life (Luke/Jesus) but to those characterized by their meekness, their patience, their humility. They are the *anawim* with Jesus himself as the ultimate 'poor man' (11:29). It is evident that 'blessed are those who hunger and thirst for righteousness' is very different from Luke's blessedness of the 'poor' and the 'hungry.' For Matthew, Christianity has broadened and deepened the meaning of the term righteousness (5:20).

Among the really new beatitudes we first look at 'Blessed are the pure in heart for they shall see God' (5:8). The qualification 'in heart' like 'in spirit' points to an interior disposition. What is in question is what we would call 'purity of intention,' demanding perfect correspondence between intention and action. The beatitudes of the merciful and the peacemakers are concerned with action: the conduct of a Christian towards a neighbour who stands in need. The best illustration of 'merciful' is Matthew's description of the last judgment: 'I was hungry and you gave me food ' (25:35-40). As for the 'peacemakers': these evoke a good work highly prized in Judaism. It was observed that, among those who need help, the most needy are often an estranged husband and wife, or friends who have fallen out. To seek to reconcile them, to restore them to peace, is one of the kindest services one can render to the neighbour.

Where Luke applied the beatitudes to Christians as a suffering minority, Matthew has introduced a distinction: he reserves the blessedness promised in the beatitudes to Christians who truly live the gospel ideal. He had re-read the beatitudes in the light of his pastoral preoccupation and he had filled them out. He takes care to remind Christians that the promises of salvation are conditional (5:20). We will not be admitted to the Kingdom unless, after the example of the Master, we have shown ourselves to be meek and humble; unless we have given proof of righteousness and loyalty; unless we have carried out what God has asked of us in particular, unless we have served our brothers and sisters in their need.

The Beatitudes are thoroughly Jewish in form and content. They challenged those who made up 'Israel' in Matthew's time by delineating the kinds of persons and actions that will receive their full reward when God's kingdom comes. They remind Christians today of the Jewish roots of their piety and challenge each generation to reflect on what persons and actions they consider to be important or 'blessed.' (Daniel J. Harrington, S.J., *Matthew*, p. 84)

THE IMMACULATE CONCEPTION OF MARY
8 DECEMBER

The feast of the Immaculate Conception can fit easily into the time of preparation for Christmas. It celebrates the way in which God prepared a dwelling for his Son in the midst of the human race, when he chose Mary and preserved her from sin. The doctrinal aspect is neatly summed up in the Collect which makes it clear that Mary, though without sin, is redeemed through the merits of Jesus Christ.

But on this day the Immaculate Conception should not be approached in too abstract a manner. It is better to let it be a joyful celebration of Mary in Advent, a feast which, in praising Mary's fullness of grace, rejoices in God's gracious decision to pour out an abundance of blessing on a people in need of God's mercy.

The chosen readings give plenty of reasons for celebration. It may be remarked how, in the Gospel narrative, 'things happen'. We meet, not a precise definition, but an angel exclaiming, 'Greetings, favoured one!' This phrase from the Gospel, which, in its more traditional form, 'Hail, full of grace', also provides the Alleluia verse, is the one on which attention is focused today. (On March 25 the same Gospel is read but with the emphasis on the Son whom Mary is to conceive.). The reading from Genesis carries the assurance that in spite of sin the human race is not to be written off, while Ephesians dwells on how it is by God's gracious choice that men and women are saved. The use of these texts for this feast implies, of course, that Mary's place in the history of salvation is part of God's own plan.

First Reading   Gen 3:9-15.20

The sad aftermath of the 'fall': the perceptive Yahwist has sketched an unforgettable picture of the tragedy of sin. The man and woman had hitherto looked eagerly to their daily encounter with their God (the clear implication of v. 8). He comes as before, strolling in the garden, eminently accessible – but they are changed; now, in their guilt, they flee his face. Humankind cannot remain hidden from God. The man's reply to the second question of Yahweh (v. 11) is his desperate attempt to place responsibility for the results of his actions anywhere but at his own door. First he blames the woman: 'the woman ... gave me'; ultimately he seeks to pin the blame on God – she is the woman 'whom you gave to be with me.' The attempt to involve God is pathetic (but it is still the way of humankind). More tragic is the breakdown of relations between humans – here the man betrays the woman. Solidarity in sin, complicity in crime, are utterly divisive.

We must seek the true meaning of this passage but we should not seek to draw from it what it does not contain. In v. 15 'woman' and 'serpent' are the characters of the story: the 'mother of all living' and the 'cunning' snake. The function of the *nahash*, a talking snake – a stage prop – is to focus attention on the command ('of the tree of the knowledge of good and evil you shall not eat' , 2:17) and to spell out that disobedience is, in effect, a vain attempt 'to be like God.' It will remain the perennial human temptation. Between woman, snake and their progeny there will be perpetual antipathy. The masculine pronoun *autos*, 'he', in the Greek version is simply an awareness that human 'seed' is in question. The Latin *ipsa*, 'she', of the Vulgate does not seem to have come from Jerome himself but reflects a later tradition. If one will use Genesis 3:15 in a messsianic and mariological context (the obvious implication of the choice of the reading on this feast) one must be aware that this is accommodation – and, as such, quite proper. But one cannot maintain that such is the meaning or intent of the Genesis text. A note of hope is sounded in v. 20: 'the mother of all living'. There is hope for the human race because God will have the last word.

Second Reading   Eph 1:3-6.11-12

Ephesians has as its central theme the wonder of grace. From the first, God had devised a merciful plan for uniting humankind with himself, through sending his Son as Saviour. Having enunciated his theme in v. 3 with a three-fold mention of 'blessing', the author proceeds in the following verses to give a description of God's blessing. It consists of God's choice that we should be holy (v. 4), our adoption as God's children (v. 5), our redemption from sin – the forgiveness of our trespasses (v. 7), the revelation of the 'mystery' or divine plan itself (vv 9-10). Mary, the singularly graced (see Lk 1:28), is surely the perfect child of God who inherits and, in her measure, mediates God's blessing.

Gospel   Lk 1:26-38

The infancy gospel of Luke, like that of Matthew, is firmly christological. Here, in 1:32-33, Jesus is described as the Davidic Messiah in terms taken from 2 Sam 7:9-16. The only specifically Christian feature is that Jesus has been identified as that promised Messiah. Luke then moves quite beyond the Old Testament level and uses the technique of Mary's question and Gabriel's answer to point to the true identity of the Messiah (1:34-35). The Messiah is God's Son and his conception is not through marital intercourse (Mary) but through the Holy Spirit (Gabriel). It is Luke's dramatic version of an early christological formula, such as that of Rom 1:3-4. The child is wholly God's work – a new creation.

If the primary emphasis is christological, a secondary aim in our passage is to affirm the status God has granted to Mary. The full stream of divine favour is centred in her. The coming of the Holy Spirit and his overshadowing of Mary highlights both the divine initiative and the beginning of the final process of salvation. Luke, writing in the light of his resurrection-faith, had discerned Mary's stature. She was mother, specially chosen, of Jesus – the Spirit-begotten. She was mother of a unique son, the one who would save his people from their sins. She was, truly, the most blessed of womankind (see 1:42).

Bibliography

T. L. Brodie, *The Gospel according to John. A Literary and Theological Commentary* (Oxford / New York: Oxford University Press, 1993).

R. E. Brown, *The Birth of the Messiah*, updated edition, New York: Doubleday, 1993.

R. E. Brown, *The Death of the Messiah*. 2 vols (New York / London: Doubleday / Chapman, 1994).

F. W. Danker, *Jesus and the New Age. A Commentary on St Luke's Gospel* (Philadelphia: Fortress, 1988).

L. Doohan, *Acts of Apostles. A Spiritual Commentary* (San Jose CA: Resource Publications, 1994).

J. A. Fitzmyer, *The Gospel According to Luke*. 2 vols. (New York: Doubleday, 1981, 1985).

W. J. Harrington, *Revelation. Sacra Pagina 16*. A Michael Glazier Book (Collegeville MN: Liturgical Press, 1993).

L. T. Johnson, *Luke . Sacra Pagina 3*. A Michael Glazier Book (Collegeville MN: Liturgical Press, 1991).

F. J. Matera, *Galatians. Sacra Pagina 9*. A Michael Glazier Book. (Collegeville MN: Liturgical Press. 1992).

J. Murphy-O'Connor, *1 Corinthians. New Testament Message 10* (Wilmington, DE: M. Glazier, 1979).

C. Osiek, *Galatians. New Testament Message 12*. (Wilmington, DE: M. Glazier, 1980).

Index to Scripture Commentary

Old Testament

New Testament

IOO YEARS WORK AT
Dominican Publications

Publishers of
Journals
& Books
since 1897

The work of Dominican Publications began in April 1897 with the first edition of *The Irish Rosary* (10,000 copies), which proved so successful that it had to be reprinted twice within days of its launch. At the beginning its focus was primarily on devotion to the Rosary, but as the years went by, it evolved into describing itself as 'A Monthly Magazine of Literature and Art for Catholics'. Other magazines followed – *The Imeldist* (1912), *The Lantern* (1934), *The Dominican Bulletin* (1940), *The Irish Spotlight* (1962) and *Faith Today* (1975) – but, like *The Irish Rosary*, these have all now ceased publication.

Entering its second century, Dominican Publications remains committed to its task: it now brings out four journals and has a regular programme of book publishing. In addition, it has begun to publish CDRoms and is also making available reproductions of works of modern religious art suitable for home or classroom.

The **Dominican Publications journals** are:

DOCTRINE &LIFE (ten times a year) which seeks to promote a dialogue between today's thinking and the inheritance of faith;

RELIGIOUS LIFE REVIEW (six times a year) which deals with matters of concern to religious;

SCRIPTURE IN CHURCH (four times a year) – an aid to understanding the Scripture readings at Mass;

Spirituality (six times a year) which aims to help lay Christian especially to deepen their Christian lives.

Book publishing in Dominican Publications centres on the topics on which the four journals focus. The main concentration is on homiletics and liturgical aids, with attention also being given to religious life, Church documents, current problems, spirituality, and biography.

Publishing on CDRom is a new departure: the first 100 issues of *Scripture in Church* are already available in that format, and the CD of *Vatican Council II: Conciliar and Post-Concilar Documents* will be published in autumn 1997 – in conjunction with Costello Publishing Company of Northport, Long Island, New York, and The Liturgical Press, Collegeville MN..

To meet the need for **works of art for the home or class room**, Dominican Publications have now made available a set of four posters on major religious themes by artists whose approach combines respect for tradition with freshness – Rachel Wroe Sawko, Patrick Pye, Albert Carpentier, and Jack P. Hanlon.

I Remember Your Name in the Night

THINKING ABOUT DEATH

Donagh O'Shea

'Those who are already familiar with Fr O'Shea's reflections in books such as *Take Nothing for the Journey* (1990) will be delighted to hear from him again.... O'Shea speaks of the moment of death; of our fears and struggles inthe face of our own impending death and that of loved ones. But he situates the death question right in the midst of life ...

'O'Shea has the gift of ebing able to be present to the joy and the sorrow hidden in the most ordinary of human experiences. The very way in which he uses language is itself a revelation ... I know of no other scholar who has succeeded in allowing the insight of Meister Eckhart to speak so simply and profoundly at the same time. O'Shea also knows how to bl;end sound psychology with common sense and place both within the context of our searching for and discovery of God.'

Eamonn Conway in *The Furrow*

144 pages

215 X 138 mm

Paperback

£7.99

Edition for USA and Canada from Twenty-Third Publications, Mystic CT

Donagh O'Shea is an Irish Dominican priest. A native of Co. Cork, he has lectured on spirituality in Italy, Ireland, Britain, Switzerland, the U.S.A., Albania and the Philippines. From 1989 to 1996, he taught in Rome – at the Regina Mundi Institute and at the Beda – and he is now novice-master for the Irish Dominicans. His three previous books have won wide acclaim – *Go Down to the Potter's House*, *Take Nothing for the Journey*, and *In a Fitful Light*.

The Spiritual Adventure of the Apocalypse

WHAT IS THE SPIRIT SAYING

TO THE CHURCHES?

William Riley

Some people approach the Book of Revelation as if it predicted the date of the end of the world. Others trawl its pages for proof that such-and-such a political figure is the Antichrist John speaks of. Still others seem to glory in what comes across as doom and gloom in the book's story.

William Riley's approach is altogether different. A Scripture teacher who knew that he was suffering the illness which finally claimed his life on 21 June 1995, he explores how reading the Apocalypse can be an authentic spring-time of the soul – not just for the individual believer but for the Church too – and can bring a message of celebration, challenge and, above all, hope. For Fr Riley, if the Apocalypse portrays evil with great force it is only as a help to perceiving more clearly the reality of God. The Seer opens up a vision of God as majestic – sovereignly ruling over cosmic forces – and offers this as an assurance that the God who may often be unseen and unheard still remains the source and goal of all things.

> 'This is exactly the kind of blend of scholarship and personal story which is needed as the end of the millennium approaches.' Wilfrid Harrington OP

William Riley (1949-1995), a native of Ohio, and a priest of the diocese of Dublin, taught Scripture at Carysfort College of Education and later at the Mater Dei Institute, both in Dublin. His books included *The Bible Group: an Owner's Manual* and *The Tale of Two Testaments*.

160 pages

215 x 138 mm

Paperback

£7.99

Edition for USA and Canada from Twenty-Third Publications, Mystic CT

Vatican Council II: Constitutions, Decrees, Declarations A COMPLETELY REVISED TRANSLATION IN INCLUSIVE LANGUAGE

General Editor: Austin Flannery OP

This is a completely revised translation of the sixteen council documents in inclusive language. Inclusive language is used throughout in passages about men and women, not, however, in passages about God except where the use of the masculine pronoun was easily avoidable.

> '... an important dimension of the project of Vatican II'.
>   Linda Hogan in *Doctrine & Life*

> '... not only appropriate, but necessary ... to be warmly welcomed.'
>   Anne Thurston in *Religious Life Review*

> '... much easier to read ... to cite without sounding odd or quaint. There is a new fluency here'.
>   Denis Carroll in *The Furrow*

> '... the virtually definitive version for the normal bookshelf ... By finding an inclusive speech-form, Fr Flannery removes any possible misconception regarding what the Council had in mind ... '
>   Louis McRedmond in *The Tablet*

xiv + 610 pages

210 x 135 mm

Paperback

£15.99

Edition for USA and Canada from Costellos Publishing Company Northport Long Island, NY.